D1523905

FLORIDA 2000

FLORIDA 2000

A Sourcebook
on the Contested
Presidential Election

edited by
Mark Whitman

LYNNE
RIENNER
PUBLISHERS

BOULDER
LONDON

Published in the United States of America in 2003 by
Lynne Rienner Publishers, Inc.
1800 30th Street, Boulder, Colorado 80301
www.rienner.com

and in the United Kingdom by
Lynne Rienner Publishers, Inc.
3 Henrietta Street, Covent Garden, London WC2E 8LU

Library of Congress Cataloging-in-Publication Data
Whitman, Mark, 1937–
    Florida 2000 : a sourcebook on the contested presidential election / by Mark Whitman.
    Includes bibliographical references and index.
    ISBN 1-58826-204-9
    1. Bush, George W. (George Walker), 1946—Trials, litigation, etc.   2. Gore, Albert,
    1948—Trials, litigation, etc.   3. Presidents—United States—Election—2000.   4.
    Contested elections—United States.   5. Contested elections—Florida.   I. Title.
    KF5074.2.W48   2003
    342.73'075—dc21
                                                                                    2003043179

British Cataloguing in Publication Data
A Cataloguing in Publication record for this book
is available from the British Library.

Printed and bound in the United States of America

The paper used in this publication meets the requirements
of the American National Standard for Permanence of
Paper for Printed Library Materials Z39.48-1992.

5   4   3   2   1

To my sister Sandy
And to the family that is more than I deserve—
Andy and Laura and Joshua and Kate,
Gary and Shana and Zachary,
And also, of course, for Dorothy

Contents

Preface

This volume will be of interest, I think, to anyone who followed the Florida election drama of 2000—and also to those who are studying this singular event in modern political and constitutional history for the first time.

I have sought to fashion a clear narrative, explicating the legal and constitutional issues raised by the 2000 presidential election as they unfolded from November 8 to December 12, and to some degree afterward. I do this largely through the introductions to each part of the book and to its documents, and then by letting important documents speak for themselves. But at the three most crucial points in the Bush-Gore controversy—the Florida Supreme Court's decision on recounts of November 22, the Florida court's contest decision of December 8, and the United States Supreme Court judgment in *Bush v. Gore*—I have added a comment section that synthesizes and evaluates the competing arguments.

The documents in the volume consist of court decisions, legal briefs, and memoranda, as well as newspaper and periodical commentary. Much, though by no means all, of the commentary is contemporaneous with the shifting developments in Florida, in order to convey to the reader the flavor of that tumultuous time. The emphasis throughout is on those legal and constitutional issues that were decisive at the various stages of the election struggle.

My point of view on some issues inevitably comes through, especially in the comment sections. But I am most interested here in laying bare the major fault lines of the Bush-Gore controversy—in pointing to the strengths and weaknesses of the pleas made by the protagonists and of the responses proffered by the courts of Florida and of the nation. This way, readers can form their own judgments.

* * *

I owe a debt to many people who helped to make this project possible, but I must start with two in particular.

Leanne Anderson, acquisitions editor at Lynne Rienner Publishers, has shown great faith in this undertaking from the beginning. Her consummate skill as an editor brought form out of my chaos, and her good cheer bucked me up at difficult moments. Every writer dreams of having such a marvelous, supportive editor.

If disposition and capacity for personal kindness were being auctioned off, Emily Daugherty's would go for untold millions. She good-naturedly put up with all my changes of text and, more amazingly, with my handwriting. Much of my satisfaction with this project comes from working with Emily.

My thanks go to a number of people I have never had the privilege of meeting. Ron Klain and Richard Cordray gave permission to print their December 12 brief, Anthony Amsterdam to print his *Los Angeles Times* essay, and Gregory Barnhart supplied me with the transcript of Judge LaBarga's November 22 hearing. Joe Knetsch led me to Lance De Haven Smith of Florida State University, Evan Kolodner of the Broward County Office of Election Supervisors, and Sarah Jane Bradshaw at the Florida State Senate, who in turn helped me to really understand Florida's elections. David Kidwell and Elisabeth Donovan of the *Miami Herald* were generous with their time, and Dennis Cauchon of *USA Today* supplied me with the invaluable results of the overvote count spearheaded by the two newspapers.

For more than three decades, the Towson University History Department has been my home under the consummate leadership first of Mary Catherine Kahl and now of Cindy Gissendanner. My colleague and close friend Myron Scholnick, in addition to being an incredibly good person, has always been my biggest booster and my greatest source of comfort at Towson. I also deeply appreciate the friendship and intellectual endeavors I have shared over many years with Laura Eldridge, Karl and Marilyn Larew, Fred and Nancy Rivers, and Garry Van Osdell. Neither this book, nor any of my others, would ever have been written without the encouragement of Patricia Romero.

David Sides of Towson's Center for Geographic Information Services did the excellent map of Florida, and I have profited greatly from the hospitality and courtesy of the staff at the University of Baltimore Law Library.

My extended family is a source of constant support and joy, especially my cousins Penny and Sol Love, Rita and Irv Sherman, and, until his death this year, Harry Frankel. Nor can I forget my beloved uncle Marvin Davis and my other Friday lunch companions: Marvin Cornblath, Ted Feldberg, Donald Klein, Tony Perlman, and Arthur Rosenbaum.

I remember always my parents and my aunt Sylvia Davis.

FLORIDA 2000

PART I

SETTING THE STAGE

It was 1 P.M. in the east on Wednesday, November 8, 2000, and never, since the age of modern radio and television communication began, had Americans waited so long to learn who their new president would be.

Richard Nixon's telegram of concession, in the cliff-hanging election of 1960, arrived in Hyannisport, Massachusetts, at 11 o'clock the morning after the vote. Hubert Humphrey conceded to Nixon in 1968 at 11 o'clock in the morning, Minneapolis time. President Gerald Ford congratulated Jimmy Carter from the White House, just after noon on the day following the election of 1976.[1]

The election of 2000, however, was taking a different and more protracted course. Vice President Al Gore was forging ahead in the popular vote, and had apparently secured 267 of the 270 electoral votes he needed to win. His margin of victory was perilously thin in Wisconsin, Iowa, New Mexico, and Oregon, yet he could afford to lose two or even three of those states and still be elected if he won the state of Florida. Governor George W. Bush, with 246 electoral votes secured, would also stand or fall on Florida's result.

And the outcome there was far from final on November 8. After an evening of television high jinks, in which commentators gave the state to Gore, declared it too close to call, then gave it to Bush, the governor emerged with a lead of 1,784 votes out of almost 6 million cast. Since this margin was less than 0.5 percent of the total, it was not enough under Florida law to make the outcome official.[2] An automatic recount was necessary, to be carried out by the same types of mechanical tabulating equipment used to count the vote originally, in all but the few counties still employing paper ballots. The stated deadline for submission of those returns to the Florida Elections Canvassing Commission, headed by Secretary of State Katherine Harris, was Tuesday, November 14.[3]

Still, most people on November 8 were certain George Bush had won.

I

The recount seemed highly unlikely to upset a margin of almost 2,000 votes, and past experience indicated Bush would benefit from the overseas absentee ballots, not due, under an agreement with the federal government, until midnight on Friday, November 17.[4] (Indeed, the machine recount did show Bush winning, if only with a plurality of 327 votes, a margin eventually boosted to 930 when the overseas ballot totals came in.)

By that time, however, forces were in motion that would transform the presidential election of 2000 from a slightly extended replay of 1960 or 1976 into a modern version of the election of 1876, the epic disputed contest between Rutherford B. Hayes and Samuel J. Tilden. On November 9, acting through the Democratic Party of Florida, the vice president's lawyers requested a manual recount of the votes in four predominantly Democratic counties: Palm Beach, Miami-Dade, Broward, and Volusia.[5] If the requests were granted, it was not immediately certain how long these recounts would take, or whether the Republicans would challenge them.

Meanwhile, in Palm Beach County, a bitter and emotional dispute flared up, beginning on election day itself, over the design of the county's election ballot and the distortion of voter preferences the ballot allegedly caused—to the terrible detriment of Vice President Gore.[6] The legal ramifications of this dispute seemed to some Gore strategists to represent their best chance of altering the result in Florida. A trial in the Palm Beach courts, however, would be more protracted than the recounts, and introduced the possibility of a judge effectively deciding the outcome of a political contest.

The Statutory Context

To get a better handle on the unprecedented situation developing in Florida on November 9 and 10, we must place these events in the unglamorous but instructive context of the state's election code.

The legislation Vice President Gore relied on in calling for his recounts was passed only in 1989. Before that time, only a court could order a manual recounting of any Florida election. But there were now new options available to a candidate, and to a political party, centered in revisions to Section 102.166 of the election code. These revisions allowed candidate or party to ask any county canvassing board for a manual recount anytime prior to the board's certification of election results, "or within 72 hours after midnight of the date the election was held, whichever occurs later."[7] This meant a candidate might validly file such a request five or six days after an election, if certification was delayed for some reason. Significantly, there was no provision in Florida law for a statewide recount.

Should a canvassing board decide to proceed with the manual count, the statute gave it two different choices. The board could immediately go through all the ballots, a likely course in a smaller jurisdiction. In the case of a very large county, however, officials were more likely to do a preliminary sample recount of "at least 1 percent of the total votes cast,"[8] from precincts the candidate got the right to designate.

Only if this sample recount uncovered "an error in the vote tabulation which could affect the outcome of the election,"[9] did the board have to take further action, and the statute gave it three conceivable options, of which further ballot counting was just one. Thus the board could:

1. Correct the error and recount the remaining precincts with the vote tabulation system,
2. Request the Department of State to verify the tabulation software (the department was given three days to respond), or
3. Manually recount all ballots.[10]

The "or" suggested those choices were mutually exclusive, but as the secretary of state's lawyers later pointed out, discovery of uncorrectable glitches under 2 could lead inevitably to 3. Yet 3 could also be the first and only choice under the statute.

Section 102.166 also laid down the procedures governing a manual recount, which did not distinguish between the sample and the exhaustive varieties, and which stipulated that "If a counting team is unable to determine a voter's intent in casting a ballot, the ballot shall be presented to the county canvassing board for it to determine the voter's intent."[11] The interpretation of these less than transparent directions bred the first, and in many ways the central legal quarrel of the Florida crisis. For now, we need only point out that the language in Section 166 could refer both to breakdowns in the state's vote counting equipment, and to close elections.

The Gore Strategy Develops

Vice President Gore was obviously focusing on the latter, and on the manual recounts he thought they should occasion. He was confident such recounts would aid his cause, especially in the four counties he wanted redone. This was not only because these counties were solidly Democratic and among the most populous in the state. In addition, all of them, except Volusia, used a system for voting that seemed at the time more likely than others to boost a candidate who was trailing—the punch-card system.

Under this system, voters register their preferences by placing a ballot card covered with detachable little rectangles into the voting device. The card contains multiple columns: The first column has numbers running down the ballot from one to twenty or so; subsequent columns take the numbers above 200.

The voting device itself is equipped with a booklet listing the candidates for each office on a separate page, with numbers next to their names. (The presidential candidates on the first page have the lowest numbers.) To the right of the names on a given page are a series of descending punch holes carved through a plastic template. If a ballot is properly aligned, the number for a presidential candidate points to that hole under which the ballot displays an identical number. As a voter turns the pages of the booklet to a different race, a new column of holes appears, over a new column of numbers on the ballot. This all moves from left to right.[12] The actual process of voting takes place using a plastic or rubber stylus which pushes the appropriate rectangle out of the ballot. Soft rubber strips under the card facilitate this process. The stylus is supposed to push the rectangles completely off the ballot card, to a collection area beneath. Indeed, written instructions posted at the polling places in 2000 warned voters to make sure those rectangles, or *chads* as they came to be called, were not still attached to the ballot. In Palm Beach County the instructions explicitly told the voter to "Be Sure...There Are No Chips Left Hanging On The Back Of The Card"[13]; the Broward County instructions simply stated that the voter should "punch the stylus straight down through the ballot card."[14] A fully punched card was read by a vote-recording machine when the machine passed a light through the open hole. Computers then coordinated the results.

This was the theory. But Gore and his strategists knew that punch-card machines were notoriously unreliable. Since their introduction in the 1960s, a cascade of complaints had descended upon these devices, originally manufactured by IBM under the name Votomatic. IBM, in fact, abandoned the production of Votomatics in 1969, and licensed five other companies to manufacture and market them.[15]

The problems continued, however, the main one being the system's congenital inability to guarantee fully punched punch cards. Historically, many ballots turned up in Votomatic cities or counties that were neither punched out nor undisturbed, but had chads on them hanging by anywhere from one to three corners. (A chad attached to the ballot card by three corners was known as a *tri-chad*; if two corners were detached, it was a *swinging chad*; a single corner attached was a *hanging chad*.) Sometimes, ballots revealed only indentations or dimples in chads not separated from the ballot cards at all. The classic dimpled ballot displayed a chad having a caved-in look if viewed from the front, or a pushed-up quality if viewed from the back.[16]

These dimpled ballots would not register on a punch-card reading machine, but the machine lacked a foolproof technology for dealing with hanging chads. It might "read" cards with two or three corners dangling, if the chads flipped open as the cards were going through and allowed light to penetrate. Otherwise, the ballots did not count. The same was true of ballots with only pinhole-sized perforations that might or might not allow penetration of light.

Some punch cards would almost certainly get counted during a machine run because their hanging chads fell off as they passed through the reading devices. (This accounted in part for the fact that over 1,200 of the 1,484 votes Gore gained during the machine recount came from the Votomatic counties of Palm Beach, Pinellas, and Duval.) There were fully punched ballots, however, that could go unread if the detached chads temporarily blocked the machine.[17]

There was plenty of raw material to work with in the punch-card counties Gore targeted. Even after the two machine runs, 28,000 ballots remained in Palm Beach, Broward, and Miami-Dade on which no preference appeared in the contest for president—so-called undervotes.[18] As a whole, the counties using the punch-card system in 2000 showed five times as many undervotes as the ones using the newer optical-scanning technology. (Volusia County, which employed optical scanners, recorded 450 undervotes, a percentage about average for such counties.)[19] The Gore team was convinced a full manual recount, particularly one based on the "intent of the voter," would validate all the ballots with detached chads, and perhaps other votes as well—most of them Democratic.

It was also clear, however, as one of Gore's lawyers noted at the outset, that the whole recount procedure they were working with was designed only "to resolve contests in sheriff . . . and county commissioner races. [It] never contemplated something the size of this."[20] Applying such a procedure to a statewide contest, in the selective way Gore sought to apply it, meant that victory could flow from ballots identical to ones for his opponent that lay untouched in the other punch-card counties, to say nothing of what might be found in the rejected ballots from counties using optical scanners.

The vice president considered the possibility of asking for recounts in all sixty-seven Florida counties; some of his advisors favored such a course. But the very absurdity of the law put him in a difficult position. Going to every one of Florida's counties would obviously create a chaotic spectacle, and some canvassing boards, especially Republican-dominated ones, would probably refuse the recount requests. "The press would treat a substantial number of refusals as a fatal loss of momentum for Gore," it was felt.[21] Furthermore, Gore was convinced he must get ahead as quickly as he could in the vote count, and put the pressure on Bush to seek full counts, before the public became fed up with his recount effort.

Hence, the vice president limited his official recount requests to the four South Florida counties, though suggesting publicly to Bush that the two endorse a full statewide recount. His actions were dictated in great part by the inadequacy of the Florida statutory structure, but he was not unaware, surely, of the practical advantages of such a course, if it wound up passing legal muster. "We thought we were pretty cute hitting the big four counties," campaign chairman William Daley later acknowledged. Dennis Whouley, Gore's top political strategist, noted, "Recounts have rules. Socrates didn't write them."[22] It did not take Socrates, of course, to spot the ethical deficiencies in the vice president's scheme.

The Butterfly Detour

At the time Gore launched his recount efforts, though, they did not seem any more crucial to the outcome in Florida than the possibility he might join a series of lawsuits filed by the aggrieved voters of Palm Beach County, beginning also on November 9.[23] The suits followed a flood of election-day complaints from people who claimed they miscast their vote for president because neither they nor anyone else could possibly follow the listing of the presidential candidates on the county's ballot. Hundreds signed affidavits to that effect in the days immediately following the election.[24]

The source of these complaints was the notorious "butterfly ballot," so named because it slated those running for president on two adjoining pages of the ballot book instead of on the single column page used in nearly all the other punch-card counties. The punch holes under which voters placed their ballot cards ran in this case between the two pages, which meant the holes were to the right of the candidates found on the left page, and to the left of those on the right page. The appropriate punch hole for a candidate alternated then between the pages, meaning Bush, at the top on the left, had the first hole, but Reform Party candidate Pat Buchanan, at the top on the right, had the second punch hole. Consequently, though the vice president was listed second on the ballot starting down the left page, his punch hole was the third one, just above the one for Socialist candidate David McReynolds (listed below Buchanan).[25]

In all fairness to the Palm Beach authorities, it should be noted that arrows on the ballot pointed from each candidate's name to the appropriate punch hole. Furthermore, the authorities confronted a difficult situation in designing the ballot, due to changes in the state constitution that made it much easier for minor-party candidates to qualify for a place on the presidential line. In 1996, four candidates were listed for president; in 2000, ten had to be fitted in.[26]

Still, the butterfly contributed to some peculiar results in the county.

The Buchanan ticket received 3,407 votes—20 percent of its overall total for Florida—as opposed to just over 500 votes in neighboring Miami-Dade County, and a little less than 800 in Broward County, both far more populous than Palm Beach. Buchanan got 0.79 percent of the vote in Palm Beach County, and 0.29 percent statewide.[27] Most significantly, he garnered some of his strongest support in Palm Beach precincts Gore won handily, the opposite of the trend in other parts of the state. In the massive, heavily Jewish condominium development of Kings Point, in Broward County, Buchanan received 1 vote for every 851 cast for Gore. At the Kings Point development in Palm Beach County, Buchanan got 1 vote for every 72 Gore votes.[28]

In addition, there were over 19,000 ballots in the county rejected as overvotes, meaning voters had punched the names of two or more presidential candidates. This was two and one-half times as many overvotes as registered in 1996. Later analysis showed that 6,330 of the overvotes went for Gore-Buchanan, around 3,000 more for Gore-McReynolds, and that these people voted Democratic in the concurrent Florida senate race by a 10-to-1 margin.[29] (In Duval County, officials took a different tack, and listed the presidential candidates on succeeding pages of the ballot book. There were almost 22,000 overvotes in Duval, over 9,000 of them in minority neighborhoods.)[30]

Since the butterfly ballot was at odds with a provision of state law requiring that the place to indicate a preference for a candidate must be set to the candidate's right, the appellants who went to court on November 9 felt they were entitled to the only remedy capable of curing the wrongs done by the ballot—a revote in all of Palm Beach County. That weekend, a petition supporting such action appeared in the *New York Times*, signed by prominent legal scholars such as Ronald Dworkin, Cass Sunstein, and Bruce Ackerman, as well as by a host of leading figures in the arts, including Arthur Miller, Toni Morrison, E. L. Doctorow, Paul Newman, and Joanne Woodward.[31]

The vice president indicated on November 9 he might intervene in the legal challenge to the butterfly ballot, and some of his advisors saw this as the "killer lawsuit" that could catapult Gore into the White House. "The level of injustice was overwhelming," recalled Ron Klain, a brilliant young lawyer who played a leading role in Gore's Florida efforts. To Klain, examining the situation in the first days after the election, the hand count was "definitely the B-track strategy." Assault on the Palm Beach County ballot "was Plan A."[32]

As the machine recount trimmed Bush's margin back toward 300, however, the manual-recount idea gained credibility. (What the Gore forces didn't know was that eighteen counties in Florida, containing a quarter of the state's ballots, never ran a *machine* recount.[33]) On Saturday, November 11,

Gore gathered his advisers at his naval observatory residence to refine post-election plans. Most urged the vice president to drop the butterfly option and concentrate on the manual recounts, especially campaign manager William Daley. In the absence of wholesale fraud or election-day violence, there was "no way," Daley said, courts would order a new election to fix what happened with the ballot. "People get screwed every day. They don't have a remedy. Ask black people. There's no way to solve this problem."[34] Daley recalled that a "lot of . . . logical geniuses were saying we could get this and get that—a special election or a reallocation of votes. Get real here. . . . No way some judge is going to name a guy president of the United States. It's not going to happen."[35]

Senator Lieberman (who walked from Georgetown for the meeting) disagreed with Daley. "There are Holocaust survivors down there who didn't get their votes counted," he argued. "We can't just walk away from them."[36] The vice president did not make an irrevocable decision on November 11, but he realized the butterfly suit was almost certainly futile.[37] He never did intervene in Palm Beach, though allies in the labor movement helped finance the private lawsuits that went forward.[38]

Bush's Preemptive Move

The recounts, then, would be the heart of Vice President Gore's effort to prevail in the 2000 election. They would focus mainly on validating undervotes in Palm Beach, Miami-Dade, and Broward Counties (which ranked second, seventh, and twelfth respectively in total percentage of undervotes for the punch-card jurisdictions). Gore and his strategists seemed to hold out little hope of rehabilitating overvotes.

But these recounts had barely begun when George Bush unveiled his approach to the 2000 election by seeking to put a stop to the whole recounting operation. Despite the public-relations risks of being the first to launch legal action, and notwithstanding the qualms of some of his states'-rights–oriented supporters, he had his lawyers join a group of Florida voters and go to federal district court on November 11, seeking an emergency restraining order and preliminary injunction against all manual recounting of votes in Florida. The lawyers maintained, for one thing, that recounting votes in only four jurisdictions violated the equal-protection clause of the Fourteenth Amendment, as they could later prove in a full-scale hearing, and that allowing those counts to go forward now would do "irreparable harm" to Governor Bush by exposing him to sensationalized news reports about vote totals that were actually invalid.[39]

Bush and the Florida plaintiffs analogized their situation to the one condemned in the reapportionment cases of the 1960s, where the United

States Supreme Court found that only the one person–one vote principle comported with the equal protection of the laws in the setting up of state legislative and congressional districts.[40] The seminal reapportionment case, *Reynolds v. Sims*, had stated that the right to vote was "'denied by a debasement or dilution of the weight of a citizen's vote just as effectively as by wholly prohibiting the free exercise of the franchise. . . . Every voter [must be] equal to every other voter in his State, when he casts his ballot.'"[41] *Reynolds*, therefore, would clearly proscribe a system where "the votes of citizens across the state of Florida [are] unconstitutionally diluted" because Vice President Gore was allowed to "conduct a manual recount of only select ballots in portions of four heavily Democratic counties."[42]

Governor Bush put forth another equal protection grievance, also drawing in part on the reapportionment parallel. He alleged that since Florida possessed no detailed statutory standards at all for hand-counting votes, "similarly-punched ballots in different [punch-card] counties may be tabulated differently."[43]

This lawsuit was part of a general strategy by the Bush campaign, spelled out, curiously enough, in a handbook on recounts distributed to Gore operatives in Florida the day after the election. "The one who is behind has to gather votes," the handbook noted. But "when you've got a lead, you sit on the ball."[44] The Bush post-election team, led by former secretary of state James Baker, vigorously pursued the latter tactic. "Once the machine recounts were completed . . . Baker wanted to send the message that the election was over and that any further recounts were attempts to undermine the system."[45] Baker and his lieutenants opposed, and decried, any and all moves by the vice president, anything that might thrust him ahead in the vote count, even temporarily, and throw Bush on the defensive. The best way to prevail, Baker believed, was to resist.[46]

Accordingly, Bush's advisers eschewed hand-count requests of their own in heavily Republican areas of Florida, promptly refused Gore's offer of a joint statewide recount, and savagely denounced the whole idea of manual counting as some kind of exotic and patently absurd way of evaluating ballots, unknown to an orderly democracy. Baker claimed such efforts were an attempt to "destroy . . . the traditional process for selecting our presidents,"[47] neglecting to mention that manual recounts of ballots were mandated in Texas, California, Indiana, and numerous other states.[48] His case was no doubt strengthened, though, by the nature of Gore's proposed recount.[49]

Joining a federal lawsuit against recounts fitted in with Baker's grand strategy, particularly since he predicted from the outset that the Bush-Gore dispute would end up in the United States Supreme Court.[50] But District Judge Donald Middlebrooks was not impressed with the plaintiffs' arguments. As applied specifically to their candidate, Governor Bush,

Middlebrooks noted "that any presidential candidate was offered an equal opportunity under [102.166] to ask for a manual recount."[51] More generally, Judge Middlebrooks read *Reynolds v. Sims* as requiring an entire structure of discrimination not present, he felt, in this instance. A law deliberately gerrymandering districts and putting voters in unequal positions represented such action. Somewhat unbalanced applications of a law valid on its face did not. "Whatever disparities may result from a county-by-county election count," the judge felt, "do not constitute a constitutional injury."[52] Such "isolated events that adversely affect individuals are not presumed to be a violation of the equal protection clause."[53] (No other court, including the U.S. Supreme Court, addressed this equal-protection argument during the protest phase of the Bush-Gore controversy.)[54]

As to the charge that Florida possessed no constitutionally adequate standards for counting votes, it was clear to Judge Middlebrooks such a contention was wholly premature, since the canvassing boards had barely started work.[55] Whatever the importance this argument would later assume,[56] the judge brushed it aside here.

The plaintiffs went to the Eleventh Circuit Court of Appeals, asking for an emergency stay against the recounts, even while they were appealing Judge Middlebrooks's decision. On November 17, though, the circuit court unanimously rejected the emergency appeals, and eventually set argument on the injunction appeal for the end of the month.[57] (The circuit court rejected the appeal on December 6 by an 8-4 vote.)[58]

Thus the recounting of votes in the 2000 presidential election went forward in the four counties selected by Vice President Gore, the recounts that would spark a political and constitutional crisis over the presidency unknown in America since the era of reconstruction. There would be two trips to the Florida Supreme Court, and two to the United States Supreme Court (the first of those leading to a clarification by the Florida Court of *its* initial decision). The crisis would be ended only on December 12, 2000, by the most controversial—though not necessarily the most influential—Supreme Court decision in a generation.[59]

Notes

(Florida documents not readily available in print or not available at all can be found at www.flcourts.org. Supreme Court briefs and oral arguments are found on-line at Supreme Court of the United States.)

1. Theodore White, *The Making of the President 1960* (New York: New American Library, 1961), p. 379; Albert Eisele, *Almost to the Presidency* (Blue Earth, Minn.: Piper Co., 1972), p. 393; Martin Schram, *Running for President 1976* (New York: Stein and Day, 1977), p. 358.

2. *The 2000 Florida Statutes,* 102.141 (4), www.flcourts.org.

3. Ibid., 102.111 (1); 102.112 (1).

4. By a consent decree with the federal government.

5. Dan Balz, "Gore Mulls Challenges," *Washington Post*, November 10, 2000, p. A1.

6. Don Van Natta Jr. and Dana Canedy, "The Case of the Butterfly Ballot," November 9, 2000, included in Correspondents of *The New York Times, 36 Days* (New York: Times Books, 2001), p. 10. I have used this source, when referring to general election coverage, as often as possible, since it is convenient for readers.

7. *The 2000 Florida Statutes*, 102.166 (4) (b).

8. Ibid., 102.166 (4) (d).

9. Ibid., 102.166 (5).

10. Ibid., 102.166 (5) (a), (b), (c).

11. Ibid., 102.166 (7) (b).

12. A good visual depiction of the punch-card device is found in Correspondents of *The New York Times, 36 Days*, pp. 46–47.

13. This is quoted, among many others, by Chief Justice Rehnquist in his concurrence in *Bush v. Gore*, 148 L Ed 2d 388, 407.

14. Richard Friedman, "Trying to Make Peace with *Bush v. Gore*," 29 *Florida State University Law Review* (2001), pp. 811, 845.

15. See Martin Merzer and the Staff of *The Miami Herald, The Miami Herald Report: Democracy Held Hostage* (New York: St. Martin's Press, 2001), ch. 4.

16. Correspondents of *The New York Times, 36 Days*, p. 90.

17. Merzer, *The Miami Herald Report*, pp. 54–55.

18. *New York Times*, November 10, 2000, p. A24 shows first Gore gains.

19. Correspondents of *The New York Times, 36 Days*, pp. 191, 285.

20. The Political Staff of *The Washington Post, Deadlock: The Inside Story of America's Closest Election* (New York: Public Affairs, 2001), p. 56.

21. Jeffrey Toobin, *Too Close to Call* (New York: Random House, 2001), p. 38.

22. David A. Kaplan, *The Accidental President* (New York: William Morrow, 2001), p. 69.

23. The first one, *Fladell v. Palm Beach County Canvassing Board*, 15th Judicial Circuit, was actually filed at 6:01 P.M. on November 8. Four other suits were filed during working hours on November 9.

24. Dexter Filkins, "Street Protests Erupt in Palm Beach," November 10, 2000, p. 20, and David Firestone, "Democrats Seek Manual Recounts, Weigh Legal Battle," November 11, 2000, p. 31, both in Correspondents of *The New York Times, 36 Days*.

25. Correspondents of *The New York Times, 36 Days*, p. 11.

26. Merzer,*The Miami Herald Report*, pp. 36–37.

27. Glenn Kessler and Dan Keating, "Numbers Add Up to More Dispute," *Washington Post*, November 11, 2000, p. A19.

28. Merzer,*The Miami Herald Report*, p. 86.

29. Dan Keating, "Florida 'Overvotes' Hit Democrats the Hardest," *Washington Post*, January 27, 2001, p. A1; Merzer,*The Miami Herald Report*, p. 43.

30. Merzer,*The Miami Herald Report*, pp. 37–38; Correspondents of *The New York Times, 36 Days*, pp. 91–92.

31. "We the People," *New York Times*, November 11, 2000, p. A27.

32. Political Staff of *The Washington Post, Deadlock*, pp. 70–71.

33. Toobin, *Too Close to Call*, pp. 64–66; Kaplan, *The Accidental President*, pp. 50–51.

34. Political Staff of *The Washington Post, Deadlock*, p. 93.
35. Kaplan, *The Accidental President*, p. 79.
36. Toobin, *Too Close to Call*, p. 56.
37. Political Staff of *The Washington Post, Deadlock*, pp. 93–94.
38. Ibid., p. 22.
39. *Siegel v. LePore*, 120 F. Supp. 2d 1041 (S.D. Fla. 2000). Two days later, citizens in Brevard County filed an almost identical lawsuit, *Touchton v. McDermott*, 120 F. Supp. 2d 1055 (M.D. Fla. 2000).
40. For background on the critical constitutional development in *Baker v. Carr*, 369 US 186 (1962), see Gene Graham, *One Man, One Vote* (Boston: Little Brown, 1972).
41. *Siegel v. LePore*, "Emergency Motion for Temporary Restraining Order and Preliminary Injunction and Supporting Memorandum of Law," p. 7, quoting *Reynolds v. Sims*, 377 US 533, 554, 557-58 (1964).
42. Ibid., p. 8.
43. *Siegel v. LePore*, 1051.
44. Political Staff of *The Washington Post, Deadlock*, p. 53.
45. Toobin, *Too Close to Call*, p. 48.
46. Political Staff of *The Washington Post, Deadlock*, p. 73.
47. Ibid., p. 74.
48. See Texas Election Code, Section 212.005 (d); California Election Code, Section 15627; Indiana Election Code, Sections 3-12, 3-13. At least seventeen other states have statutes allowing manual recounts of punch-card tabulation systems.
49. See Kaplan, *The Accidental President*, ch. 3.
50. Toobin, *Too Close to Call*, p. 47.
51. *Siegel v. LePore*, 1051, fn. 11.
52. Ibid.
53. Ibid., 1051-1052, fn. 11, quoting from *Baker v. Curry*, 802 F. 2d 1302, 1314 (11th Cir. 1986). *Baker* itself was quoting from *Gamza v. Aguirre*, 619 F. 2d 449, 453 (5th Cir. 1980). I have quoted directly from *Gamza*.
54. See Part 2.
55. *Siegel v. LePore*, 1053.
56. See Part 6.
57. *Touchton v. McDermott*, 234 F. 3d 1130 (11th Cir. 2000); *Siegel v. LePore*, 234 F. 3d 1162 (11th Cir. 2000).
58. *Touchton v. McDermott*, 234 F. 3d 1133 (11th Cir. 2000); *Siegel v. LePore*, 234 F. 3d 1163 (11th Cir. 2000).
59. On this point see John Yoo, "In Defense of the Court's Legitimacy," in Cass Sunstein and Richard Epstein (eds.), *The Vote: Bush, Gore, and the Supreme Court* (Chicago: University of Chicago Press, 2001).

Bad Intent

Andrew Sullivan

The Bush plea to Judge Middlebrooks was but the first stage of a highly charged, yet highly technical, controversy over the nature of
recounts in Florida: when they were appropriate, when "chads" should
and should not be counted as votes, and what authority is properly
exercised over elections by the Florida secretary of state.

Even as this scene was unfolding, however, one of the nation's
most brilliant and most provocative essayists argued that the divide
between Gore and Bush was more a philosophical and an ethical one
than a legal one.

Andrew Sullivan is now senior editor of *The New Republic,* and
was formerly editor of the magazine. Born and educated in England, he
graduated with first-class honors from Oxford, and has a Ph.D. in
political science from Harvard. Sullivan has written extensively in
defense of the gay lifestyle, most notably in his *Virtually Normal* of
1995.

Note: If you make a mistake, return your ballot card and obtain another.
AFTER VOTING, CHECK YOUR BALLOT CARD TO BE SURE
YOUR VOTING SELECTIONS ARE CLEARLY AND CLEANLY
PUNCHED AND THERE ARE NO CHIPS LEFT HANGING ON THE
BACK OF THE CARD

—Voting instructions,
Palm Beach County, Florida

ATTENTION READERS: I hope you can understand the above text. It's
not exactly opaque; in fact, the critical text is in screaming bold capital let-

The New Republic, December 4, 2000, p. 10. Reprinted by permission of *The New Republic*, LLC.

ters.... They are the only instructions...in bold capitals. The central rationale of the Gore campaign's attempt to force hand recounts in Florida is therefore obvious. It is that even though there are clear and accurate instructions how to vote, and even though there is no evidence of fraud or voting-machine failure, that's still not good enough. Even under these palpably fair circumstances, the voters deserve a second and third chance.

So this is what the meaning of the word "vote" now is.

When all this is over, assuming it ever is, it will be worth examining the philosophical underpinnings of the Gore campaign's current argument about voting in Florida. The position, so far as I can glean, is that an election is about "the votes of all people who *attempted* [my emphasis] to exercise that vote." A vote should be counted, in other words, even if the voter blithely ignores clear voting instructions, even if he doesn't punch a hole forcefully enough, even if the only indicator of his vote is the merest dent in a piece of paper—the legendary "dimpled chad."

In the current atmosphere, it's easy to overlook the implications of this stance—especially since the Republicans have been engaging in plenty of ugly, partisan hypocrisy of their own. But there is a real issue here about what voting actually means. To some, voting is a right that should be guaranteed regardless of any incompetence, error, failure, or irresponsibility on the part of the voter. What matters is not the vote as such but the intent of the voter. Presumably, this is why members of the Gore campaign have made the argument that, if the "will of the people" is considered, Al Gore will win Florida and the presidency. The Rousseauian "will of the people" is the corollary to the narrower phrase "intent of the voter." That's why plenty of Democrats, Hillary Clinton now among them, want to abolish the electoral college, since its formalism might undercut the popular "will." That's why, as I write, hundreds of election workers in Palm Beach, Broward, and Miami-Dade Counties are holding ballots up to the light, running their fingers over them, twisting them in the air to catch shadows, and so on. They are discerning the Holy Grail of democratic politics—the will of the people.

Others have a different view. They argue that American democracy is not a Rousseauian exercise in popular will. It's a far stricter, Lockean, Anglo-American system based on the letter of the law and a successful vote cast by a rational, responsible voter. In this constitutional system, the "will of the people" is an irrelevant abstraction. After all, half the people don't even bother to vote—and, since that's their choice, there's no need to be overly concerned about it. And the other half don't constitute some mystical force called the "general will." The 100 million voters, in this reading, are merely 100 million citizens making discrete decisions, the motives for which are rightly ineffable.

I include myself among the hard-asses holding this view, which has a clear upshot: that a strict, clear, technical standard for a vote should be maintained at all costs. That's why I believe, contra the Democrats, that Florida's hand recounts in selective counties should have been halted pronto and that, contra the Republicans, the strictest standards should be applied to overseas military ballots as well—even if it means throwing many of them into the trash. That's why I support [the] entirely reasonable interpretation of Florida law…that manual recounts should only be conducted if the machines have clearly malfunctioned….

This is a genuine philosophical disagreement—and it matters. It matters because the Gore campaign's endgame is of a piece with its dragging the Clintonized Democrats back to the left. It's clear, for example, that Gore's passionate faith in affirmative action and hate-crime laws stems from the same outlook. What matters, to Gore, is justice. And by justice he means not the strict application of formal legal norms but the flexibility of those norms in the hands of well-meaning people to get the just result: "law which has meaning," as he recently put it. So, even if there's no evidence that universities are racist in denying places to minority applicants, the admissions boards should still ignore technical things like test scores and admit enough minority students to achieve fairness. Similarly with the criminal law: Where once we simply determined whether a crime was committed or not, now we inquire further into the intent of the criminal to see whether his bigotry demands greater punishment. Otherwise, we are told, justice in its fullest sense will not be done. From affirmative action and hate-crime laws it's a small step to ensuring that all voters, however negligent, have their intent, however vague, reflected in the final result of an election. Call it affirmative action voting—the apotheosis of modern liberalism.

This is a far more important issue than who wins the election. What matters now is not who wins but how he wins. If Gore wins this way, the main result, apart from a right-wing backlash of untold ferocity, will be a blow to the careful formalism of our electoral system. It will open the floodgates for an onslaught of lawyers into every nook and cranny of our electoral system, in races up and down the country. After that, the electoral college will be targeted. A Gore victory through judicially imposed, loosely interpreted hand counts in South Florida will resonate across the country as the triumph of a liberalism that has replaced responsibility with victimhood, law with legalism, character with partisanship. Rather than challenging voters to a new civic responsibility, the Democrats are defining down democracy to include those who cannot even be held responsible for following a simple ballot instruction. The sad truth is that Gore is now undermining the very ethic of responsibility he once defended. I hope, for his sake, that this isn't the way he wins.

The Butterfly Debacle

Political Staff of the Washington Post

The ballot problem in Palm Beach County wound up having little effect, legally, on the 2000 election. It was a disheartening experience, however, for those citizens who felt their vote had gone to waste.

The frustrations of dealing with the "butterfly" are captured in the *Washington Post*'s account of the election, *Deadlock,* the first and still one of the very best chronicles of the Bush-Gore struggle.

The Bermans are two of the 14,000 retired people who live in Century Village, a sprawling, sun-baked complex, part barracks, part country club—and one of the largest, purest concentrations of Democratic votes on the planet. There are state party chairmen in America who don't have the pull of the party boss at Century Village. A Democrat running statewide in Florida can take an 8,000- or 10,000-vote cushion out of just this complex—and there are others approaching its scale all down the Gold Coast of South Florida. That margin is then whittled away by Republican retirees on the Gulf Coast, by farmers in central Florida and by the Deep South conservatives in northern Florida. This is the basic dynamic of all statewide races—southeast Florida versus the rest of the state, with the central Florida suburbs gaining more power every year.

Rachel Berman awoke at 6 a.m. on Election Day to take her daily two-mile walk. Paul rose an hour and a half later, when he heard his wife's key in the lock. Today would be a good day, they thought. They wanted to vote for Gore—but even more, they wanted to vote for Lieberman, "my *lands-*

Excerpted from the Political Staff of *The Washington Post, Deadlock: The Inside Story of America's Closest Election,* published by Public Affairs, pp. 67–70. Reprinted by permission.

man," as Paul Berman called the first Jew on a major party ticket. He was not alone. The old hands in Palm Beach County would credit Lieberman with catalyzing one of the strongest Democratic turnouts in the county's history.

From their apartment, the Bermans could see the large clubhouse, a two-story brick and stucco building a brisk six-minute walk away, where half of Century Village voted. The clubhouse polling station was in a large room that served as bingo hall, dining room and ballroom, where the Bermans like to do the polka and the Lindy Hop on the parquet dance floor.

That morning the lines to vote were "unbelievable," Paul Berman recalled. "Everybody showed up." After standing in line for 20 minutes, the Bermans reached the registration table, only to be asked for identification, which they didn't have. No matter. They decided to go swimming first—it was not yet 10:30 a.m.

They stood in line again, and this time, they were given cards to insert in the Votomatic machines. "I was voting straight Democratic," Rachel Berman said later. "So I don't know whether there was one hole or two holes. I saw Gore, I punched Gore."...

Paul Berman did not notice anything odd until he was patting his "I voted" sticker onto his polo shirt. There was a commotion. Gradually, as he sorted out the buzz, Paul realized that he had been so intent on voting for Lieberman that he had voted twice. "I voted for Gore, but I also voted for the vice president. I punched two holes instead of one....I said, 'Oh my God, I think I did it wrong.' All I had to do was just punch Gore. It would have been sufficient. But I saw Lieberman—so I punched it, too."

Democratic officials all over the state were bombarded with complaints, and at 11:24 a.m., an attorney for the party sent a fax to Theresa LePore asking her to order deputy supervisors to put up signs in polling places, and issue instructions, clarifying the butterfly ballot. Three and a half hours later, the party faxed another request to LePore, this time requesting special attention to whether the punch holes lined up properly with the ballot.

"Theresa was in a coma," Gore's Florida strategist, Nick Baldick, said later.

Phone lines to elections headquarters in West Palm Beach rang and rang unanswered. When Lois Frankel, the Democratic leader of the Florida House of Representatives, drove to LePore's office around 2 p.m., she recalled, LePore told her: "There's no way to communicate. We have over 500 precincts and the only way we can communicate is they call us."

"Well, they can't call you because the lines have been jammed all day," Frankel answered. So LePore sat down to draft a memo. "ATTENTION ALL POLLWORKERS," the memo began, in bold, underlined letters.

"Please remind ALL voters coming in that they are to vote only for one (1) presidential candidate and that they are to punch the hole next to the arrow next to the number next to the candidate they wish to vote for." "How are we going to get them out?" Frankel remembered asking. "I've no way to get them out," LePore answered.

Was Gore's Strategy in Florida Constitutional? The Forgotten Circuit Court Dissents

As noted, after Judge Middlebrooks's decision in the injunction case, the constitutionality of recounting a statewide election in only four counties was not addressed by any other court during the protest and recount phases of the Florida election, which lasted until November 26. After that, for reasons we will examine later, this issue became largely moot.

On December 6, however, during the last phases of the 2000 election controversy, several judges of the Eleventh Circuit Court of Appeals, most notably Ed Carnes and Gerald Tjoflat, took on the matter of selective counting, as they dissented from the circuit court's final denial of the Bush injunction request. (Somewhat inaccurately, though prophetically as it turned out, Judge Carnes focused not on undervotes, but on total no-votes—overvotes and undervotes.)

Though coming too late to be of any practical relevance, the dissents make a vigorous case against the legality of the basic approach to recounting adopted by Vice President Gore.

Dissenting Opinion of Judge Gerald Tjoflat
in *Touchton v. McDermott*

If [as Vice President Gore essentially maintains] the vote tabulating machines serve merely as a screening device in counting valid votes, then the legislature, in enacting sections 102.166 (4)-(7), inaptly refers to the process of manually counting dimple votes as a "recount." In fact, a county's *initial* vote count (including the automatic recount) is not complete until all ballots containing non-votes in any race have been examined manually. Nevertheless, section 102.166 (4) provides that such a manual examination of ballots will be conducted only at a candidate or political party's request, and only in those specific counties chosen by the candidate or political party.... [I]t precludes the counting of remaining votes except in those counties selected by a candidate or his party. Under this "selective dimple model," dimple votes cast in a county where no "recount" is requested are simply not counted.... The model, therefore, lends itself to several undesirable results.

Since the selective dimple model leaves to the candidates the decision of whether and where dimple votes should be included in the final vote tally, the system encourages candidates to cherry-pick—to carefully select the counties in which to request that ballots be manually examined for dimple votes. Under the selective dimple model, a candidate will choose the counties based on: (1) the percentage of the total machine-tabulated vote received; (2) the size of the county, measured by the total number of ballots cast in the election; and (3) the political makeup of the canvassing board in the county. A candidate will want dimple votes counted in counties where he captured a greater proportion of the machine tabulated vote than did his opponent, because the candidate can expect that he will likely take a similar

---

From Dissenting Opinion of Judge Gerald Tjoflat in *Touchton v. McDermott*, 234 F. 3d 1133, 1143–1145, 1150–1151.

proportion of the dimple votes. A candidate will favor counties where the most ballots were cast because those counties will have the most dimple votes. The political composition of the county canvassing board will be critical to a candidate in making selective manual count requests for two reasons. First, the election statutes give the canvassing board unfettered discretion to honor a candidate's request to manually examine ballots. Second, if the canvassing board grants the request, the election system affords the canvassing board unfettered discretion to set the standards for determining which markings on a ballot demonstrate voter intent sufficient to constitute a vote. Thus, a candidate is more likely to have his request for a manual count granted, and to receive favorable interpretations of voter intent, in counties where the candidate shares a political party affiliation with the majority of the canvassing board.

[Furthermore] section 102.166 (5) allows the county canvassing board to conduct a recount only if the results of the recount "could affect the outcome of the election." Seemingly, the candidate who received the most votes state-wide according to the machine tabulation could never demonstrate that a manual recount of any county could affect the outcome of the election, since adding dimple votes would only serve to increase that candidate's margin of victory. Thus, it is doubtful that a county canvassing board would, in its discretion, grant such a candidate's request for the sample manual recount. Arguably, however, granting the candidate's request could affect the outcome of the election if his opponent is granted full recounts in other counties, and thereby gains a significant number of votes. Given that the canvassing board has limited time to certify the election results, and that one board may not know whether another county will manually recount its ballots, I question exactly what remains to guide a canvassing board in its decision to grant or deny a manual count.

The selective dimple model also encourages candidates to manipulate the timing of manual recount requests, so as to use the statutory limitations period to foreclose his opponent from making his own requests for manual counts. Since the manual recount statute cuts off a candidate's right to request a manual examination of ballots, a candidate who stays his request until the midnight hour may pin his opponent against the statutory deadline. Thus, by gaming the timing and location of recount requests under the selective dimple model, a candidate can maximize the count of dimple votes cast for him, while minimizing the number of dimple votes counted for his opponent....

These observations underscore the adversarial structure of the Florida scheme which allows candidates to play games with individual rights. The selective dimple model puts voters in no better a position than children in a schoolyard game yelling, "Pick me, pick me!" The candidates, as team captains, will only choose those who are sure to help them win. Smaller, less populated counties—like frail schoolchildren—have almost no chance of being picked. At the end of choosing teams, those who aren't chosen simply don't get to play. This scheme clearly contravenes the long-settled principle that "[q]ualified citizens not only have a constitutionally protected right to vote, but also the right to have their votes counted." *Duncan v. Poythress*, 657 F. 2d 691, 700 (5th Cir. Unit B 1981).... The Florida vote counting model...works to deprive voters of their right to vote based on their county of residence and thereby denies them equal protection of the laws.

Dissenting Opinion of Judge Ed Carnes
in *Siegel v. Lepore*

[T]he 3 counties chosen by the [Democratic] Party on a statewide basis [for recounting] are the most populous and vote-rich of all the punch-card counties, and in each of them the Party's nominee received substantially more votes than his principal opponent.

Not only that, but we also see from the data...another conspicuous fact. The 3 counties the Florida Democratic party selected for manual recounts are 3 of the 4 punch card counties that gave its nominee the highest percentage of the vote cast among the two opposing Presidential candidates. Those percentages are as follows: Broward (68.55%); Palm Beach (63.81%); and Miami-Dade (53.18%). No other punch card county gave the Party's nominee a greater percentage of its vote than Broward and Palm Beach Counties, and only one punch card county gave the Party's nominee a greater percentage of its vote than Miami-Dade County did. That lone exception is sparsely populated Jefferson County which, although favoring the Party's nominee with 55.10% of its vote, cast a total of only 5,519 votes for the nominees of both major parties (compared, for example, to the 618,335 votes cast for them in Miami-Dade County). Because so few votes were cast in Jefferson County, that county offered little prospect for finding enough uncounted votes to make a difference. In effect, the voters of Jefferson County were too few in number to matter in view of the Party's objective, which was to change the election result that had been reported to that date.

Given the theory of the recount—finding intended votes that were not counted by the punch card system—the most relevant data of all would be the percentage of votes that were intended but not counted. We do not have

From Dissenting Opinion of Judge Ed Carnes in *Siegel v. Lepore,* 234 F. 3d 1163, 1202–1204, 1206.

that, but...[w]e do have the "no vote" data, which shows the difference between the total number of voters who cast a ballot and the total votes cast for any Presidential candidate. [T]he no vote data shows the number of ballots in which no vote for President was counted either because the tabulating machine did not pick up from the punch card any vote for President, or because it picked up two or more votes for President on the same card resulting in no vote for President being counted....

If Palm Beach, Miami-Dade, and Broward Counties had been selected for manual recounts because of problems resulting in no vote for President being picked up by the tabulating machines, those 3 counties would have the highest no vote rates. They do not. [T]here are 7 punch card counties with a higher percentage of no votes in the Presidential race than Palm Beach County, yet none of them was selected for manual recounts.... Ten punch card counties have a higher percentage of no votes than Miami-Dade County, but none of them was selected for a manual recount. And as for Broward County, there were 17 punch card counties with a higher no vote rate that were not selected for manual recounts. In fact, Broward is tied for the fourth smallest percentage of no votes for President among all of the 24 punch card counties, yet the Florida Democratic Party still selected it for a manual recount.

One of the many affidavits the Florida Democratic Party submitted in the district court stated that "two groups of citizens, the elderly and minorities, are more prone to have problems on this system than the rest of the population."... Perhaps that opinion rests upon derogatory stereotypes that federal courts should not countenance. Even assuming, however, that there is some factual basis for that opinion and that we should consider the possibility, the problems that any group, including the elderly and minorities, have with punch card voting should be captured to some extent in the no vote data.... But as we have seen, the Party's selection of the 3 counties cannot be justified on the basis of that data.

Moreover, [ranking of] the punch card counties by percentage of population over the age of 65, shows that 7 of those counties that were not selected for manual recounts have a greater percentage of their population in that age category than Palm Beach County does; 11 not selected for manual recounts have a greater percentage in that age category than Broward County does; and 13 of them have a greater percentage in that age category than Miami-Dade County does. The Florida Democratic Party's selection of punch card counties for manual recounts could not have been based upon the percentage of elderly in each county's population.

As for "minorities" having more problems with punch card voting, it is unclear exactly what the Florida Democratic Party's affiant meant by "minorities." [I]f he meant to include both blacks and Hispanics in that grouping, Miami-Dade County's population does have a higher percentage of minorities than any other punch card county. But...6 punch card counties that were not selected for manual recounts have a higher percentage of minorities in their populations than Broward County, which was selected. And...8 punch card counties that were not selected for manual recounts have a higher percentage of minorities in their population than Palm Beach County which was also selected.

So, the facts we have about the Florida Democratic Party's selection of the counties in which a manual recount would be undertaken in order to ensure that voters were not disenfranchised by systemic problems with punch card technology or by carelessness, are these. The selection was not based upon the rate of punch card error—the no vote rate—nor was it based upon the relative percentage of senior citizens or minorities in each county's population. Instead, the defining characteristic of the 3 punch card counties chosen to undertake a manual recount is that they are the 3 most populous counties in the state, all of which gave the Party's Presidential nominee a higher percentage of the vote than his opponent.

Of course, none of this is surprising. We expect political parties to act in their own best political interest, and the 3 most populous counties that had voted for its nominee presented the Florida Democratic Party with its best prospects for turning the election around. It would not have served the Party's goal of electing its nominee for President for it to have sought the intended but unsuccessful votes in those punch card counties that went for the other party's nominee, Governor George W. Bush. The votes in 17 of the 24 punch card counties favored Governor Bush.... Making sure that every intended vote was counted in those 17 counties that favored Bush over Gore, over two-thirds of the total number of punch card counties, was not the way for the Florida Democratic Party to get its candidate elected....

If Florida enacted a statute that provided a manual recount procedure for correcting the undervote caused by the use of the punch card voting system, but provided that the corrective procedure could be invoked only in the 3 most populous counties of the state, no one would question that such a provision would be unconstitutional....

The reason we would or should be unanimous in holding such a law unconstitutional is that states cannot treat votes differently depending upon the counties in which the voters live.... [This] hypothetical statute is not far removed from the statute that Florida [actually] does have.

PART 2

THE FIRST SHOWDOWN

The Florida recount process started as early as November 11, and by November 13 it was clear the federal district court would not stop it. But the recounts would very quickly become entangled in the web of Florida law and practice.

The Florida courts had decided that county canvassing boards possessed broad discretion to accept or reject a recount request, according to their interpretation of Section 166.[1] On Thursday, November 9, Volusia County exercised its discretion and decided to do a full manual recount starting on Saturday. Palm Beach County agreed to start a sample recount the same day. Such actions seemed to endorse the view that a close election was sufficient reason for recounting ballots, though Volusia County had experienced some quickly corrected machine trouble on election night.

The Palm Beach canvassing board found Gore had gained 19 votes in the four precincts counted, and at 2 A.M. on Sunday, November 12, voted 2-1 to do a complete hand recount, starting on Tuesday, November 14.[2] The dissenter was Judge Charles Burton, the board's chairman, who, after hearing the views of a lawyer from the state department's division of elections who was present at the meeting, felt the board should not go forward with any recounts until it had plumbed the meaning of Section 166's indefinite references to close elections and machine malfunctions. "I was concerned," Burton later said, "about whether we could lawfully go forward, based on the fact we were dealing with voter error, versus machine error."[3]

That Sunday, Judge Burton did some research in his chambers, and found that as chair of the Palm Beach canvassing board he could request a legal opinion about the validity of the county's recount.[4] Burton immediately wrote to Clayton Roberts, head of the division of elections, and a key subordinate of Secretary Harris. The next day he also wrote to Attorney General Robert Butterworth, Gore's campaign chairman in Florida, who had urged the board by fax to request an opinion from him. Burton asked each:

> Would a discrepancy between the number of votes determined by a tabulation system and by a manual recount of four precincts be considered an "error in voting tabulation" which could affect the outcome of an election within the meaning of Section 102.166(5), Florida Statutes, thereby enabling the canvassing board to request a manual recount of the entire county, or are "errors" confined to errors in tabulation system/software?[5]

Meanwhile, the Broward County canvassing board met on November 13. Its sample recount found only four additional votes for Gore, and, partly for this reason, the board voted 2-1 not to proceed with a full recount. But one of the Democratic members of the canvassing board, Judge Robert Lee, voted against proceeding because he was aware of a memorandum from the secretary of state's office that provided an emphatic answer to Judge Burton's question.[6] The memo was addressed to Republican state chairman Al Cardenas, who had made inquiries of Clayton Roberts almost identical to the ones Burton raised. Cardenas was persuaded to do this on the afternoon of Sunday, November 12, by Frank Jimenez, who had just taken a leave of absence as Governor Jeb Bush's acting general counsel to work on the presidential recount. Jimenez acted after learning from Clay Roberts that Burton's request had not yet arrived. (It was found on Sunday night.)[7]

Roberts's memo to Cardenas staunchly denied the validity of the kind of recount Gore was anticipating, and the canvassing boards were beginning to do. Read in the overall context of Section 102.166, Roberts claimed, the phrase "error in the vote tabulation" actually referred to an error in the vote tabulation *system* of a precinct or of a county, a failure of the electronic equipment to properly do its job. "An 'error in the vote tabulation' means a *counting error* in which the *vote tabulation system* fails to count properly marked [optical-scanner ballots] or properly punched punchcard ballots."[8] These errors came solely from mechanical defects, such as a glitch in the "reporting software of the voting system,"[9] and had nothing to do with close elections per se.

Thus the inability of a vote counter "to read an improperly marked [scanner ballot] or improperly punched punchcard ballot is not an 'error in the vote tabulation' and would not trigger the requirement for [a] county canvassing board to take [any] of the actions"[10] listed in Section 102.166. For Roberts, hanging chads that had possibly gone uncounted were no justification for a recount, though he does not relate this contention to the improperly executed punchcards that *did* get counted by a properly functioning machine.

This legal position was not without merit. Still, Roberts and Secretary

Harris were Republicans and Bush loyalists, who were undoubtedly out-
raged by the selective pattern of recounts that had emerged. Harris served
as co-chair of Governor Bush's Florida campaign. Furthermore, she took as
her key advisor during the recount crisis a powerful lawyer-lobbyist named
"Mac" Stipanovich, who had ties to Governor Jeb Bush, and who embarked
on this assignment at the behest of George Bush's team in Florida. His constant advice to the secretary was to "bring the election to an end, force it
down the funnel, bring it in for a landing."[11]

Stipanovich refused later to say whether he fed information to George
Bush or his brother. "[Tallahassee's] a small town. I know a lot of people
and I talk to them all the time."[12] Asked whether he was aware of Harris's
instruction to her aides to avoid contact with the Bush campaign,
Stipanovich replied, "She couldn't give me instructions. I didn't work for
her."[13]

By November 14, Judge Burton had received his reply from Roberts,
containing the same sentiments expressed in the memo to Cardenas, though
it did not refer specifically to "improperly punched" ballots.[14] But when the
Palm Beach board met that day, Burton also possessed the memorandum
from Attorney General Butterworth. Butterworth took sharp issue with his
Republican colleagues.

Section 102.166, he noted, spoke of an "error in the vote tabulation,"
not an error in the vote tabulation "system," as the Roberts opinion tried to
assume.[15] "The opinion ignores the plain language of the statute."[16] A mistake in vote totals "might be caused by a mechanical malfunction in the
operation of the vote counting system, but the error might also result from
the failure of a properly functioning . . . system to discern the choices of the
voters as revealed by the ballots."[17] That was why the statute gave a canvassing board several possible courses of action should an "error" occur,
though the secretary deliberately sought to "blur [these] distinctions."[18] Not
only statutory language, but judicial precedent pointed to a broad tolerance
for voter miscues. Roberts's opinion failed "to acknowledge the longstanding case law in Florida which has held that the intent of the voter as shown
by their ballots should be given effect," that where "a ballot is marked so as
to plainly indicate the voter's choice and intent, it should be counted as
marked unless some positive provision of law would be violated."[19]

Getting wind of the Butterworth opinion, Judge Lee changed his vote
on November 14, and Broward County commenced a full manual recount.[20]
Palm Beach initially decided to do the same, but then voted to suspend all
counting while the board sought a declaratory judgment from the Florida
Supreme Court telling its members whether the secretary of state or the
attorney general was right.[21] The Democratic Party of Florida immediately
went to circuit court on November 14, and asked Judge Jorge LaBarga to
order resumption of the counting. LaBarga had responded the same day to a

citizen suit challenging the entire Palm Beach manual recount by holding
that the board possessed authority to do the count and submit it to Secretary
Harris. "If she decides to accept [it], fine. If she doesn't, then you need to
talk to her about it."[22] The judge did not interfere, however, with Palm
Beach's decision to withhold action until the state supreme court answered
its question.[23]

Hence, on November 15, Palm Beach officials filed their emergency
petition with the supreme court, asking it to adjudicate between the Harris-
Roberts and Butterworth opinions. "The dispute squarely presented by this
case," the petition claimed, "—whether the Palm Beach County canvassing
board may proceed with a manual recount of the ballots cast for President
of the United States—has assumed . . . national significance, because it
affects the ultimate tally of votes certified by Florida voters to the electoral
college, in an election in which the results literally hinge upon the outcome
in Florida."[24]

The result of this litigation appeared to be of no significance to Miami-
Dade County. The county canvassing board finally met on November 14,
and after agreeing to and conducting a sample recount that showed a shift
of six votes to Gore, voted not to do a full recount.[25]

The Other Question: Deadlines

While all of this was going on, the legality of the recounts became closely
bound up with another question: whether their legal status really made any
difference. As Judge Burton and other observers could see, the Palm Beach
recount, even if approved, figured to go on well past the November 14
deadline for submission of election returns. The same was true of Broward
County's recount, and possibly of Volusia's.

But Burton was unclear whether this meant late returns could never be
accepted. For while Section 102.111 of the election code did say "returns . .
. not received by the Department of State by 5 P.M. of the seventh day following an election,...*shall* be ignored,"[26] the succeeding section of the
code provided that if returns were "not received . . . by the time specified,
such returns *may* be ignored"[27] (though the section also imposed a $200-a-
day fine for late returns).[28]

Hence, on November 13, Burton had addressed a second inquiry to
Clayton Roberts, wanting to know what the conjunction of subsections 111
and 112 meant for the legal deadline, whether the Department of State
might certify election results submitted after November 14, as a result of
approved manual recounts.

The department's response was again immediate and emphatic, mirror-
ing, perhaps, Harris's and Roberts's political orientation, but also reflecting

their belief that manual recounts of the type the Democrats envisioned could not possibly be legal. "[I]f the Palm Beach County canvassing board fails to certify the county returns . . . by 5:00 P.M. of the seventh day following the election, the votes cast in Palm Beach County will *not* be counted in the certification of the statewide results."[29] Section 102.111 was "explicitly mandatory" on this point, and while 102.112 gave a little leeway, it actually covered only "unforeseen circumstances not specifically contemplated by the legislature," such as "Hurricane Andrew."[30]

The secretary's office informed the other counties conducting recounts of her views, and Volusia, though making great progress on its hand count, went to circuit court; the county sought a temporary injunction requiring Harris to accept recount totals submitted after 5 P.M. on November 14. (To be on the safe side, Volusia originally filed its suit on November 9.) Since the secretary's office was in Tallahassee, proper jurisdiction lay in the Leon County circuit. Palm Beach County joined the suit, as did Vice President Gore and the Florida Democratic Party. George Bush entered on the side of Secretary Harris.

Judge Terry Lewis's decision on November 14 did not grant the injunction. But by putting 111 and 112 in the overall context of Florida election procedures, Judge Lewis found the latter definitely controlling, and the secretary's discretion under it less unyielding than her November 13 communiqué asserted.

The first point became evident, the judge thought, when one laid the deadline statutes alongside Section 102.166, particularly the provision allowing a candidate seventy-two hours after an election (at a minimum) to request a manual recount. Considering the possible need for a sample count, and evaluation of its results, "it is easy to imagine a situation where a manual recount could be lawfully authorized, commenced, but not completed within seven days of the election."[31] Indeed, "only in sparsely populated counties could a Canvassing Board safely exercise what the Legislature has clearly intended to be an option where the Board has a real question as to the accuracy of a vote."[32]

Furthermore, Judge Lewis noted that through the consent decree with the federal government, Florida authorities had agreed to wait until ten days after a national election before declaring overseas absentee ballots due, meaning they would fully certify the election returns of 2000 only on November 18, not November 14. "The Secretary explains this anomaly by inferring a requirement to do one certification of results seven days after the election and a 'supplemental certification' ten days after the election. There is, however, no statutory provision that provides for such a supplemental certification."[33]

Since all of this proved 102.112 took precedence over 102.111 (which Judge Lewis barely mentioned in his opinion), it was certainly within the broad "discretion" of the secretary of state to accept, or not accept, supplemental election returns submitted after the statutory deadline. But for her to decree "ahead of time that such returns *will* be ignored, . . . unless caused by some Act of God, is not the exercise of discretion. It is the abdication of that discretion."[34] The proper exercise of discretion, Judge Lewis ruled, "contemplates a decision based upon a weighing and consideration of all attendant facts and circumstances."[35]

> [W]hen was the request for recount made? What were the reasons given? When did the Canvassing Board decide to do a manual recount? What was the basis for determination that such a recount was the appropriate action? How late were the results?
>
> Obviously, the list of scenarios is almost endless and the questions that would need to be asked in properly exercising discretion as to whether to ignore or not ignore late filed returns are numerous. The Secretary may, and should, consider all of the facts and circumstances.
>
> The County Canvassing Boards are, indeed, mandated to certify and file their returns with the Secretary of State by 5:00 P.M. today, November 14, 2000. There is nothing, however, to prevent the County Canvassing Boards from filing with the Secretary of State further returns after completing a manual recount. It is then up to the Secretary of State, as the Chief Election Officer, to determine whether any such corrective or supplemental returns filed after 5:00 P.M. today, are to be ignored.[36]

Judge Lewis's reasoning made it clear that even under the secretary's interpretation of 102.166, a mandatory deadline could wreak havoc. Thus if a candidate asked for a recount in a large county, based on machine error, at midnight on the Friday after an election, the canvassing board would have to complete its sample by the next afternoon if it hoped to meet the seven-day deadline, yet needed to ask the secretary of state's office for verification of the election software, since 166(10) gave the secretary "3 working days" to respond to such a request. And it was entirely possible (as the secretary's lawyers well knew) that her office would find the error in the tabulation software beyond repair. Then, the "or" in 102.166 notwithstanding, a full hand count was supposed to commence, after the seven-day deadline for submitting vote returns had passed.

Some of the language in Lewis's opinion could be read as requiring Secretary Harris to wait until she actually received a late return before deciding whether to accept it (e.g., "It is *then* up to the Secretary of State," "[T]he Secretary cannot decide ahead of time what late returns should or should not be ignored").[37] Other language, though, indicates the secretary may review the "decision" of the county canvassing board to undertake a recount (e.g., "What was the basis for determination that such a recount was the appropriate action?").

Secretary Harris Acts

The secretary assembled all the totals sent to her by the afternoon of November 14. These included the full hand recount from Volusia County, which appealed Judge Lewis's decision in the morning, then met the 5 P.M. deadline. That evening, in deference to the judge's orders, Harris requested "counties contemplating manual vote recounts to submit a written statement to me of the facts and circumstances justifying any belief on their part that they should be allowed to amend the certified returns previously filed by them in accordance with law."[38] The query was aimed at Palm Beach and Broward Counties, though Miami-Dade also took up the secretary's offer and asked to add results of the sample done just as the deadline passed.

It was not hard to guess how Secretary Harris would utilize her authority, considering the view she took of manual recounts. Her replies to the counties on November 15 listed the "Facts and Circumstances Warranting Waiver of [the] Statutory Deadline" for receiving returns; deriving from Florida case law, these now expanded to include "proof of voter fraud that affects the outcome of [an] election," "substantial noncompliance" with election law, and "a mechanical malfunction of the *voting tabulation system.*"[39]

Balanced against this were "facts and circumstances" clearly ruling out the activities under way in Palm Beach and Broward Counties, and even providing a hedge against possible action in the butterfly controversy.

Facts & Circumstances Not Warranting Waiver of Statutory Deadline

2. Where there exists a ballot that may be confusing because of the alignment and location of the candidates' names, but is otherwise in substantial compliance with the election laws.
3. Where there is nothing "*more than a mere possibility that the outcome of the election would have been affected.*"[40]

There was no attempt to square this last "circumstance" with the language in 102.166 providing for a full manual recount because of "an error in the vote tabulation which could affect the outcome of the election"; that passage was obviously thought irrelevant to the controversy at hand.

At a press conference on the evening of November 15, Secretary Harris underlined the fact that she had "exercise[d] my discretion"[41] in rejecting the boards' requests, and her lawyers consistently defended her actions in those terms. In fact, she could, probably should, have concluded that Florida law, as she interpreted it, gave her *no* discretion to accept the canvassing boards' petitions, or their recounts, since the recounts were illegal.

Harris's view of the election statute, in Judge Richard Posner's words, allowed her "discretion to disregard results *not* barred by the statute" (such as late returns occasioned by a machine breakdown), but *"compelled* [her] to ignore [results the statute] barred."[42]

Harris and her lawyers also neglected what was their strongest justification for refusing to allow time for the particular recounts involved in 2000, even if those recounts were adjudged legal. They might have maintained from the outset, as eventually they did, that in the case of elections for president, the secretary of state's discretion concerning deadlines was limited by a provision of federal law stipulating that only if a state arranged for the final settlement of all disputes concerning presidential electors by December 12 could the state put its slate of electors beyond challenge from any opposing slate, once the certified returns were sent to Congress.

This provision was part of the Electoral Count Act of 1887, passed in the wake of the Hayes-Tilden affray eleven years earlier. Section 5 of the act (as later codified in Part 3 of the United States Code) stated:

> If any State shall have provided, by laws enacted prior to the day fixed for the appointment of the electors, for its final determination of any controversy or contest concerning the appointment of all or any of the electors of such State, by judicial or other methods or procedures, and such determination shall have been made at least six days before the time fixed for the meeting of the electors [that time was December 18 in 2000], such determination made pursuant to such law so existing on said day, and made at least six days prior to said time of meeting of the electors, shall be conclusive, and shall govern in the counting of the electoral votes . . . , so far as the ascertainment of the electors appointed by such State is concerned.[43]

No one had fully explored at this stage whether Section 5 embodied a requirement of federal law, whether Florida, through its legislature, had decided this deadline must be observed, or whether adhering to the deadline might simply be within the discretion of a secretary of state, to protect the state's interests. (There was no Florida statute on the subject.) But Harris's lawyers, it turned out after November 15, felt the deadline was mandatory, probably as a matter of federal law.

Under any circumstances, this could have been the ideal justification for Harris's actions. Florida law gave an "unsuccessful candidate,"[44] or a disgruntled voter, ten days from the time of the certification deadline to move on to the next stage of the electoral process, and file an election contest suit in a Florida circuit court under Section 102.168 of the state code.[45] The county canvassing board, the defendant in such a proceeding, had ten days to respond to the complaint.[46]

This meant that even under the secretary's "discretionary" November 14 deadline, and her rigid refusal to allow recounts to run past that date, it would take an expedited briefing and deposition schedule to keep a contest trial from starting on December 4, just eight days before the December 12 guarantee date, with appeals to follow. Indeed, had Harris used common sense, and allowed amended returns to come in until midnight, November 17, since final certification did not commence until then anyway, she could surely have claimed she was doing all in her power to reconcile the demands of the Electoral Count Act with respect for the popular will, even granting the manual recounts in Palm Beach and Broward Counties were a valid expression of that will. Surely, a deadline much beyond November 18 was highly implausible. Yet the counties could never have completed their recounts by midnight of November 17—or of November 19—and the effect of those final totals on the outcome in Florida, however a court finally treated the matter, would have had to go over to a contest phase.[47]

To the Florida Supreme Court

After rejecting all the appeals for extensions, Secretary Harris and her two colleagues on the state canvassing commission certified the Florida election results received by 5 P.M. on November 14. A complete certification, Harris stated, would take place after the counting of the overseas absentee ballots.[48] Knowing the Gore forces would appeal her actions, she filed a petition in the Florida Supreme Court to halt any further hand counts "pending final resolution as to whether any basis exists to modify the certified results after the statutory deadline."[49] (It was refused.)

On November 16, Gore and the Democratic Party did indeed go to court again. They appealed to Terry Lewis, claiming Harris violated his previous order by "arbitrarily"[50] deciding to ignore amended returns. The Florida attorneys considered summoning Secretary Harris herself as a witness, but the campaign leadership in Washington vetoed the idea. Thus the lawyers called no witnesses at all, to Judge Lewis's annoyance.

The next morning, Lewis issued a brief, taut opinion upholding Secretary Harris's actions. He stressed that his previous order granted "to the Secretary, as the Chief Election Officer, broad discretionary authority to accept or reject late filed returns"; and on the admittedly *"limited evidence presented*, it appears that the Secretary has exercised her reasoned judgment to determine what relevant factors and criteria should be considered, applied them to the facts and circumstances pertinent to the individual counties involved, and made her decision. My order requires nothing more."[51]

The plaintiffs went immediately to Florida's First District Court of Appeals and asked that body to send their appeal of Judge Lewis's decision to the state supreme court, under so-called pass through arrangements provided in the Florida constitution.[52] The court of appeals did so, and on the afternoon of November 17, the supreme court accepted the case and combined it with the Palm Beach County declaratory judgment case filed on November 15. The previous day, the court had issued an interim order in that case; based in part on Judge LaBarga's authority, it permitted hand counts to move forward in Palm Beach, pending judgment, and the board resumed counting on the evening of November 16.[53]

Gore's lawyers had decided not to ask the Florida Supreme Court for an injunction to stop the complete certification of the Florida vote while it heard their appeal of Judge Lewis's decision. The attorneys were certain they could not demonstrate the "irreparable harm" needed for such an order, though it meant that over the weekend Bush would reap the public-relations benefits of a certification ceremony. But on their own initiative, the justices combined their November 17 acceptance of the appeal with an order forbidding Secretary Harris from finishing certification of Florida's presidential results "until further notice of this court"[54] (meaning the overseas absentee totals would remain temporarily uncertified). This was the first sign of the court's displeasure with the secretary of state.

To complicate matters further, the Miami-Dade canvassing board met on November 17 and decided to do a full manual recount.[55]

Notes

1. *Broward County Canvassing Board v. Hogan*, 607 So. 2d 508, 510 (Fla. 4th DCA 1992).
2. Don Van Natta Jr. and Rick Bragg, "Scrutiny and Disagreements Accompany Hand Recount," *New York Times*, November 13, 2000, p. A18. (A truncated version is found in Correspondents of *The New York Times, 36 Days* [New York: Times Books, 2001], p. 48.)
3. "Contest Trial Before Judge Sauls," p. 277, www.flcourts.org.
4. Jeffrey Toobin, *Too Close to Call* (New York: Random House, 2001), p. 91.
5. Letter from Judge Charles Burton to Clayton Roberts, November 13, 2000, *Palm Beach County Canvassing Board v. Harris*, Florida Supreme Court, "Emergency Petition for Extraordinary Writ," Appendix A; Letter from Judge Charles Burton to Attorney General Robert Butterworth, November 13, 2000, *Harris v. The Circuit Judges* et al., Florida Supreme Court, "Emergency Petition for Extraordinary Relief," Appendix 11.
6. Dana Canedy, "After a Partial Recount, Broward County Drops the Whole Idea," November 14, 2000, in Correspondents of *The New York Times, 36 Days*, p. 65.
7. Toobin, *Too Close to Call*, pp. 74–75.
8. Division of Elections, Advisory Opinion DE 00-11: "Definitions of Errors in Vote Tabulation," November 13, 2000, reprinted in E. J. Dionne and William Kristol (eds.), *Bush v. Gore: The Court Cases and the Commentary* (Washington, D.C.: Brookings Institution Press, 2001), p. 11 (italics added).

9. Ibid.
10. Ibid.
11. David A. Kaplan, *The Accidental President* (New York: William Morrow, 2001), p. 108.
12. The Political Staff of *The Washington Post, Deadlock: The Inside Story of America's Closest Election* (New York: Public Affairs, 2001), p. 85.
13. Kaplan, *The Accidental President*, p. 109.
14. Advisory Opinion DE 00-13: "Manual Recount Procedures and Partial Certification of County Returns," November 13, 2000, reprinted in Dionne and Kristol (eds.), *Bush v. Gore*, pp. 12–14.
15. Florida Attorney General Advisory Legal Opinion, "Manual Recount of Ballots, Error in Vote Tabulation," November 14, 2000, reprinted in Dionne and Kristol (eds.), *Bush v. Gore*, p. 15.
16. Ibid.
17. Ibid.
18. Ibid.
19. Ibid., p. 17.
20. *Palm Beach County Canvassing Board v. Harris*, Florida Supreme Court, "Petitioner Broward County Canvassing Board's and Broward County Supervisor of Election's Initial Brief on the Merits," p. 3.
21. Don Van Natta Jr., "Palm Beach Panel Votes to Recount," November 15, 2000, in Correspondents of *The New York Times, 36 Days*, p. 73.
22. Ibid., p. 74.
23. *Palm Beach County Canvassing Board v. Harris*, "Emergency Petition for Extraordinary Writ," p. 7.
24. Ibid., p. 1.
25. Serge Kovaleski, "Larger Recount is Denied," *Washington Post*, November 15, 2000, p. A 22.
26. *The 2000 Florida Statutes*, 102.111 (1) (italics added), www.flcourts.org.
27. Ibid., 102.112 (1) (italics added).
28. Ibid., 102.112 (2).
29. Division of Elections, Advisory Opinion DE 00-10: "Deadline for Certification on County Results," reprinted in Dionne and Kristol (eds.), *Bush v. Gore*, p. 9 (italics added).
30. Ibid., pp. 9, 10.
31. *McDermott v. Harris*, "Order Granting in Part and Denying in Part Motion for Temporary Injunction," 2nd Judicial Circuit, reprinted in Dionne and Kristol (eds.), *Bush v. Gore*, p. 21.
32. Ibid.
33. Ibid., p. 22.
34. Ibid.
35. Ibid.
36. Ibid., pp. 22–23.
37. Ibid., p. 23 (italics added).
38. "A Statement from the Secretary of State," November 15, 2000, *Palm Beach County Canvassing Board v. Harris*, "Intervenors' Supplemental Appendix," Exhibit G.
39. Katherine Harris to Judge Charles Burton, November 15, 2000, "Intervenors' Supplemental Appendix," Exhibit F, p. 2 (italics added). Harris wrote very similar letters to Chairman Lee of the Broward County board and Chairman King of the Miami-Dade board.

40. Ibid. (italics added). The quotation in 3 is from *Broward County Canvassing Board v. Hogan*, 607 So. 2d 508, 510 (1992).

41. "Intervenors' Supplemental Appendix," Exhibit G.

42. Richard Posner, *Breaking the Deadlock* (Princeton, N.J.: Princeton University Press, 2001), p. 102 (italics added).

43. 3 USC Section 5.

44. *The 2000 Florida Statutes,* 102.168 (1).

45. Ibid., 102.168 (2).

46. Ibid., 102.168 (6).

47. See Part 5 for a further discussion of this.

48. The Political Staff of *The Washington Post, Deadlock*, p. 105.

49. *Harris v. The Circuit Judges* et al., "Emergency Petition for Extraordinary Relief," p. 11.

50. *McDermott v. Harris*, 2nd Judicial Circuit, "Order Denying Emergency Motion to Compel Compliance with and for Enforcement of Injunction," p. 1.

51. Ibid., pp. 1–2.

52. Florida Constitution, Article V, Section 3 (b) (5).

53. *Palm Beach County Canvassing Board v. Harris*, Interim Order, November 16, 2000.

54. *Palm Beach County Canvassing Board v. Harris*, Stay Order, November 17, 2000.

55. Sue Anne Pressley, "Miami Panel Backs Recount," *Washington Post*, November 15, 2000, p. A12.

4

Joint Brief of Vice President Gore and the Florida Democratic Party

The Gore and Harris briefs to the Florida Supreme Court differed irreconcilably in their views on the proper exercise of secretarial discretion, because they differed fundamentally on the purpose of manual recounts in Florida.

Gore's lawyers affirmed Attorney General Butterworth's analysis of 102.166, that recounts were available to correct voter error as well as in the case of machine failure. And this being so, they argued, Secretary Harris had absolutely no discretion to refuse amended returns when they were the fruit of a legally mandated manual recount.

The Gore legal team even pointed to provisions of Florida law demonstrating in their view that no deadline at all could constrain the need for definitive and accurate results. The $200-a-day fines, therefore, did not apply to canvassing boards striving to complete authorized recounts.

IIA. The Secretary Has No Discretion To Reject the Results of a Manual Recount

At the outset, there is a fundamental defect in the Secretary's position and in the analysis used by Judge Lewis: in the circumstances of this case, the Secretary *has no discretion at all* to refuse to take into account the results of a manual recount. In arguing to the contrary, the Secretary necessarily is contending that she may disregard properly cast votes, or may halt the tabulation of votes, even if ongoing recounts are in the process of demonstrating that valid ballots were not tabulated *and that the wrong candidate is*

From Joint Brief of Vice President Gore and the Florida Democratic Party, www.flcourts.org, pp. 32–37.

being certified as the winner. Not surprisingly, this approach is not compelled by the statutory language, is flatly inconsistent with the statutory structure, and is precluded by the fundamental purposes of Florida election law.

II-A-1. The Secretary's view that Section 102.111 or Section 102.112... allows her to exclude manually recounted votes – and to permit certification while a manual recount is pending – cannot be reconciled with the basic statutory structure. The law expressly contemplates that the results of a manual recount will trump a machine vote tabulation.... The Secretary appears to recognize as much. She does not deny that she must include manually recounted votes that are tabulated *prior* to 5 p.m. of the seventh day following the election; indeed, she certified the results of a manual recount in Volusia County.... Instead, her position is that, although manually recounted votes ordinarily are controlling, she has discretion to exclude these votes if they are returned to her office after that time.

This position, however, makes no sense at all. Florida law provides that a request for a manual recount may be filed at any time prior to certification of the election results; in addition, by providing that a manual recount may be limited to sample precincts before a county-wide manual recount is authorized, the Legislature plainly contemplated that some time might go by before the recount was conducted. Indeed, the Legislature surely knew that, where large counties are concerned, it may be *inevitable* that it will take more than a week for a manual recount to be requested, authorized, and completed. Against this background, it simply cannot be the case that the Legislature provided for full manual recounts to determine the accurate and controlling vote tally, while allowing the Secretary to certify a winner prior to when the recount could be completed.

Moreover, county canvassing boards order full manual recounts when they find, based on a review of a sample of the county's precincts, "an error in the vote tabulation which could affect the outcome of the election." It would make no sense for the Legislature to allow the Election Canvassing Commission to certify the winner of an election based upon vote counts found to be potentially erroneous at the very time that corrected vote counts were being produced.

Read together, Sections 102.112 and 102.166 are most naturally understood to dictate that all manually recounted votes be tabulated and that certification be delayed pending the completion of a manual recount that was requested on a timely basis.... To instead read Section 102.112 as permitting the Secretary to exclude votes because a manual recount is not final within one week of the election would run afoul of the black-letter rule that a "statute must be read with reference to its manifest intent and spirit and cannot be limited to the literal meaning of a single word. It must be construed as a whole and interpreted according to the sense in which the words are employed, regard being had to the plain intention of the Legislature." *Werhan v. State*, 673 So. 2d 550, 554 (Fla. App. Dist. 1996).... In fact, Sections 102.111 and 102.112 plainly are meant to apply in the ordinary case when a recount is not proceeding; read in context, these provisions appear intended only to penalize unreasonably dilatory county canvassing boards and not to disenfranchise the voters in such jurisdictions. This point is further suggested by Section 102.112 (2), which provides that members of County Canvassing Boards may be fined $200 for each day that returns are late. Although the provision states that the Elections Canvassing Commission "shall" fine members, it cannot plausibly be suggested that fines are appropriate when certification is delayed for reasons beyond the members' control – for example, during the pendency of a statutorily mandated recount....

Other provisions of the statute confirm that the Secretary's approach is illegal. The statutory provision dealing with certification of elections states that the Elections Canvassing Commission is to certify the returns "as soon as the *official results* are compiled." Section 102.111, Fla. Stat. (2000) (emphasis added). And by statute, the "official return of the election" ...includes "[t]he return printed by the automatic tabulating equipment *to which has been added the return of* write-in, absentee, and *manually counted votes*." Section 101.561 (8) (2000), Fla. Stat. (emphasis added). It therefore is clear that the "official" results that are used in certifying the election include manually counted votes – making it improper to exclude such votes and certify the election before the manual recount is completed.

II-A-2. In addition, the Secretary's position is shockingly inconsistent with "the public policy of Florida" (*Bayne v. Glisson*, 300 So. 2d 79, 82 (Fla. App. 1974) and the essential purpose of the State's election laws: effectuating the will of the electorate. This Court has held repeatedly that, "[b]y refusing to recognize an otherwise valid exercise of the right to a citizen to vote for the sake of sacred, unyielding adherence to statutory scripture, we would in effect nullify that right." *Boardman v. Esteva*, 323 So. 2d 259, 263 (Fla. 1976).

5

Brief of Secretary of State Katherine Harris

Secretary of State Katherine Harris's lawyers defended her broad discretionary powers, especially in the area of elections. Such power commanded great deference, and courts could interfere with it only if exercised in a wholly "arbitrary" manner. Yet the reasonableness of Harris's actions in refusing late returns was closely bound up, the brief suggested, with her correct understanding of Florida law, which forbade manual recounts altogether when voting equipment was working "as intended."

Only before the Florida Supreme Court did Harris offer the contention she should have offered on November 13 or 15. Any holdup in submitting election results, her lawyers now argued, collided with the deadline specified in the Electoral Count Act. That deadline, they made clear, was mandatory. A full airing of 2000 election issues, then, might have to await the contest phase, which, the brief suggested, contained procedures for dealing with such issues.

C. Florida Law Provides Strict Statutory Deadlines for Certification of Election Results to Which the Secretary Properly Adhered....

C-2. Sound Practical and Policy Reasons for the Deadline Exist.

The legislature had good reasons to set strict time limits for the certification of elections. Likewise, the Secretary's respect for those time frames. The time period allows for finality in an election....

From Amended Answer Brief of the Secretary of State, www.flcourts.org, pp. 19, 24–26, 28–30, 33–34, 37, 38–39.

If the certification of presidential electors is contested pursuant to a state's statutory election contest procedures, the determination made as of six days prior to the meeting of the electoral college – *at whatever stage the contest proceeding is in, is conclusive.* 3 U.S.C. § 5. (Italics added.) To delay certification affects the ability to have an election contest heard and possibly appealed and to implement whatever remedy the court might fashion. Each day that certifications are not made and the right to contest is not triggered, the likelihood of a court's ability to effectively deal with a legitimate election failure is adversely affected. If an election contest cannot be heard by a court through contest proceedings and the results are not certified, there will be no appointment of the presidential electors short of extraordinary legislative intervention....

C-3. To the Extent Florida Law Allows Late-filed Certification, it Places the Discretion to Accept or Reject the Late Filing with the Secretary....

[I]f the term "may" in section 102.112 were found to grant additional powers to the Secretary, such authority would obviously be discretionary. One simply cannot read a statute that states in one provision that "all missing counties shall be ignored" and in another warns county boards that if returns are not filed on time they may be ignored, to mean that the Secretary must accept any and all late-filed returns. This would in essence rewrite the directive that the Secretary shall and/or may reject late returns to mean that she shall not or may not reject the returns. This construction turns the statute on its head and should not be adopted....

Because rejection of the late returns was either absolute requirement or a discretionary act of the Secretary, the only issue before the Court is whether there was any basis to consider a late return, and, if so, whether the Secretary's exercise of discretion was within the bounds of law. The standard of review for such decisions is very limited: "It is well established that courts have the right to review and grant relief [only] from administrative action which is arbitrary, capricious, unreasonable, discriminatory, or oppressive, or which constitutes an abuse of discretion." *Martin Memorial Hosp. Ass'n v. Department of Health & Rehabilitative Servs.*, 584 So. 2d 39, 40 (Fla. 4th DCA 1991)....

In sum, Judge Lewis' determination that the decision as to whether to accept late filed election returns was within Secretary Harris's discretion was correct and should be upheld.

C-4. The Secretary Properly Rejected the Proposed Late Filings....

[T]he Secretary found that requests based solely on an expressed desire to conduct manual recounting were insufficient to justify delay where there was no contention that (i) the tabulating equipment was malfunctioning, (ii) ballots had been damaged so as to be unreadable by tabulating equipment, or (iii) there was any reason to believe that properly executed ballots would not be tabulated by the equipment. This decision was based on the Secretary's reasoned interpretation of the Florida statutes governing manual recounting as not allowing for a recount in such a circumstance.... As previously discussed, Florida law does not authorize a local canvassing board that has chosen to employ automated tabulation equipment to order a manual recount when the equipment is operating as intended. To the extent that the local boards are conducting such recounts, they are acting outside the scope of their statutory delegations of authority. Certainly, the Secretary was reasonable in not compounding this error by ignoring a statutory deadline to allow the local boards more time to conduct the inappropriate recounting....

The Petitioners assert ... that the Secretary must postpone the certification of this statewide election until completion of manual recounts in selected counties. This assertion is illogical and inconsistent with the statute. Petitioner has confused a pre-certification election protest (section 102.166) with a post-certification election contest (section 102.168) ... two distinct and different processes....

It is also not clear that the manual counting requested would accurately reflect the will of the voter. Manual counting of ballots that were designed to be counted by a computer necessarily interjects an element of subjectivity into the counting process and creates a significant potential for human error. The possibility for human error and bias, coupled with the lack of any uniform and objective standards, makes the proposition that manual counting will increase accuracy dubious at best. Additionally, the selective recounting of ballots only in selected counties, all of which overwhelmingly supported the same presidential candidate, has the potential to skew the election results unfairly. Based on these considerations, it was determined that, on balance, the desire of the local canvassing boards to conduct manual recounting even though there had been no technical failure in the counting apparatus did not justify violation of the statutory deadline.

6

Brief of Intervenor George W. Bush

While not directly a party to *Palm Beach County Canvassing Board v. Harris,* or its companion cases, George Bush inevitably intervened in the dispute, and where manual recounts were concerned, his lawyers put a different slant on the matter. Gore maintained that because such recounts were valid, even in the absence of machine breakdowns, the secretary of state had no right to refuse to accept them beyond the statutory deadline. The secretary's lawyers claimed she possessed such discretion, especially since the recounts she was rejecting were improper.

The Bush lawyers, by contrast, argued that even if the hand counts in south Florida were legal, and even if the secretary of state possessed discretion over election matters in general, her discretion could not extend to late acceptance of these recounts, because the state's election scheme specifically precluded such action. Even Section 102.112, they noted, set a definite deadline of November 14 for receipt of election returns. Yet the Florida legislature was surely aware of the possibility of manual recounts when it set that date, because the counts were also part of the law it wrote.

This logic seemed to mean there was no effective difference between 111 and 112, erasing the discretionary power over recounts claimed for the secretary of state by her lawyers.

The Bush intervenors also brought their two-pronged equal-protection claim to the state supreme court for consideration, arguing that the Florida recount statute, "as applied," counted the votes of citizens differently depending upon where they lived, and laid down no consistent standards for officials conducting the recounts. This analysis occupied less than a page, however.

From Brief of Intervenor George W. Bush, www.flcourts.org, pp. 7–10, 13, 17–20, 44.

I. The Injunction Petitioners Seek
Is Inconsistent with the Text, Structure,
and Intent of the Statutory Scheme....

While the Petitioners' argument is sometimes framed as challenging the Secretary's exercise of her discretion under the Election Code, it is, in fact, a direct challenge to the statute itself and a request for the Court to rewrite the law. Simply put, they ask this Court to revise the statute's plain directive that late-filed returns "may be ignored" to read instead that the Secretary *"may not* ignore" late-filed returns if the county board is conducting a manual recount. Petitioners are not coy about seeking a statutory revision to eviscerate the discretion vested by the plain language of the statute....

The only reason offered by the three county boards for offering extraordinarily late election returns is that they are conducting a full manual recount, which, like all manual recounts, can only be conducted if there is an error "which could affect the outcome of the election." But the legislature expressly contemplated manual recounts in close elections and, with full knowledge of their potential logistical difficulties, nevertheless *required* canvassing boards to file their returns within seven days and expressly authorized the Secretary to ignore returns where they violate that mandatory duty. While it will be the rare case where the Secretary can be said to abuse her discretion to ignore late-filed returns—because the statute does not set forth any factors or standards cabining that discretion—she is certainly not required to accept late-filed returns when the legislature has *expressly contemplated* the county board's proffered justification for tardiness and nonetheless authorized the Secretary to ignore them. Again, the circumstance that petitioners feature as a reason specifically justifying the manual recounts here—that the result of the election might turn—is the very predicate for conducting *all* manual recounts. Yet it defies common sense to suppose...that the legislature silently excepted such recounts from the normal statutory deadline....

Indeed, we submit that it would be an abuse of discretion to accept late-filed returns in these circumstances because the Secretary would be overriding the balance struck by the legislature between finality and the desirability of manual recounts. [Italics added.]

Petitioners' only response is to hypothesize an inherent conflict between conducting manual recounts and meeting the statutory deadline. They thus contend that the legislature simply could not have contemplated ignoring returns in counties which find it impracticable to do a manual recount within seven days. But the statute's language and structure make clear that this analysis is wrong....

Further evidence that the legislature expected timeliness in submission of returns is found in the requirement that county board members who delay the submission of returns in order to conduct manual recounts must nonetheless be personally fined $200 per day for every day beyond the deadline. As Petitioners themselves note, it is not remotely "plausible" that a legislature would fine county board members for conducting manual recounts necessary to assess the "electorate's...will." Indeed, if the legislature believed that manual recounts beyond the deadline were absolutely necessary to accurately calculate the number of votes cast, it would have been extraordinarily inequitable for the legislature to *punish* board members who are simply carrying out this important constitutional and public duty. Contrary to Petitioners' assertion, however, public policy concerns do not authorize this Court to rewrite a second provision in the statute by amending "shall" be fined to "shall not" be fined....

In short, Petitioners seek to turn the process of statutory interpretation on its head...substitu[ting] the certification process of Section 102.111 and Section 102.112 for the contested election process of Section 102.168 as the means for determining the accuracy of vote tallies....

Moreover, even after the Court...completed the extended journey of revisions through the election code that Petitioners urge... (We must assume that even Petitioners agree that some deadline at some point is appropriate prior to the Inauguration itself)... we [would] still not have arrived at the destination which [they] claim equity demands: an accurate *statewide* compilation of votes for presidential candidates. If, as Petitioners claim, machine reading of ballots will "predictably misread" the valid ballots cast, the Court will not know which "candidate for 'President' receive[d] the highest number of votes" even *after* the manual recounts in [the] three [selected] counties are completed. There will still be 63 counties [of course] which have not conducted a manual recount. And, if Petitioners are correct, it would be intolerable to allow such a close election to turn on the "potentially erroneous" results produced by...machine counts. Yet Petitioners, notwithstanding their devotion to manual recounts in all circumstances, did not request that all Florida counties conduct manual recounts, as was their right....

[Thus], allowing these three [additional] counties, and only these three counties, to include manual recounts will inevitably *skew* the results in a partisan manner that favors Democrats....

In a *county* election, no court would permit a recount in only four of 67 precincts, particularly if those precincts were selected by one political party and were composed predominantly of members of one party. It follows *a fortiori* that this Court may not *require* such a partisan, skewed recount in the name of "accuracy," particularly in the face of explicit statutory requirements foreclosing such a "remedy."...

This scheme, as applied, [also] violates the United States Constitution.

[I]t dilutes the votes of Florida voters, both within and without the counties that are manually counted, by counting their votes differently based upon where they reside, in violation of the Due Process and Equal Protection Clauses of the Fourteenth Amendment.... Second, because the manual recount statute prescribes no meaningful standards for officials conducting such recounts, it permits the invasion of the liberty interest in voting in an arbitrary and capricious manner.

7

Decision: *Palm Beach County Canvassing Board v. Harris*

In a decision issued on the evening of November 21, the Florida Supreme Court sided unanimously with Gore, and Butterworth. The court held that manual recounts were permissible under 102.166 to mine undervotes, even where there were no machine breakdowns. Curiously, the opinion does not mention the "voter intent" provision of 102.166 in reaching its conclusion. Indeed, the words in 101.5614 that the justices do quote to justify hand recounts for close elections refer actually to ballots so "damaged or defective . . . that [they] cannot be counted properly by the automatic tabulating equipment," a point of considerable importance later.

The court also held that 102.112 trumped 102.111, and because manual recounts to correct voter error were valid, a secretary of state's discretion to refuse recounts in a presidential election, or to level fines against a canvassing board, was limited in essence to seeing that adjudication met the December 12 deadline of the Electoral Count Act. The justices refused, however, to countenance Harris's belated use of the deadline to justify her actions in this case, since she had not invoked it at the outset of the election dispute.

Furthermore, the *Harris* opinion did not address the question of whether the Florida legislature had set such a deadline for presidential elections; it seemed to treat the deadline simply as something the secretary could permissibly choose to honor. Indeed, the Electoral Count Act is mentioned only in a footnote in the opinion, and Section 5 is not explicitly mentioned at all. (Gore's lead counsel, David Boies, was said to have admitted at oral argument that December 12 was an absolute

---

From Decision: *Palm Beach County Canvassing Board v. Harris,* 772 So. 2d 1220, 1228–1231, 1234–1240.

deadline for settling controversies. The record seems more mixed, however, for Boies said at one point that an election contest "if there is one takes place between [December 12] and December 18" [*New York Times,* November 21, 2000, p. A19].)

The Florida court did not tackle, or even mention, the equal-protection arguments raised by Bush, claiming, erroneously, in a footnote that neither party had challenged the constitutionality of Florida's election laws.

Invoking what it regarded as its "equitable powers," the court extended the deadline for sending recounts to the Florida Elections Canvassing Board to November 26.

IV. Legal Opinion of the Division of Elections....

The issue in dispute here is the meaning of the phrase "error in the vote tabulation" found in section 102.166 (5). The Division opines that an "error in the vote tabulation" only means a counting error resulting from incorrect election parameters or an error in the vote tabulating software. We disagree.

The plain language of section 102.166 (5) refers to an error in the vote tabulation rather than the vote tabulation system. On its face, the statute does not include any words of limitation; rather, it provides a remedy for any type of mistake made in tabulating ballots. The Legislature has utilized the phrase "vote tabulation system" and "automatic tabulating equipment" in section 102.166 when it intended to refer to the voting system rather than the vote count. Equating "vote tabulation" with "vote tabulation system" obliterates the distinction created in section 102.166 by the Legislature.

Sections 101.5641 (5) and (6) also support the proposition that the "error in vote tabulation" encompasses more than a mere determination of whether the vote tabulation system is functioning. Section 101.5614 (5) provides that "[n]o vote shall be declared invalid or void if there is a clear indication of the intent of the voter as determined by the canvassing board." Conversely, section 101.5614 (6) provides that any vote in which the Board cannot discern the intent of the voter must be discarded. Taken together, these sections suggest that "error in the vote tabulation" includes errors in the failure of the voting machinery to read a ballot and not simply errors resulting from the voting machinery....

Although error cannot be completely eliminated in any tabulation of the ballots, our society has not yet gone so far as to place blind faith in machines. In almost all endeavors, including elections, humans routinely correct the errors of machines. For this very reason Florida law provides a human check on both the malfunction of tabulation equipment and error in failing to accurately count the ballots. Thus, we find that the Division's opinion regarding the ability of county canvassing boards to authorize a manual recount is contrary to the plain language of the statute....

VI. Statutory Ambiguity

The provisions of the code are ambiguous in two significant areas. First, the time frame for conducting a manual recount under section 102.166 (4) is in conflict with the time frame for submitting county returns under sections 102.111 and 102.112. Second, the mandatory language in section 102.111 conflicts with the permissive language in 102.112....

VII. Legislative Intent

Legislative intent—as always—is the polestar that guides a court's inquiry into the provisions of the Florida Election Code. Where the language of the Code is clear and amenable to a reasonable and logical interpretation, courts are without power to diverge from the intent of the Legislature as expressed in the plain language of the Code. As noted above, however, chapter 102 is unclear.... In light of this ambiguity, the Court must resort to traditional rules of statutory construction in an effort to determine legislative intent.

First, it is well-settled that where two statutory provisions are in conflict, the specific statute controls the general statute. In the present case, whereas section 102.111 in its title and text addresses the general makeup and duties of the Elections Canvassing Commission, the statute only tangentially addresses the penalty for returns filed after the statutory date, noting that such returns "shall" be ignored by the Department. Section 102.112, on the other hand, directly addresses in its title and text both the "deadline" for submitting returns and the "penalties" for submitting returns after a certain date; the statute expressly states that such returns "may" be ignored and that dilatory Board members "shall" be fined. Based on the precision of the title and text, section 102.112 constitutes a specific penalty statute that defines both the deadline for filing returns and the penalties for filing returns thereafter and section 102.111 constitutes a non-specific statute in this regard. The specific statute controls the non-specific statute.

Second, it also is well-settled that when two statutes are in conflict, the more recently enacted statute controls the older statute. In the present case, the provision in section 102.111 stating that the Department "shall" ignore returns was enacted in 1951 as part of the Code. On the other hand, the penalty provision in section 102.112 stating that the Department "may" ignore returns was enacted in 1989 as a revision to chapter 102. The more recently enacted provision may be viewed as the clearest and most recent expression of legislative intent.

Third, a statutory provision will not be construed in such a way that it renders meaningless or absurd any other statutory provision. In the present case, section 102.112 contains a detailed provision authorizing the assessment of fines against members of a dilatory County Canvassing Board. The fines are personal and substantial, i.e., $200 for each day the returns are not received. If, as the Secretary asserts, the Department were required to ignore all returns received after the statutory date, the fine provision would be meaningless. For example, if a Board simply completed its count late and if the returns were going to be ignored in any event, what would be the point in submitting the returns? The Board would simply file no returns and avoid the fines. But, on the other hand, if the returns submitted after the statutory date would not be ignored, the Board would have good reason to submit the returns and accept the fines. The fines thus serve as an alternative penalty and are applicable only if the Department may count the returns.

Fourth, related statutory provisions must be read as a cohesive whole. As stated in *Forsythe v. Longboat Key Beach Erosion Control Dist.*, 604 So. 2d 452, 455 (Fla. 1992), "all parts of a statute must be read together in order to achieve a consistent whole. Where possible, courts must give effect to all statutory provisions and construe related statutory provisions in harmony with another." In this regard we consider the provisions of section 102.166....

Section 102.166 states that a candidate, political committee, or political party may request a manual recount any time before the County Canvassing Board certifies the results to the Department and, if the initial manual recount indicates a significant error, the Board "shall" conduct a countywide manual recount in certain cases. Thus, if a protest is filed on the sixth day following an election and a full manual recount is required, the Board, through no fault of its own, will be unable to submit its returns to the Department by 5:00 p.m. on the seventh day following the election. In such a case, if the mandatory provision in section 102.111 were given effect, the votes of the county would be ignored for the simple reason that the Board was following the dictates of a different section of the Code. The Legislature could not have intended to penalize County Canvassing Boards for following the dictates of the Code.

[Furthermore], when the Legislature enacted the Code in 1951, it envisioned that all votes cast during a particular election, including absentee ballots, would be submitted to the Department at one time and would be treated in a uniform fashion.... Section 101.68 (2) (d) expressly states that "[t]he votes on absentee ballots shall be included in the total vote of the county."...

The Legislature thus envisioned that when returns are submitted to the Department, the returns "shall" embrace all the votes in the county, including absentee ballots. This, of course, is not possible because our state statutory scheme has been superseded by federal law governing overseas voters; overseas ballots must be counted if received no later than ten days following the election (i.e., the ballots do *not* have to be received by 7 p.m. of the day of the election, as provided by state law). In light of the fact that overseas ballots cannot be counted until after the seven day deadline has expired, the mandatory language in section 102.111 has been supplanted by the permissive language of section 102.112....

Under this statutory scheme, the County Canvassing Boards are required to submit their returns to the Department by 5 p.m. of the seventh day following the election. The statutes make no provision for exceptions following a manual recount. If a Board fails to meet the deadline, the Secretary is not required to ignore the county's returns but rather is permitted to ignore the returns within the parameters of this statutory scheme. To determine the circumstances under which the Secretary may lawfully ignore returns filed pursuant to the provisions of section 102.166 for a manual recount, it is necessary to examine the interplay between our statutory and constitutional law at both the state and federal levels.

VIII. The Right to Vote

The text of our Florida Constitution begins with a Declaration of Rights, a series of rights so basic that the founders accorded them a place of special privilege.... Courts must attend with special vigilance whenever the Declaration of Rights is in issue.

The right of suffrage is the preeminent right contained in the Declaration of Rights, for without this basic freedom all others would be diminished. The importance of this right was acknowledged by the authors of the Constitution, who placed it first in the Declaration. The very first words in the body of the constitution are as follows:

SECTION 1. Political power.—*All political power is inherent in the people*. The enunciation herein of certain rights shall not be construed to deny or impair others retained by the people.

Art. I., § 1, Fla. Const. (emphasis added). The framers thus began the constitution with a declaration that all political power inheres in the people and only they, the people, may decide how and when that power may be given up.

To the extent that the Legislature may enact laws regulating the electoral process, those laws are valid only if they impose no "unreasonable or unnecessary" restraints on the right of suffrage.... Because election laws are intended to facilitate the right of suffrage, such laws must be liberally construed in favor of the citizens' right to vote:

> Generally, the courts, in construing statutes relating to elections, hold that the same should receive a liberal construction in favor of the citizen whose right to vote they tend to restrict and in so doing to prevent disfranchisement of legal voters and the intention of the voters should prevail when counting ballots....It is the intention of the law to obtain an honest expression of the will or desire of the voter. *State ex. rel. Carpenter v. Barber*, 198 So. 49, 51 (Fla. 1940).

Courts must not lose sight of the fundamental purpose of election laws: the laws are intended to facilitate and safeguard the right of each voter to express his or her will in the context of our representative democracy. Technical statutory requirements must not be exalted over the substance of this right....

IX. The Present Case

The trial court below properly concluded that the County Canvassing Boards are required to submit their returns to the Department by 5:00 p.m. of the seventh day following the election and that the Department is not required to ignore the amended returns but rather may count them. The court, however, erred in holding that the Secretary acted within her discretion in prematurely rejecting any amended returns that would be the result of ongoing manual recounts....

We conclude that, consistent with the Florida election scheme, the Secretary may reject a Board's amended returns only if the returns are submitted so late that their inclusion will preclude a candidate from contesting the certification or preclude Florida's voters from participating fully in the federal electoral process. The Secretary in the present case has made no claim that either of these conditions apply at this point in time (In its December 11 clarification, the court stated, "In this case, as of the date that the Secretary rejected the amended returns on November 14, 2000,...neither of the circumstances set forth above had been considered.")....

X. Conclusion

According to the legislative intent evinced in the Florida Election Code, the permissive language of section 102.112 supersedes the mandatory language of section 102.111. The statutory fines set forth in section 102.112 offer strong incentive to County Canvassing Boards to submit their returns in a timely fashion. However, when a Board certifies its returns after the seven-day period because the Board is acting in conformity with other provisions of the Code or with administrative rules or for other good cause, the Secretary may impose no fines. It is unlikely that the Legislature would have intended to punish a Board for complying with the dictates of the code or some other law.

Because the right to vote is the preeminent right in the Declaration of Rights of the Florida Constitution, the circumstances under which the Secretary may exercise her authority to ignore a county's returns filed after the initial statutory date are limited [to the ones specified].... But to allow the Secretary to summarily disenfranchise innocent electors in an effort to punish dilatory Board members, as she proposes in the present case, misses the constitutional mark. The constitution eschews punishment by proxy....

In the present case, we have used traditional rules of statutory construction...to the extent necessary to address the issues presented here. We decline to rule more expansively, for to do so would result in this Court substantially rewriting the Code. We leave that matter to the sound discretion of the body best equipped to address it—the Legislature.

Because of the unique circumstances and extraordinary importance of the present case...and because of our reluctance to rewrite the Florida Election Code, we conclude that we must invoke the equitable powers of this Court to fashion a remedy that will allow a fair and expeditious resolution of the questions presented here. [An accompanying footnote states, At oral argument, we inquired as to whether the presidential candidates were interested in our consideration of a reopening of the opportunity to request recounts in any additional counties. Neither candidate requested such an opportunity.] Accordingly, in order to allow maximum time for contests pursuant to section 102.168, amended certifications must be filed with the Elections Canvassing Commission by 5 p.m. on Sunday, November 26, 2000, and the Secretary of State and the Elections Canvassing Commission shall accept any such amended certifications received by 5 p.m. on Sunday, November 26, 2000, provided that the office of the Secretary of State, Division of Elections, is open in order to allow receipt thereof. If the office is not open for this special purpose on Sunday, November 26, 2000, then any amended certifications shall be accepted until 9 a.m. on Monday, November 27, 2000....

It is so ordered. No motion for rehearing will be allowed.

Wells, C.J., and Shaw, Harding, Anstead, Pariente, Lewis and Quince, J.J., Concur.

Reactions to *Palm Beach County Canvassing Board v. Harris*

The reaction to the Florida Supreme Court opinion was fervent and sometimes hysterical on the part of Republican politicians and conservative columnists. The Democrats praised it unreservedly. Two of the nation's leading constitutional scholars reacted in more measured tones, however, though they differed in their assessments.

Michael McConnell of the University of Utah Law School, now a Bush appointee as judge on the Tenth Circuit Court of Appeals, was bothered as much by what he saw as the dangerous impracticality of the Florida decision as by its reasoning. (Judge McConnell is the author of seminal studies of establishment of religion, free exercise of religion, and of the original intent of the Fourteenth Amendment's framers with regard to school segregation.)

Cass Sunstein of the University of Chicago Law School did not wholly endorse the Florida opinion, but he defended the honesty and the plausibility of the arguments on both sides of the dispute. Coeditor of a distinguished constitutional-law casebook, Sunstein's work frequently examines the structure of legal process, as in his recent work, *One Case at a Time.*

Supremely Ill-Judged

Michael McConnell

One sentence of the Florida Supreme Court's decision on hand recounts tells it all: "The will of the people, not a hyper-technical reliance upon statutory provisions, should be our guiding principle."

That is like saying, of a disputed umpire call in the World Series: "Athletic superiority, not a hyper-technical reliance upon the rules of baseball, should be our guiding principle." In our system, the will of the people is manifested through procedures specified in advance. When those rules are changed in mid-stream, something has gone terribly wrong.

Article II of the U.S. Constitution provides: "Each State shall appoint, in such Manner as the Legislature thereof may direct, a Number of Electors...." The Florida legislature has enacted a detailed election code, including an unambiguous deadline of seven days after the election for counties to report their results....

If any counties fail to report on time, one section of the law states that "all missing counties shall be ignored," and another that "such returns may be ignored." As the Florida Supreme Court pointed out on Tuesday night, these provisions are inconsistent. But the court purported to reconcile the "shall" with the "may" by holding that late returns may not be ignored. It did this because it believed that enforcement of the statutory deadline would be "a drastic measure," and that to "disenfranchise electors" on account of the statutory deadline would be "unreasonable" and "unnecessary."

But since the legislature made the rules, and no one claimed they were unconstitutional, the court's opinion about their wisdom or necessity should have been irrelevant. Presumably, the rules could work to one side's advantage in one election and the other side's advantage in another election. Can

Wall Street Journal, November 24, 2000, p. A16. Reprinted by permission.

you imagine the screams from the Gore campaign if votes cast in favor of George W. Bush had been counted after a statutory deadline?

In any event, the deadline is far from "unnecessary." Under Florida law, all voters have 10 days after the initial certification of election results to contest it. (In my opinion, perhaps contrary to the Republicans' arguments, the manual recounts can proceed and, if they are validated and demonstrate a change in the result, could be the basis for such a contest. Despite their high potential for arbitrariness and even fraud, manual recounts, like deadlines, are a feature of the Florida law.) Those contests will take time to adjudicate....

That is why the Florida statutory scheme, so casually dismissed by the court, made sense. Under that scheme, counties have seven days to certify an initial result. Voters then have 10 days to file protests. That gives a total of 17 days for counts and recounts, and leaves about a three-week period for full consideration of contests.

The Florida Supreme Court, by fiat, has reduced the time for review of these difficult questions by at least eight days. Now, contests can be initiated as late as Dec. 6, 10 days after the court's arbitrary deadline. Electors must be chosen by Dec. 12. That leaves less than a week for the real issues of this election to be adjudicated. It is hard to see how that can be done, at least with any pretense of fairness.

At this point—and thanks in no small part to the Florida Supreme Court's decision to supersede the statute—there are two possible scenarios, neither of them happy. In one scenario, the Democrats succeed in treating virtually all the [disputed] ballots as valid votes, despite their inherent ambiguity. If that occurs, it will be evident to the American people that the results of the Florida count did not reflect "the will of the people," but only the inexorable process of finding more Gore votes, no matter what.

In the second scenario, each disputed ballot will receive due attention.... [The] ultimate decisions will be made by the county boards of canvassers, with appeals to the courts. That will take time, almost certainly longer than the six days the court's decision allows. Under this scenario, the process will not be complete by Dec. 12.

Under either scenario, the Florida legislature will be tempted to interfere, to ensure that the Florida vote tally is conducted in accordance with the law. Since the legislature is a political body, with a Republican majority, such a step will be enormously controversial. It should only be a last step, to be entertained only if the alternative is either manifest error or inability to choose electors. It would have been far better for the Florida Supreme Court to resist the temptation to rewrite the state's laws, and to leave in place a system that—however imperfect—could have reached a result that fair-minded Americans could view as legitimate.

One Fine Mess

Cass R. Sunstein

THE HORROR. That seems to be most pundits' verdict on this post-campaign campaign. Both candidates, sober-minded observers agree, have behaved terribly, trying to twist and mangle the law to their own selfish ends. "Al Gore and George W. Bush," admonished *The Boston Globe,* "should, for once, start acting like statesmen." And then there's Florida's sorry excuse for election law. "I mean, Florida election law," griped CBS News legal analyst Andrew Cohen, "if [there's] nothing else we can agree on, we can agree that it was just absolutely a disaster."

Actually, we can't, and we shouldn't. The last three weeks have been trying, but not because Florida is a banana republic and not because of anything the Gore and Bush campaigns have done in court. In fact, the great neglected story of November has been the eminent reasonableness of almost every legal position the Gore and Bush campaigns have taken, and the eminent reasonableness (if ambiguity) of the very Florida election law both campaigns are fighting over.

It's possible to disagree with the legal arguments put forward by the two camps; but they are neither reckless nor absurd, and the frequent suggestion that they are says more about the instinctive cynicism of many commentators than about the arguments' legal merits. The Gore campaign's request for manual recounts...was widely condemned as illegitimate, a form of sour grapes. But Florida law explicitly authorizes manual recounts, and the Gore campaign was well within its rights to insist on them. Whether or not manual recounts are reliable, or more reliable than machine counts, Florida law makes them fully available to disappointed candidates.

By the same token, it was quite reasonable for the Bush campaign and Florida's much-reviled secretary of state, Katherine Harris, to interpret

The New Republic, December 11, 2000, pp. 15–16. Reprinted by permission of *The New Republic,* LLC.

Florida law as forbidding Harris to receive returns after November 14. A provision of Florida law plainly says that if county returns are not received by that day, "all missing counties shall be ignored, and the results shown by the returns on file shall be certified." To be sure, a separate provision proclaims that such returns "may be ignored," but that provision could easily be read to allow the secretary of state to ignore late returns.

The Gore lawyers disagreed. They argued that the "may be ignored" provision, because it was enacted by the legislature more recently, trumps the "shall be ignored" one. And they claimed, rightly, that even if late returns "may be ignored," the secretary of state cannot do so arbitrarily. She has to explain herself. Most important of all, Florida's explicit and detailed provisions for manual recounts would be rendered meaningless in populous areas, where recounting is slow, if the secretary of state were free to "ignore" returns filed after a week's time. In these circumstances, the Florida Supreme Court's decision to read the "may be ignored" language together with the manual-recount provision, to ensure that manually recounted votes are not "ignored," was entirely justifiable....

Are both sides right? Of course not. But both sides are making sensible arguments that have substantial legal merit; they're not clogging up the courts with fanciful, transparent sophistries—which is the impression you might get from watching television. In fact, Gore and Bush both have arguments so serious that their lawyers might be remiss if they *didn't* bring them to court. How can both sides have strong arguments? Because, on many key questions, Florida election law is unclear.

Which is why trashing Florida election law is rapidly becoming a new national sport. To be sure, if we were sending the election law of one U.S. state to a fledgling democracy to show how things should be done, we probably wouldn't choose Florida's. But the pundits who keep bemoaning the lack of clarity of the Sunshine State's electoral statutes should remember a couple of things. First, on the vast majority of issues, Florida election law is quite clear; it's served the state fairly well through many campaigns. Yes, the unbelievably anomalous election of 2000 has exposed several pressure points—provisions that reasonable people can read in different ways. But legislatures have limited foresight; they can never predict every circumstance that will arise when there's a near tie. Even well-crafted laws are potentially ambiguous; if they were self-explanatory, we wouldn't need a judiciary to interpret them.

Indeed, the real lesson here is not that Florida law is a complete mess but that an independent arbiter (such as a judge) imposes a needed discipline on what people say and how they say it. Unlike in the political arena, where both sides have engaged in gross hyperbole and never-ending spin, in the legal domain both sides—in their briefs and inside courtrooms— have restricted themselves to solid arguments about hard questions. If only those outside the courtroom—for instance, the press—would do the same.

9

Comment:
Was the Secretary Right
About Manual Recounts?

Mark Whitman

102.166 Protest of election returns . . . .
(5) If the manual recount indicates an error in the vote tabulation which
could affect the outcome of the election, the county canvassing board
shall:
  (a) Correct the error and recount the remaining precincts with the
  vote tabulation system;
  (b) Request the Department of State to verify the tabulation software;
  or
  (c) Manually recount all ballots . . . .
(7) Procedures for a manual recount are as follows: . . .
  (b) If a counting team is unable to determine a voter's intent in casting a ballot, the ballot shall be presented to the county canvassing
  board for it to determine the voter's intent.

One simple but crucially significant fact stands out from these early developments in Florida of November 8 to November 21. If everyone had agreed
with Secretary Harris about the reasons for ordering, or not ordering, hand
recounts, when they were legally appropriate and when they were not, the
constitutional drama of 2000 would never have taken place at all.

It is important, therefore, to take a closer look at Section 102.166 of
the state's election code. What can its general background, its legislative
history, and a parsing of its language, tell us about the validity of Harris's
(and Gore's) position?

The Legacy of 1988

The secretary's briefs accurately noted that widespread machine glitches in
the 1988 United States Senate contest between Connie Mack and Buddy
McKay brought on the legislation of which the recount provision in 166
was a part, the Voter Protection Act of 1989. In numerous precincts in

Bradenton during this election, the machines mangled warped and soggy ballots fed into them. A software failure in Ft. Pierce resulted in a situation where the voting machines counted all the Democratic ballots but rejected all the Republican ones.[1]

In addressing these problems, the Voter Protection Act increased the secretary of state's authority to monitor quality control of the state's voting devices, especially when they employed "mechanical, electromechanical, or electronic apparatus."[2] The Department of State assumed the power, among other things, to "establish minimum standards for hardware and software for electronic and electromechanical voting systems,"[3] to "adopt rules prescribing standards for ballots used in [such systems],"[4] and to conduct an audit every five years of all voting equipment.[5] The legislation also demanded competitive bidding for the purchase of election hardware and supplies costing over $1,000.[6]

Newspaper coverage of the legislation focused on its aim of "protect[ing] voters from computer fraud," and the centralization of authority thought necessary to achieve this purpose.[7] Indeed, the principal opposition to the bill came from county election officials who feared "the expansion of power at the state level and the diminishing role of local authority."[8] A group of election supervisors from north Florida lamented to the legislation's senate sponsor, "We do not deserve the treatment we have received with this bill."[9] Their opposition carried little weight, for the Voter Protection Act passed unanimously in the Florida Senate, 98-11 in the house.[10] (A more successful, if decidedly more limited, opposition was mounted by lobbyists for punch-card ballot manufacturers, who got their product removed from the competitive-bidding provision of the law.)[11]

Parsing the Words

This general background tends in the direction of the secretary's point of view. But it is just that—general—and nowhere provides us with any specific exposition of Section 15 of the Voter Protection Act, which constitutes the amended form of 102.166. And nothing in the legislative history of the act tells us a word about how Florida's legislators conceived the recounts they were establishing. The secretary's briefs do not claim otherwise. Thus, the actual language of 102.166 is all we have to go on in determining its meaning and import. As is so often the case, that language presents a mixed bag.

The central dispute over 166 focused, of course, on whether recounts could be launched on a sample basis, and then possibly extended, for the purpose of uncovering votes adjudged valid, even though a properly functioning machine had not counted them; or whether an error in the vote tabulation referred only to machine failures, and not to the "inability of a voting [machine] to read an improperly marked [optical-scanner ballot] or [an] improperly punched punchcard ballot."[12]

The key words at the beginning of subsection 5—"Error in the vote tabulation"—do not definitively settle the issue, since, as Attorney General Butterworth suggested, they are not accompanied by the word "system," a term with which the legislators were certainly familiar. They use "vote tabulation system" in fact in 5 (a) of 166; and a closer look at this first remedial option available after an "error in vote tabulation" is discovered by a canvassing board tends, not surprisingly, to favor Harris's position.

Thus, before it went to the secretary of state for software verification, or manually recounted all ballots, 5 (a) gave a board the power to "*correct the error*" it found in the sample count, but then to "*recount the remaining precincts*" with the electromechanical equipment ("the vote tabulation system"). This is the only reference back to the "error" invoked at the beginning of the subsection , and it does not seem to square with the Gore-Butterworth view of that error. For Section 5 (a)'s definition is clearly not an "error" in vote *totals* brought about during the sample recount by the addition of ballots the machines had missed. Otherwise, what would be the point in such an instance of "correcting the error" by updating the precinct results, and then returning to the same method of counting votes that presumably produced that error?

Taken by itself, 5 (a) is best read as referring to an error in the vote tabulation network—in the compilation and addition software, the computers, or the machine readers—that the sample recount was launched to check into, and which county officials can fix before rerunning the rest of the precincts. Furthermore, such a view of the language is consistent with the other possible steps the county board is directed to take in 5 (b) or 5 (c).

But the overall architecture of the manual-recount process, especially as revealed in 166.7 (b), points in a different direction. For 7 (b) requires that when a "counting team is unable to determine a *voter's intent in casting a ballot*, the ballot shall be presented to the county canvassing board *for it to determine the voter's intent.*" If recounts stemmed only from suspicion of or confirmation of machine breakdowns, there would be no need for counting teams or canvassing officials to bother about this. As Michael McConnell points out, "Since a ballot cast in full compliance with the voting instructions is highly unlikely ever to raise questions about voter intent, this suggests that manual recounts are expected to include some ballots that were not in compliance with the instructions. This does not necessarily mean that dimples should be counted . . . but it does provide support for the Florida [Supreme Court's] conclusion that manual recounts should include some ballots that were rejected by the machines."[13]

It can be argued that 7 (b) comes into play only *after* a canvassing board has ordered a full recount in a jurisdiction, that the board has no business looking for voter intent until it has discovered a glitch in the machines.[14] But the statute, as we have seen, does not differentiate between standards used in a sample, and those used in a full recount. Indeed, if this bifurcated view is correct, and only evidence of machine failure justifies full manual recounts, the Florida legislature would have created an election system under which a candidate who lost by a handful of votes has no redress, when the machines do not misbehave. Yet the candidate might have won the election had there been significant mechanical problems (even if correction of them did not help him), since a recount structure focusing on the intent of the voter would then kick into play, counting hundreds (or thousands) of ostensible "no votes" that otherwise remained untouched.

Judged by the whole, the Florida recount system certainly is designed to deal with machine breakdowns or glitches under 166.5 (a), (b), and (c). The suspicion of electromechanical failure would properly set off a sample recount, even in an election that was not particularly close, and then the appropriate steps would follow: correct the mistake, go to the secretary of state, or manually recount all ballots (perhaps more than one of these). But a razor-thin election of itself might also call for a sample and then possibly a full recount under 166.5 (c), buttressed by 166.7 (b). If this view of the law is correct, as Gore maintained, it is hard to see how a secretary of state would have any justification for spurning hand counts in a close presidential race, especially from large counties, except under circumstances very much like those described in *Palm Beach County v. Harris*. It is true this would be telling Secretary Harris what she "must" do. But any official who has discretion to do or not to do something can abuse that discretion on occasion. And a court order correcting the abuse would very often demand that something be done. Of course, by the terms of the supreme court opinion in *Harris*, it would not have been an abuse of discretion for a future secretary of state to refuse exactly the type of returns being proffered in 2000.

Parsing the Court

The vice president's view of 166 is certainly plausible. Still, Secretary Harris's interpretation is by no means without merit. As such, it was subject to a considerable degree of deference from the courts under state administrative law. Florida precedent did not follow the standard of administrative procedure laid down by the United States Supreme Court, under which judges must accept agency rulings so long as they were based on any "permissible construction of [a] statute."[15] But case law in the state did provide that "the judgment of officials duly charged with carrying out the election process should be presumed correct if reasonable and not in derogation of the law"; an agency's interpretation could be overturned only if it was "unreasonable . . . , or . . . clearly erroneous."[16]

Of course, reasonableness is an elastic concept, and the Florida justices may have felt Harris's interpretation of 102.166 was so at odds with the "count every vote" emphasis they saw in statutory and decisional law as to render it aberrant. But the Florida Supreme Court's decision on this point needs to be evaluated finally, it would seem, in the same context in which parts of the United States Supreme Court decision in *Bush v. Gore* were later evaluated. Some praised the U.S. Supreme Court, whether rightly or wrongly, for doing what it had to do in December to avoid a national crisis, even at some sacrifice of doctrinal consistency.[17] Similarly, whether correct or not, the Florida justices in *Palm Beach v. Harris* were probably doing what they had to do to keep from ending the 2000 election through affirmance of a legal memorandum they were sure was incorrect, issued by a state official who was also an openly partisan politician (and whose advisor was the Bush campaign's designated emissary).

The desire to keep Harris out of the Bush-Gore dispute may also explain why the Florida court set its own November 26 deadline for submission of the recounts, instead of remanding the case to the secretary of state (albeit with instructions designed to ensure a November 26 deadline). In this instance, however, the court offered no explanation for eschewing traditional procedure; it made no reply to Bush's contention that it was "without authority . . . to substitute a judicially-created deadline for the date selected by the legislature."[18]

The justices later claimed, in their December 11 clarificatory opinion, that setting such a date merely restored to "Palm Beach County, and potentially other counties," the time they lost in combating the Department of State's legal errors.[19] When the Division of Elections' opinion appeared on November 13, "the counties had at least until Saturday, November 18, to complete the manual recounts and certify the amended results."[20] In such a situation, the November 26 date (decreed on November 21) "gave the counties no more time to complete the recount than they would have had if the [Division of Elections] had not forestalled their efforts."[21] Hence, the date did not constitute "a 'new' deadline and has no effect in future elections."[22]

There is evidence suggesting this explanation was supposed to go into the November 21 opinion, but was unaccountably omitted.[23] Hence, whatever its virtues or defects, such a defense arrived too late to justify the Florida Supreme Court's position in the litigation that followed.

The most surprising omission in *Palm Beach v. Harris* is the failure to face any equal-protection issues. The justices claimed, of course, that the matter was not even before them. "Neither party has raised as an issue on appeal the constitutionality of Florida's election laws."[24] But this was not actually the case, as we have seen. It was true that neither the Bush brief

nor Secretary Harris's had explored equal protection with any thorough-
ness. And the matter was downplayed at oral argument by Bush attorney
Michael Carvin.

JUSTICE PARIENTE. Well . . . let me ask . . . , is there a constitutional attack
on this statute being made?

MR. CARVIN. Well, we don't think you need reach the question, but yes.

JUSTICE PARIENTE. Well, is that because you're requesting the federal court
to reach it and you don't think that the state court has it within its jurisdiction to decide whether a statute is being constitutionally applied?

MR. CARVIN. Oh, no, clearly state courts have that power. I'm simply
making the point that there's a much simpler basis for deciding this case
than going all the way to the U.S. Constitution, which is state law.[25]

Nonetheless, the way was legally open for jurists so devoted to procedures for divining the true will of the people to have proclaimed here what
a majority of them proclaimed in the later contest opinion. "[I]t is absolutely essential . . . that a manual recount be conducted for all legal votes in this
State, . . . in all Florida counties where there [is] . . . a concern that not
every citizen's vote was counted."[26] Had the court ruled this way on
November 21, it would have been impossible to order sixty-three counties
in Florida to commence recounts, and extend the protest period into
December (which is probably why the vice president was not interested in
pursuing this subject at all in oral argument). Yet it might well have been
open to Gore to file an immediate contest action contending that, whatever
his errors, the complete count required by the justices was simply not
doable during the protest phase *because* of the secretary of state's erroneous interpretation of Florida law, and that a recount, therefore, must be
granted as contest relief.

Notes

1. "Senate Staff Analysis and Economic Impact Statement," pp. 1–2, Florida
Archives on Voter Protection Act, Florida Department of State, Bureau of Archives
and Record Management (hereafter, Florida Archives).
2. *Voter Protection Act*, 97.021 (26), Florida Archives.
3. Ibid., 101.105 (1).
4. Ibid., 101.5609 (8).
5. Ibid., 101.591 (1).
6. Proposed as 101.293 (1).
7. Don Pride, "Vote Fraud Bill Advances," *Tampa Tribune*, May 27, 1989,

Florida Archives.

8. Senator Norman Ostrau to Jane Carroll, May 11, 1989, p. 1, Florida Archives.

9. North Florida election supervisors to Senator George Stuart, April 26, 1989, p. 2, Florida Archives.

10. *Journal of the Senate*, June 2, 1989, p. 970; *Journal of the House of Representatives*, June 2, 1989, pp. 1546-1547, Florida Archives.

11. Pride, "Vote Fraud Bill Advances."

12. Division of Elections, Advisory Opinion DE 00-11: "Definitions of Errors in Vote Tabulation," November 13, 2000, reprinted in E. J. Dionne and William Kristol (eds.), *Bush v. Gore: The Court Cases and the Commentary* (Washington: Brookings Institution Press, 2001), p. 11.

13. Michael McConnell, "Two-and-a-Half Cheers for *Bush v. Gore*," in Cass Sunstein and Richard Epstein (eds.), *The Vote: Bush, Gore and the Supreme Court* (Chicago: Chicago University Press, 2001), pp. 106–107.

14. Richard Posner, *Breaking the Deadlock* (Princeton, N.J.: Princeton University Press, 2001), p. 101.

15. *Chevron U.S.A. v. Natural Resources Defense Council*, 467 US 837, 843 (1984).

16. *Krivanek v. Take Back Tampa Political Committee*, 625 So. 2d 840, 845 (1993); *Las Olas Tower Co. v. City of Fort Lauderdale*, 742 So. 2d 308, 312 (1999).

17. See Part 6.

18. *Palm Beach County Canvassing Board v. Harris*, Florida Supreme Court, "Answer Brief of Intervenor/Respondent George W. Bush," p. 17.

19. *Palm Beach County Canvassing Board v. Harris*, 772 So. 2d 1273, 1290 (2000).

20. Ibid.

21. Ibid.

22. Ibid.

23. Jeffrey Toobin, *Too Close to Call* (New York: Random House, 2001), p. 136.

24. *Palm Beach County Canvassing Board v. Harris*, 772 So. 2d 1220, 1228, fn. 10.

25. Oral Argument in *Palm Beach County Canvassing Board v. Harris*, reprinted in the *New York Times*, November 21, 2000, p. A19.

26. *Gore v. Harris*, 772 So. 2d 1243, 1253 (2000).

PART 3

COUNTING THE VOTES

On November 22, 2000, the hand counting of the ballots in Palm Beach, Broward, and Miami-Dade Counties could go forward without the fear of certain rejection by the secretary of state—at least until November 26.

From the beginning of the recounts, though, critical disputes had arisen about *how* the ballots in Florida should be assessed, what standards should govern the search for voter intent. Vice President Gore and his attorneys pushed persistently and urgently for the most liberal, inclusive standard—both before and after November 22.

The Early Struggles over Standards

This issue surfaced immediately in Palm Beach County. After completing its sample recount of November 10 and 11, the county canvassing board announced its intention of following for its full recount the standard adopted by the board ten years earlier, the only written attempt in the state of Florida to define the intent of the voter. The rule allowed any "chad that is hanging or partially detached" to count as a vote, "since it is possible to punch through the card and still not totally dislodge the chad" (others of which may have fallen off anyway).[1] However, a chad "fully attached, bearing only an indentation, should not be counted as a vote," since the indentation (or dimple) "may result from a voter placing the stylus in the position, but not punching through."[2] The Palm Beach board had, in fact, used this standard through most of the sample recount, after experimenting briefly with a "sunshine rule," under which a ballot counted if officials could detect light through its detachable rectangles.[3]

Even at this early stage, the Democrats were starting to feel a detached-chad standard was not liberal enough, either as a matter of law or of expediency. They went to the Palm Beach County Circuit Court and asked Judge Jorge LaBarga to clarify and to loosen up the criteria used in the recounts. Their counsel denounced the Palm Beach rules, or any other "per se rule" delimiting attempts to "determine [a] voter's intent . . . pursuant to . . . 102.166."[4] Counters must follow a standard "based on the totality of the evidence in the four corners of the punchcard ballot," and not automatically exclude "a definite indentation on a punch card."[5] In short, Gore's lawyers wanted a system that would make it possible, even easy, to count dimpled ballots.

This was not the customary practice in punch-card jurisdictions. Only Texas law, ironically, sanctioned such a practice in explicit terms,[6] though in the 1996 case of *Delahunt v. Johnston*, the Massachusetts Supreme Court had decided a congressional primary by counting ballots with dimples,[7] and, three years earlier, the supreme court of South Dakota laid down a voter-intent standard favoring such ballots.[8] An Illinois Supreme Court decision of 1990 suggested dimples might count, hence could not automatically be discarded by a trial judge.[9]

On November 15, Judge LaBarga issued a declaratory order that patted the Palm Beach canvassing board on the back, yet pushed it in the direction of a totality of the circumstances standard. The canvassing board, he held, "has the discretion to utilize whatever methodology it deems proper to determine the true intention of the voter and it should not be restricted in the task."[10] Yet, "the present policy of a per se exclusion of any ballot that does not have a partially punched or hanging chad, is not in compliance with the law."[11] Still, the board was entitled "to consider those ballots and accept them or reject them."[12]

When the Palm Beach canvassing board got clearance from the Florida Supreme Court the next day to begin its full recount, it promulgated a new counting standard, which was actually more rigorous than the one used before, yet still sought to follow Judge LaBarga's orders. A ballot automatically counted now only if the chad was hanging by two corners or more, not simply by one, as the 1990 guideline directed. But, "In accordance with the Honorable Judge LaBarga's ruling, this policy does not exclude any ballots bearing only one corner punched or an indentation (dimple)."[13] Such ballots "may be counted as a vote if there is clear evidence of a voter's intent to cast a vote as determined by the discretion of the Canvassing Board."[14]

The first part of the new standard represented an attempt to bring Palm Beach County into line with the policy adopted by Broward County when it began counting on November 15, its county canvassing board having decreed "that, in all cases, in order for a vote to be counted, a ballot [must] have at least two (2) corners of the chad detached."[15] But after Broward circuit judge John Miller, following Judge LaBarga, told the county's officials they must not limit themselves "to just one or two criteria," and must examine "the totality of the ballot,"[16] the canvassing board announced on November 19 that the "two-corner rule is no longer being applied to restrict . . . determination of voter intent"[17]—though, as in Palm Beach, two-corner punches automatically counted.

Both jurisdictions followed the same basic procedure for hand counting the 463,000 votes in Palm Beach and the 588,000 in Broward. Volunteer teams of two were authorized to approve any ballots with chads hanging by two or three corners. Ballots with chads attached by three corners, or that were dimpled, or perforated, could count or not count, according to the team's evaluation of voter intent. A Republican and a Democratic monitor tracked the decisions of the two counters, however, and unless all four agreed on a ballot, the matter went to the canvassing board for resolution. Many times, the observer-monitor groups disagreed about whether something seen on a presidential ballot was a dimple or merely a nick or scratch.[18]

Besides Judge Burton, the Palm Beach County canvassing board consisted of Supervisor of Elections LePore and County Commissioner Carol Roberts. All were Democrats. The Broward County canvassing board had two Democrats—Judge Robert Lee, its chairman, and County Commissioner Suzanne Gunzburger. Supervisor of Elections Jane Carroll, a Republican, resigned during the recount; her replacement was Judge Robert Rosenberg of the county court, also a Republican.

It quickly became clear, even as the Florida Supreme Court was deciding the fate of the recounts, that these two sets of officials took very different views of the elusive element of intent. Gore strategists were even more certain by the time the full recounts began that only an ample supply of dimpled ballots, and possibly ballots with other markings, could bring victory. But the canvassing board in Palm Beach bitterly disappointed their hopes. Not only did it reject many punch cards adjudged to have marks on them made by something other than a stylus; even ballots with genuine dimples counted in very small numbers. A dimpled vote for president was valid, under the board's criteria, only if the members found a pattern of dimples for other offices—at least 20 percent of the punches, apparently, though there was no absolute number. The board rejected ballots on which the voter had dimpled the presidential column but punched through in the others. A pattern of pinholed perforations also counted, and a clean punch in a column trumped anything else in that column, allowing some overvotes to be retrieved. (Later studies showed, however, that only 12 overvotes were recovered in Palm Beach, all for Gore.)[19] Under this regimen, the vice president had gained a total of three votes in Palm Beach County by November 20, with 20 percent of the precincts counted.[20]

Gore's lawyers went back to Judge LaBarga on November 20, requesting an emergency hearing to clarify his November 15 order. They now sought an injunction flatly requiring the Palm Beach canvassing board "to count indentations as votes, absent other evidence on the face of the ballot that clearly indicates a voter's intention to abstain."[21]

A Strategic Crossroads

The hearing before LaBarga took place after the Florida Supreme Court decision in *Palm Beach County Canvassing Board v. Harris*, raising the stakes considerably on its outcome. Gore's attorneys, Gregory Barnhart and Ben Kuehne, brought up various practical justifications for counting dimples in the presidential race, matters developed in greater detail at the contest trial. They pointed to the figures showing vastly higher undervote rates in the punch-card counties.[22] And in response to the discovery that many voters were making a dimple only in the presidential column and punching out the rest of the offices, Barnhart and Kuehne presented an affidavit from Supervisor LePore's predecessor in Palm Beach, Jackie Winchester, claiming that the difficulty experienced with punch-card machines "on the left side of the ballot . . . is because perhaps [of] the way in which the ballot is angled into the ballot counting machine, and so you have more problems as it goes down."[23]

None of this was supposed to represent a strong or a developed case, however, for the Gore lawyers were mainly concerned with convincing Judge LaBarga that dimpled ballots must count as a matter of law. Their principal reliance was on some words in Section 101.5614 of the election code that the Florida Supreme Court missed in its decision. The court had quoted 5614 (5): "No vote shall be declared invalid or void if there is a clear indication of the intent of the voter as determined by the canvassing board"; then, using their own words, the justices paraphrased 5614 (6) as providing "that any vote in which [a] Board cannot discern the intent of the voter must be discarded."[24] But Part 6 of 5614, Gregory Barnhart noted, actually read, "If it *is impossible to determine the elector's choice*, the elector's ballot shall not be counted."[25]

This put ballot-counting standards in a different light, Barnhart thought. The Florida legislature had in truth "giv[en] us a presumption . . . in favor of the voter, not a presumption against the voter. . . . If it's possible to determine the voter's choice, we must count the vote."[26] By contrast, the current Palm Beach standard carried with it "a presumption of unlawfulness and irregularity unless the voter clearly and convincingly can show otherwise."[27] This amounted to another version of the "per se exclusionary test" found "unlawful" on November 15.[28]

In deciding the Palm Beach dispute, however, Judge LaBarga stuck with the Florida Supreme Court's reading of 5614 (6) and put his own spin on (5), as indicated by his pointed use of italics. These succeeding portions of Florida law, he held, provided "that 'no vote shall be declared invalid if there is a clear indication of the intent of the voter *as determined by the canvassing board,*'" and "'that any vote in which the board cannot discern the intent of the voter must be discarded.'"[29]

He did not think it necessary, therefore, to be any more exact in setting standards than he had been a week earlier, certainly not as exact as Barnhart and Kuehne wanted him to be, though he repeated that "the canvassing board, as previously articulated . . . , cannot have a policy . . . of per se exclusion of any ballot; each ballot must be considered in light of the totality of the circumstances."[30]

Still, Judge Burton and his colleagues felt free to stick to the techniques they used before November 22. By November 25, the day before the deadline for submission of amended returns, Vice President Gore had picked up 8 votes in the county.[31]

He fared better in Broward County, for authorities there used a different and more capacious approach to dimples. The canvassing board decided such indentations could count in the presidential race, even if the voter had punched through the other choices, if that voter designated a straight party ticket.[32] Broward County completed its recount just after midnight on Saturday, November 25, with Gore picking up 567 votes.[33]

The Miami Imbroglio

Miami-Dade County did not lay down explicit guidelines for counting ballots, but a series of dramatic events quickly overshadowed the issue of procedure. On the morning of November 22, the day after the supreme court set its deadline, the canvassing board decided it could not possibly complete the manual recount, since only 99 of 614 precincts were done. Thus, the board agreed that morning to count only the 10,750 undervotes in the county. To save time, apparently, it decided not to check any of the county's 17,850 overvotes. This omission may also have been due to the fact that very few overvotes were turning up as valid choices for either Bush or Gore. (The *USA Today–Miami Herald* survey of 2001 showed only twenty such ballots, sixteen for Gore, four for Bush.)[34]

The Miami board quickly changed its tune, however. Judge Lawrence King, the board chairman and a Democrat, had earlier stated his belief that such a partial recount was illegal,[35] as it almost surely was under 102.166, and he reiterated this view at an afternoon meeting of the group. Supervisor of Elections David Leahy (an independent) was now convinced even a count of undervotes could not be finished, as was King.[36] With the concurrence of Judge Myriam Lehr, another independent, the Miami-Dade County canvassing board shut down its manual recount. (Its ultimate legal position was that all ballots must in fact be counted.)

Democrats argued the canvassing board was intimidated by howling mobs, organized by the Bush forces, that congregated outside the county operations center and stormed into the public areas of the building, making it necessary for police to patrol the building prior to the climactic afternoon meeting.[37] Evidence indicated that these were not just ordinary Floridians petitioning their government. Gore advisers spotted in the Miami crowd staff members from the offices of Representative Tom DeLay, of Senator Fred Thompson, and of four other Republican congressmen, none from Florida.[38] Supervisor Leahy admitted the protests were one factor influencing his decisions. "This was perceived as not being an open and fair process. That weighed heavily on our minds."[39]

Whatever their feeling about all the hubbub, however, the Miami canvassing board made a decision that was logistically inevitable. Indeed, when the vice president went to court on November 23, arguing that Miami-Dade officials were legally obligated to complete a manual recount once they ordered it, the Third District Court of Appeals agreed this was technically true, but held the board exempt from performing a fruitless task. Since the canvassing board had declared that a "complete manual recount" was necessary, and "that . . . it would be impossible to complete the recount before the deadline set forth by the Supreme Court," action could not lie against them.[40]

The Overseas Ballots

Meanwhile, the Bush camp took advantage of the hold on final certification of the overseas absentee ballots, many of them, of course, from military personnel, to add some votes of their own. The 630 votes already gained when the canvassing boards counted the ballots on November 18 were the result, we now know, of a devious two-tiered strategy the governor's lawyers in Florida had employed.[41]

For this original count, the Gore strategy was to insist on strict compliance with Florida law, which required a postmark on the envelope containing an overseas absentee ballot to show it had been mailed by November 7. Federal rules on these ballots were more permissive, allowing them to be postmarked, or signed and dated inside by election day. A memorandum on this subject by the vice president's key advisor on overseas ballots, Mark Herron, acknowledged that a signature and a date might pass muster, even without a postmark, yet finally stated, "With respect to those absentee ballots mailed by . . . qualified electors overseas, only those ballots mailed with an American Post Office, Foreign Post Office, or foreign postmark shall be considered valid"; the memo did not discourage Gore lawyers from adopting the policy, "No postmark . . . no vote."[42]

Bush's strategists acceded to such an approach in counties that were Gore strongholds. In counties where Bush was strongest, however, they implored canvassing officials to ignore lack of postmark, or other deficiencies, and to credit the ballot, especially when it was from a member of the military. The Bush pleas were not without success. In three Florida panhandle counties, for example, sixty-three military ballots without postmarks were counted, where they would likely not have been counted in Broward or Palm Beach Counties.

Furthermore, as the count was ending, the Republicans got hold of the Herron memo, and launched a national media offensive, deploring the preoccupation with narrow technicalities that had kept more men and women in uniform from expressing their will (and to which they had sometimes acquiesced). Under such pressure, Senator Lieberman agreed in a television interview on Sunday, November 19, that overseas military ballots deserved "the benefit of the doubt."[43] Twelve Republican-leaning counties reopened their books, and by Thanksgiving had added 105 votes to the Bush lead, at a time when newspaper surveys of the recount showed it dipping to 154.

Later evidence showed that in counties won by Bush, 1,053 overseas absentee packets displayed characteristics such as lack of both a proper postmark and a dated signature, a United States postmark, or want of a witness's signature. Five hundred and thirty of the ballots were counted, just over 50 percent. In counties won by Gore, 810 overseas ballots had the same characteristics. Only 150 (18 percent) got counted. (We do not know how those 680 people voted, since the actual ballots themselves are routinely separated from the envelopes containing voter information.)

The First Act Finale

Palm Beach County struggled to meet the supreme court deadline, but on the afternoon of November 26, Judge Burton faxed a letter to Harris, asking for a little time beyond 5 P.M. to complete its work. The secretary refused, and at 7:30 P.M., using Palm Beach's unamended return, she certified Bush as the winner by 537 votes—2,912,970 to 2,912,253. Palm Beach completed its manual recount anyway that evening, though not presenting its final totals until later. The number of votes Gore picked up would be disputed: Bush lawyers said it was 176; the Gore attorneys said 215.[44]

The next step was for Governor Jeb Bush to send off to the National Archives in Washington by registered mail an official certificate of ascertainment naming the state's presidential electors, as required by the Electoral Count Act. Even in the performance of this purely ministerial function, a heightened sense of uncertainty prevailed.

> The Bush team feared that this was a moment of extreme danger. . . . If Gore subpoenaed the ascertainment before it could leave Florida, George W. Bush's electors would not become official in the eyes of the federal government.
> [Thus, Jeb Bush's aides] decided to give the certificate to a staff member entirely unrelated to the election dispute—someone the Gore team would never think of serving with a subpoena. This staff member took the document home and slept with it. Then, the next morning, she took it straight to the post office and mailed it.
> When she arrived at the office that morning, deputy counsel Reg Brown asked how it had gone. Fine, she said. In fact, the nice clerk at the post office had offered her an option that was better than registered mail—Express Mail.
> The people on the Florida governor's legal team rushed out the door to the post office. They flashed all sorts of identification, begged and pleaded and cajoled, until finally the clerk let them retrieve the package. They tore off the Express Mail packaging and relabeled it as registered mail. At last, George W. Bush's deciding votes were on their way to Washington.[45]

Notes

1. "Contest Trial Before Judge Sauls," p. 411, www.flcourts.org.
2. Ibid.
3. *Florida Democratic Party v. Palm Beach County Canvassing Board*, 15th Judicial Circuit, "First Amended Complaint for Declaratory Judgment and Petition for Writ of Mandamus," pp. 6–7.
4. Ibid., pp. 12–13.
5. Ibid., pp. 13, 7.
6. John Mintz, "Only Texas Law Provides for Inclusion of Indented Ballots," *Washington Post*, November 24, 2000, p. A1.
7. *Delahunt v. Johnston*, 671 N.E. 2d 1241 (1996).
8. *Duffy v. Mortenson*, 497 N.W. 2d 437 (1993).
9. *Pullen v. Mulligan*, 561 N.E. 2d 585 (1990).
10. *Florida Democratic Party v. Palm Beach Canvassing Board*, "Declaratory Order."
11. Ibid.
12. Ibid.
13. Hearing Before Judge Jorge LaBarga, November 22, 2000, p. 40. Courtesy of Gregory Barnhart.
14. Ibid.
15. Quoted in *Palm Beach County Canvassing Board v. Harris*, Florida Supreme Court, "Petitioner Broward County Canvassing Board's and Broward County Supervisor of Election's Initial Brief on the Merits," p. 7.

16. Ibid., p. 8. Judge Miller did not issue a written opinion.
17. *Palm Beach County Canvassing Board v. Harris*, "Petitioner Broward County Canvassing Board's Reply Brief," p. 1.
18. See Judge Burton's testimony, "Contest Trial Before Judge Sauls," pp. 248–250; David Gonzalez and Dana Canedy, "Local Officials and Courts Clear the Way for Recount," *New York Times*, November 16, 2000, p. A27; April Witt, "Broward Says Recount Is On," *Washington Post*, November 16, 2000, p. A26.
19. See Judge Burton's testimony in hearing before Judge LaBarga, pp. 41-47; Testimony in Contest Trial, pp. 250–251, 255–259, 263–264. *USA Today-Miami Herald* Survey of Overvotes—County Summary, p. 2. Courtesy of Dennis Cauchon.
20. *Washington Post*, November 21, 2000, p. A15.
21. *Florida Democratic Party v. Palm Beach County Canvassing Board*, "Order on Plaintiff's Emergency Motion to Clarify Declaratory Order of November 15, 2000," p. 2.
22. Hearing Before Judge LaBarga, pp. 23–24, 35–36.
23. Ibid., p. 110.
24. *Palm Beach Canvassing Board v. Harris*, 772 So. 2d 1220, 1229 (2000).
25. *The 2000 Florida Statutes*, 101.5614(6) (italics added), www.flcourts.org.
26. Hearing Before Judge LaBarga, p. 14.
27. Ibid., pp. 13–14.
28. Ibid., p. 24.
29. *Florida Democratic Party v. Palm Beach County Canvassing Board*, "Order on Plaintiff's Emergency Motion," p. 3.
30. Ibid., p. 6.
31. *New York Times*, November 25, 2000, p. A1.
32. Roberto Suro, Jo Becker, and Serge Kovaleski, "For Bush and Gore, Another Day in Court," *Washington Post*, November 24, 2000, pp. A1, 37.
33. David Firestone, "Recounts Give Gore 466 More Votes as Litigation Expands," November 26, 2000, Correspondents of *The New York Times, 36 Days* (New York: Times Books, 2001), pp. 158, 159.
34. Political Staff of *The Washington Post, Deadlock* (New York: Public Affairs, 2001), p. 138. *USA Today-Miami Herald* Survey of Overvotes—County Summary, p. 1.
35. "Contest Trial Before Judge Sauls," pp. 576–577.
36. Political Staff of *The Washington Post, Deadlock*, pp. 142–143; Jeffrey Toobin, *Too Close To Call* (New York: Random House, 2001), pp. 156–157.
37. Dexter Filkins and Dana Canedy, "Chaotic Protest Influences Miami-Dade's Decision," November 24, 2000, reprinted in Correspondents of *The New York Times, 36 Days*, pp. 134, 135.
38. Political Staff of *The Washington Post, Deadlock*, pp. 140–141.
39. Filkins and Canedy, "Chaotic Protest," p. 135.
40. *Miami-Dade County Democratic Party v. Miami-Dade County Canvassing Board*, 773 So. 2d 1179, 1180 (2000).
41. This development is explored in a study, parts of which are reprinted in the documents associated with this part. David Barstow and Don Van Natta Jr., "How Bush Took Florida: Mining the Overseas Absentee Vote," *New York Times*, July 15, 2001, pp. A1, 15, 16.
42. Robert Zelnick, *Winning Florida: How the Bush Team Fought the Battle* (Stanford: Hoover Institution Press, 2001,) p. 75; Political Staff of *The Washington Post, Deadlock*, p. 127; see also, David Kaplan, *The Accidental President* (New York: William Morrow, 2001), pp. 157–163.

43. Richard Berke, "Lieberman Put Democrats in Retreat on Military Vote," *New York Times*, July 15, 2001, p. A14.

44. Several newspaper reports on November 27 put the figure at 155. In the contest trial, Gore lawyers maintained the total of additional votes was 215. Bush attorneys said it was 176. The supreme court of Florida apparently accepted the 215 figure.

45. Political Staff of *The Washington Post, Deadlock*, p. 153–154.

Delahunt v. Johnston: The Crucial Precedent?

Gore's lawyers understandably relied on the Massachusetts Supreme Court decision in *Delahunt v. Johnston* for the proposition that dimpled ballots satisfy the standard of voter intent necessary to count them as valid. Yet the facts of the 1996 congressional primary involved in Delahunt's case, as developed in the Plymouth County Superior Court, reveal a situation very different from the one in Florida.

The vast majority of the dimples successfully disputed by Delahunt in superior court—more than enough to provide the margin of victory—came from the town of Weymouth, where a whopping 23 percent of the ballots turned up as nonvotes. This was by far the highest percentage of such votes in any punch-card community (except for the small town of Orleans, also protested in court).

Furthermore, the race for the Democratic nomination between Delahunt and Johnston was the only contested one on the ballot in Weymouth, making it almost unthinkable that so many people would have gone to the polls—during a driving rainstorm—and failed to register a choice for Congress.

Though a firm Gore supporter, William Johnston was naturally unenthusiastic about the landmark decision bearing his name. Johnston had been a state representative and director of the Massachusetts Department of Health and Human Services when he ran for Congress. In 2000, he became chairman of the Massachusetts Democratic Party.

Delahunt v. Johnston

The parties were candidates in the September 17, 1996, primary for the nomination of the Democratic Party for the office of United States Representative for the Tenth Congressional District. After the initial tabulation of the votes, the defendant Johnston was declared the winner with 266 more votes than the plaintiff Delahunt. Recounts were undertaken, pursuant to recount petitions filed in several municipalities, and, on September 30, 1996, Johnston was again declared the winner with 175 more votes than Delahunt.

On October 2, 1996, Delahunt commenced this action....

The critical question in this case is whether a discernible indentation made on or near a chad should be recorded as a vote for the person to whom the chad is assigned. The trial judge concluded that a vote should be recorded for a candidate if the chad was not removed but an impression was made on or near it. We agree with this conclusion.

We apply the standard that has been expressed in our cases concerning the counting of punch card (and other) ballots.... "The cardinal rule for guidance of election officers and courts in cases of this nature is that if the intent of the voter can be determined with reasonable certainty from an inspection of the ballot, in the light of the generally known conditions attendant upon the election, effect must be given to that intent and the vote counted in accordance therewith, provided the voter has substantially complied with the requisites of the election law; if that intent cannot thus be fairly and satisfactorily ascertained, the ballot cannot rightly be counted." *O'Brien v. Election Comm'rs of Boston*, 257 Mass. 332, 338, 153 N.E. 553 (1926). Our review of a voter's intent is a question of law that we decide de novo.

From *Delahunt v. Johnson,* 671 N.E. 2d 1241 (1996).

We find unpersuasive Johnston's contention that many voters started to express a preference in the congressional contest, made an impression on a punch card, but pulled the stylus back because they really did not want to express a choice on that contest. The large number of ballots with discernible impressions makes such an inference unwarranted, especially in a hotly contested election.

It is, of course, true that a voter who failed to push a stylus through the ballot and thereby create a hole in it could have done a better job of expressing his or her intent. Such a voter should not automatically be disqualified, however, like a litigant or one seeking favors from the government, because he or she failed to comply strictly with announced procedures. The voters are the owners of the government, and our rule that we seek to discern the voter's intention and to give it effect reflects the proper relation between government and those to whom it is responsible.

Once one accepts, as we have, the presence of a discernible impression made by a stylus as a clear indication of a voter's intent, our task is to assess each of the 956 ballots. We have done so and have agreed with the trial judge's conclusions on all but twenty-eight ballots. Our totals concerning the contested ballots show that Delahunt gained 659 votes, Johnston gained 283 votes, and fourteen ballots were blank. This resulted in a net gain of 376 votes for Delahunt which more than offset Johnston's 175 vote lead before the contested ballots were counted.

Dimpled Chads Cost Me an Election

Phillip W. Johnston

My family refers to the experience as our "hideous debacle"; it was that and more. When my 1996 primary race for the 10th Congressional district in Massachusetts ended with a judge's decision to overturn my initial victory, I never wanted to hear the term "chad" again.

This month I was in Tampa, Fla., working for Al Gore. After returning home on Election Day to attend Ted Kennedy's victory party, I was appalled to learn that those accursed punch-tab ballots that had helped to destroy my hopes of holding a seat in Congress were going to decide who would be the next occupant of the White House.

It was neither my fault nor that of my opponent, Bill Delahunt, that the Democratic voters in our district were so closely divided. On primary night, I was the apparent winner by 288 votes. Mr. Delahunt petitioned for a recount in two areas where he had done well; both used punch-tab ballots. I counter-petitioned in three areas that I had won, all of which also had punch tabs. I won the recount by 175 votes. The recounts involved judgments about chads: punch dots that voters may have only partially pierced.

Mr. Delahunt then sued in a state court, hoping to have more than 900 ballots ruled valid that had been called "blank" by the local election officials. These were dimpled, or indented, ballots—one of the types now causing problems in Florida. The judge went into her private chambers, counted the ballots, came out and overturned the election by 108 votes. She did not explain the standard she used to determine what constituted a vote, but it appeared that she had accepted any mark on the ballot. A few days later the State Supreme Court upheld her decision, and my campaign was over. Mr. Delahunt went on to win a seat in Congress.

Originally published in *The New York Times*, November 18, 2000, p. A31. Reprinted by permission.

Some of the painful lessons I learned in Massachusetts apply to today's conflict in Florida.

First, ballots that are subject to judgment calls by election officials and judges taint the electoral process. In Florida, disputed punch-tab ballots and butterfly ballots can be read in different ways by different observers. In Massachusetts, the courts have not been consistent on punch-tab ballots; six months before the decision in my race, another judge had ruled that light must be showing through a punch in order for it to count as a vote. The truth is that there are no generally accepted standards, and the punch-tab ballot doesn't make it easy to formulate them. This kind of ballot should simply be banned in all states.

It bothered me, too, that my entire district was never recounted. In the Florida situation, the suggestion that the entire state should be recounted by hand and that the candidates should abide by the outcome strikes me as eminently reasonable.

As for settling disputes about individual ballots, either local election officials who are trained in the field or three-judge panels should be responsible. Confidence in the integrity of the system would be undermined greatly if any individual judge selected the next president of the United States.

The silver lining in all this recent turmoil is that the flaws in our electoral process—the inconsistent standards, the confusing ballots, the lack of accountability and the potential for conflicts of interest—are all now exposed. Let us hope that Americans will demand quick reforms. Meanwhile, my heart goes out to the presidential candidates and their families. Whatever happens, the loser in this election will never feel that he was dealt with fairly.

11

Judge Charles Burton Testifies in Judge Jorge LaBarga's Court

The hearing before Palm Beach Circuit Court Judge Jorge LaBarga on November 22 (the second such hearing in eight days) was the Democrats' last chance to pull ahead in the recount before the November 26 deadline. Judge Charles Burton was the chief witness at the hearing, and, after carefully reviewing with him the criteria being used in the Palm Beach recount, Gore's counsel, Miami attorney Ben Kuehne, cleverly maneuvered the judge into a significant admission: that his board's standards resembled the "clear and convincing" test both Kuehne and Gregory Barnhart had argued was incompatible with Florida law.

However, Bush's ubiquitous lead counsel in Florida, Barry Richard, got Burton to back off from this admission, and raised questions as well about whether counting dimples would not actually invalidate ballots that the canvassing board had previously credited to Gore (or Bush).

Despite its importance, the atmosphere of the hearing was relaxed, a reminder that this particular phase of the Bush-Gore struggle was a contest between old friends from the Florida bar.

Cross Examination: By Mr. Kuehne

Q. Hi, Judge Burton.

A. How you doing, Mr. Kuehne?

Hearing Before Honorable Judge Jorge LaBarga, November 22, 2000, pp. 55, 59–61, 73–74, 78–79, 81–86. Courtesy of Gregory Barnhart.

Q. Good, thanks.
    This is your first Canvassing Board opportunity?

A. Absolutely.

Q. And that came to you because of the routine assignment as a new coun-
    ty court judge when the Canvassing Board was impaneled?

A. Correct....

Q. It sort of goes to, no disrespect, but the first judge on the totem pole?

A. The low man on the pole, yes, sir.

Q. And that was you?

A. Yes, sir....

Q. [Y]ou certainly have heard before today the references to the Judge
    Miller hearing where he directed the [Broward County] Canvassing
    Board... to [consider] totality of the ballot....

A. Yes....

Q. Had you seen the transcript before?

A. No, sir, I had not.

Q. Do you need to look at the transcript to help confirm, in fact, that that's
    what the Broward County judge said?

A. Mr. Kuehne, I have known you long enough that if you say it, I have no
    doubt that it's true....

Q. Now, you've mentioned a couple of times, and I just want to make sure
    that we understand it, that you're looking for a consistent pattern of
    impression when you don't have the two corners separated from the
    card, it that right?

A. Correct.

Q. Are you looking for that same consistent pattern of impression when
    you have one corner separated from the card?

A. I would say that we're trying to look at the card to see if there is any consistency with the card. In other words, if it's a one-cornered chad punched out and the rest of the card is all punched out, no, we're not giving it much thought.

   We're trying to see why this person seemed to have a problem punching out a card. You know, I have a machine with me. It's fairly simple to punch through, so. We're trying to figure out why this person had a problem. And if they consistently had the problem, we're acknowledging that showed intent. If it happened once and the rest of the time everything is punched out, we've made a determination that it doesn't show intent.

   I don't know if that's right or wrong. I'm just saying that's how we've been doing it....

Q. [So] it's clearly a vote if there are two corners out?

A. Yes.

Q. And if there are less than two corners out, then you have to go through some analysis?

A. Yes.

Q. And that analysis requires that you look at the rest of the card to see if the voters have done that same thing before?

A. That's true.

Q. Now, do you presume, as a Canvassing Board, that any marks on the card are made by the voter?

A. I don't know that we've ever thought about it. I think that certainly is more true with respect to a card that was cast at some election office versus an absentee ballot, yes.

Q. Let's put absentees to the side.

A. Okay.

Q. So markings that would be made with the security and regularity of ballot cards are made by the voter?

A. Yes....

Q. [So], finally, let me close by asking you, Judge Burton, when you are discarding or not counting these ballots, do you have any evidence that the voter did not intend to cast the ballot?

A. [D]o I have any evidence? No. The only assumption, I think, we are making as a group is that if they've been able to punch out every other hole, we're assuming they didn't have the intent to vote.

Q. And the application you're using is unless you're clearly convinced the voter intended to vote, that will not be counted as a valid ballot?

A. Correct, because I think while it is important certainly to try to include everyone's vote, I don't think this board is trying to give a person a vote they didn't intend to make. And I don't know what their intent was. You know, that's the difficult process.

Q. But as I understand, is that the standard you're using, the Canvassing Board is using, looking at the card, that piece of paper, and using a clear and convincing standard, does that card clearly and convincingly tell us, the Canvassing Board, that the person voted?

A. Yes....

Cross Examination: By Mr. Richard

Q. Good morning, Judge.

A. Good morning, sir.

Q. Did there come a time that this Board had any conversation in which you said let's decide what the legal standard is that we're going to follow; and then you said, well, we're going to follow a clear and convincing standard; and then you said what would that standard cause us to do; and that's how you came upon the operation you currently have? Is that what you did?

A. I know I came in with a proposal based on...the standard we were going to apply, yes.

Q. Let me put it another way. I heard you describe for us in some considerable detail the policies, or the procedures, or the practices that you've adopted in an effort to attempt to decide card by card what the intent of the voter is?

A. Yes, sir.

Q. So it appears to me that what you've done is you've followed a procedure that has been motivated by the effort to determine the intent of the voter rather than by some abstract legal standard that counsel has called clear and convincing, is that a fair statement?

A. Yes, sir, I believe that is fair.

Q. So if you found an instance in which the three of you reached unanimity, that you were comfortable as to the candidate that this voter intended to vote for, you wouldn't say this doesn't meet the clear and convincing standard, therefore we're going to disqualify it, would you?

A. No, sir....

Q. Now, you testified that if you had a card in which votes were cast for two candidates in the same race, that you would disqualify that card, is that correct?

A. That would be considered an over vote. You can only vote for one.

Q. Now, if the Court were to instruct you that dimples were to be given the same dignity as punch-outs, and you were to have a card in which [in] the same column there was a punch-out for one candidate and also a dimple chad for another candidate in the same race, would you then feel compelled to disqualify that card as being an over vote?

A. I would say that if the Court were to say one impression or one dimple is the same as a punch-out, you can make the decision that that's an over vote.
      On the other hand, I can also see the argument, well, if it's punched out, that should be given more weight. So I don't know. But, yes, I could see how it would be....

Q. Well, I'm asking you for a hypothetical here if the Court were to deprive you of the discretion to make that decision and were to instruct you from the bench that dimples are to be given the same dignity as punch-outs, would you then feel the necessity to disqualify those cards in which there were both in one column?

A. Well, I'm always mindful to follow a judge's order. If the judge were to tell me they're of identical and equal weight, then I would say yes.

Q. Has that occurred? Have you had cards where there was a
     punch-out and a dimple in the same column?

A. We have—I believe we have counted the punch-out as a vote.

Q. Yes.

A. Right.

Q. You're not under instructions to do otherwise.

A. Correct.

Q. But you had cards where you found that?

A. We have had cards where we have had a clearly punched hole and
     some type of impression, a dimple, whatever on another candidate, yes.

Q. More than once?

A. Yes.

Q. Often?

A. We've had some strange ballot cards, so, yes. I don't know how many.
     I'm not keeping track....

Q. Have the three members of the Board been able to achieve unanimity
     with some frequency in the determination as to the voter's intent?

A. I think for the most part we have.

Q. Often?

A. The majority I believe have been unanimous. That we did a unanimous
     decision as to the vote.

Q. Am I correct that the Supervisor and the Commissioner are
     Democrats?

A. You know, I—so I've heard.

Too Close to Call

Jeffrey Toobin

Jeffrey Toobin's outstanding book on the Florida election contains an especially vivid and incisive account of the events surrounding the Miami-Dade County Canvassing Board's decision to shut down its manual recount, and the relation of those events to the political and social culture of the city of Miami.

A former assistant United States attorney, and an associate counsel in the Iran-Contra investigation, Jeffrey Toobin has written highly acclaimed volumes on the Clinton impeachment and the O. J. Simpson trial.

Radio has unique power in Miami's Cuban-American community. Several Spanish-language stations devote themselves entirely to talk about politics, and play a critical role in shaping the agenda of the city, region, and state. No print or television outlet can match radio's influence. (Notably, Miami doesn't even have one English-language station devoted to politics.) The most powerful station is Radio Mambi, a 50,000-watt behemoth that pulsates with anti-Castro invective twenty-four hours a day. The station's office is located in the biggest building on Calle Ocho, the legendary artery of Cuban Miami, and is decorated with pictures of pre-revolutionary Havana and posters saluting the veterans of the Bay of Pigs.

The principal owner and on-air voice of Radio Mambi is Armando Perez-Roura, a seventy-year-old Cuban exile and major political figure in Florida. On the Sunday before the 2000 election, Perez-Roura introduced George W. Bush to a rally of five thousand people. There Perez-Roura inveighed the crowd to remember Elian Gonzalez when they went to the polls. "We must punish the enemy with our votes," he vowed. Perez-Roura had played this kind of role many times for the Bush family. His autobiography includes photographs of him on *Air Force One* and in the Oval Office with the first President Bush. Jeb Bush, who is fluent in Spanish, makes frequent on-air appearances with Perez-Roura. At the last rally before the election, Al Cardenas, the chairman of the state Republican party, saluted Perez-Roura as "the Cuban-American community's Rush Limbaugh."...

But Armando Perez-Roura, Sr., was more than just a fiery partisan like Limbaugh. He was known for his ability to bring his listeners into the streets, and Miami political protests had a history of violence—threats, beatings, and even bombings. Perez-Roura had never been known to incite specific acts of violence, but his word unquestionably carried an edge of menace.

It was because of Perez-Roura's authority over the streets that [an adviser to George Bush] Roger Stone and his wife, Nydia (also from a Cuban exile family, and her husband's translator), came to pay homage when the recount in Miami began. The visit to Radio Mambi kicked off a series of visits by the Stones to exile-radio broadcasters in Miami to make sure that the Cuban community could be counted on in the days ahead. Reassured, Stone left the rest of the battle to the lawyers, for the time being....

On Monday [November 20], the vote counting began [in Miami-Dade County], with each of the twenty-five [counting] tables monitored by both Democratic and Republican lawyers. Later that day, a local judge rejected a Bush lawsuit to invalidate the hand count. The following day, Tuesday, November 21, the Florida Supreme Court gave Gore his smashing victory, ordering the hand count to proceed and setting a new deadline of Sunday, November 26, for certification of the vote. The supreme court's decision also set the stage for the most dramatic events of the post-election period— the scene at Miami's Clark Center on Wednesday, November 22....

In the two weeks since the election, partisans from around the country had been converging on Florida. Generally, the migratory patterns reflected the candidates' priorities in the recount. [Ron] Klain had said [from the start], "We need lawyers"—so the Democrats recruited many attorneys, who took time off from their jobs and volunteered to take affidavits, organize court cases, and do whatever was necessary. At Gore's express directive, however, the shock troops of the Democratic Party—civil-rights, union, and other activists—were instructed to stay away. The vice president saw the recount as a legal, not political, process.

Republicans had plenty of lawyers, too, of course, but they also had a pipeline of operatives heading south, conforming with the Bush strategy of using protests as well as litigation to send its message. Some of the people arriving in Florida were well known, like Roger Stone, but also in the

group were many young and determined congressional aides who had come
to Washington since the House went Republican in 1994. Nearly a hundred
of them made their way to the Clark Center shortly after dawn on
Wednesday....

What really distinguished the scene on Wednesday, though, was the
atmosphere in front of the Clark Center. Through the preliminary skirmish-
es over the recounts, this area on the fringe of downtown Miami had been
quiet, with many reporters but no large demonstrations. From the start,
Wednesday was different. Early that morning, Armando Perez-Roura of
Radio Mambi had sent a local activist who sometimes worked for him as a
reporter to broadcast from the plaza. Evilio Cepero urged Perez-Roura's listeners to join the protest, addressing the growing crowd with a mega-
phone.... Cepero's motives were straightforward. As he told *The New York
Times*, "We were trying to stop the recount; Bush had already won." From a
building across the street, Roger Stone communicated with his people on
the ground by walkie-talkie. Many held signs that became familiar in
Florida over these weeks: SORE/LOSERMAN, they said, in a parody of
the blue-and-white Gore/Lieberman signs used in the Democratic campaign. They chanted, "Remember Elian!"

At around six-thirty on Wednesday morning, elections supervisor
David Leahy arrived at his office to consider the ramifications of the
Florida Supreme Court decision. The court had set a deadline of November
26, which was five days before Leahy thought the board could finish count-
ing all 653,963 votes. When the full canvassing board reconvened at 8
A.M., Leahy had a proposal to deal with the problem.

Judge King called the session to order in the large room on the eighteenth floor where the twenty-five counting tables were set up before him.
(On the Gore side [sat] Jack Young, the recount specialist....) Leahy's idea
was simple. Instead of recounting all the votes by hand, the board should
only look at the 10,750 undervotes. That would give the county a "good,
clear count" by the Sunday deadline. " I think it's doable. I think we can
accomplish it," Leahy said. The Bush lawyers objected, asserting that the
board had to count all the votes or none of them. The Republican lawyer
Miguel DeGrandy inflamed the situation even more by suggesting that a
continuation of the recount [in this way] would discriminate against
Hispanic voters, on the ground that the [full] 1-percent recount, which
would be included in the final vote totals, covered areas where few
Hispanics lived. It was a dubious assertion, but it was sure to motivate the
throngs of Cuban-Americans gathering inside and outside the Clark Center.

Notwithstanding the Bush lawyers' arguments, the two judges joined
Leahy and agreed to count just the undervotes. Because the number of
votes at issue had declined so dramatically, Leahy said the twenty-five
pairs of counters could be dismissed. The board itself would count the

votes. Almost in passing, Leahy suggested that the board move upstairs one flight to the nineteenth floor, where the counting machines and his own office were located. "My recommendation would be to move up to the tabulation room," he said, where observers from each party could be "behind us watching us make decisions." Again, there was no dissent—at first.

Several hundred spectators had assembled in the common area on the eighteenth floor, and as the board members moved upstairs, a sizable number—perhaps fifty—of Republican protesters followed them up on the elevators. There was far less room for the public on the nineteenth floor, only a T-shaped elevator vestibule facing a glass wall that looked out over the offices of the supervisor of elections. The tabulation room, where the counting would take place, was at the other end of the building, and it could barely be seen from behind the glass wall. As the vestibule filled with people, the atmosphere grew tense, then angry. The Republicans wanted to observe the vote counting on nineteen as they had on eighteen. But Leahy was allowing only a pair of observers from both sides in the tabulation room. "Hopefully, the mood out front will settle down," Leahy said.

But the mood didn't settle down. "Until the demonstration stops, nobody can do anything," Leahy said. Reporters, too, were demanding greater access to the tabulation room on the nineteenth floor. At about 10:30 A.M., in light of the protest, the board shut down again and decided to reconvene on the eighteenth floor, after a short recess.

Lawyers from both sides continued to move to and from the tabulation room, but the crowd around the elevator was not allowed inside. This group included the hard core of the Republican congressional aides, who were shouting in the hallway, "They're stealing the election!" "Let us in!" "We want to see the votes!" Several started banging on the doors.

Shortly before eleven, Joe Geller, the Democratic Party chair, arrived on the nineteenth floor, hoping to resolve a minor mystery in the election. On the Miami-Dade ballot, Bush's votes were punched into the fourth hole in the ballot and Gore's into the sixth. However, Geller and others had noticed an unusual number of votes in the seventh hole, which made no sense to him, because it corresponded to no candidate. Geller had a theory that the holes were punched because Gore voters had improperly inserted their cards into the machine. Geller went to the window on the nineteenth floor to get a sample ballot so he could make a test. A clerk slipped him a ballot through the bank teller-style opening in the glass wall.

A voice shot out: "He stole a ballot!" The crowd converged on Geller. "He's stealing a ballot!" "Thief!" Geller fought his way to the elevator, but a group of what would become known as the Brooks Brothers mob followed him downstairs. In the lobby, the group surrounded Geller and refused to allow him to return to the Democratic staging area. Finally, a group of police officers arrived and separated Geller from his pursuers. He explained that he only had a sample ballot, and a little while later, the officers walked Geller to his car. (Geller's theory about the ballot placement turned out to be a viable one, but even he didn't think that the number-seven-hole votes could be counted for Gore.)

Back upstairs, the crowd was still chanting, adopting such Old Left favorites as "No justice, no peace!" and "The whole world is watching!" [Republican] Congressman [John] Sweeney [of New York] was overheard yelling, "Shut it down!" (Later, the congressman explained, rather implausibly, that he meant shut down the count until more people could watch, not shut it down for good.) After Geller had safely escaped, sometime after eleven, Jack Young went back up to the nineteenth floor, where he believed the canvassing board would be reconvening shortly. When he tried to make his way through the Republican protesters, he and his colleagues were jostled, held, and harassed. At the window, Young was told that the board had decided to reconvene back on the eighteenth floor.

It wasn't until 1:30 P.M.—by which time the protests inside and outside the building had been roiling for several hours—that the board members finally took their places back on the eighteenth floor. Judge King began by recognizing David Leahy, who, it turned out, had had a major change of heart since the morning. Earlier, the elections supervisor had said that a recount of the 10,750 undervotes was "doable." Now, Leahy reconsidered. "I can't sit here and tell you that if we begin the process it will be concluded," he said. "We simply cannot get it done." Judge King agreed. "After discussing with staff and the very people that would have to do this process," he said, "we were in a different situation...than we were this morning when we made that decision, a radically different situation." [King also said, "We cannot meet the deadline of the Supreme Court of the state of Florida, and I feel it incumbent upon this canvassing board to *count each and every ballot.*" *Deadlock*, pp. 142-43 (italics added).]

Jack Young was allowed to sputter some objections, but to no avail. Within a half-hour, the board had voted three to nothing to count no more votes—neither the undervotes nor anything else.

Arguing About the Overseas Absentee Ballots

The *New York Times* study of the overseas absentee ballots took six months to complete and was not published until July 15, 2001.

Times journalists and researchers examined 2,490 absentee packets from Americans living abroad in the process of finding the 680 seriously flawed applications that were approved. As noted, it is impossible to ascertain how these improperly counted ballots might have affected the Florida election. An analysis by Professor Gary King of Harvard, commissioned by the *Times,* estimates that Governor Bush's margin of victory in the November 26 certification would have dwindled to 245 votes had the flawed applications been discarded. This is necessarily hypothetical, however.

Accompanying the main article in the *Times* were several shorter pieces dealing with related aspects of the overseas ballot controversy. A particularly intriguing one concerned Senator Lieberman and the military vote.

Mining the Overseas Absentee Vote

David Barstow and Don Van Natta Jr.

Having assumed that Mr. Bush would win easily among overseas voters, the Gore strategy was predicated on knocking out overseas votes and fighting for the strictest readings of state law. Never mind Mr. Gore's repeated pledge to count every vote; his strategists calculated simply that the fewer overseas ballots counted the better.

It was left to Mark Herron, a Tallahassee election law specialist, to teach the Gore legal recruits the basics of overseas ballots, and on Wednesday, Nov. 15, Mr. Herron circulated a five-page memorandum that listed legal grounds for protesting overseas ballots when the canvassing boards reviewed them just two days later....

But the Bush lawyers had a strategy memorandum of their own...that also set out detailed instructions for challenging overseas ballots. The 52-page document included all the information Bush lawyers might need to make their case before the canvassing boards....

Unlike the single-minded approach of the Gore memorandum, the Bush instructions set forth a more adaptable, tactical approach aimed at achieving the largest possible net gain from overseas voters. Specifically, the Bush lawyers were told how to challenge "illegal" civilian votes that they assumed would be for Mr. Gore and also how to defend equally defective military ballots, the document shows.

The clearest illustration of the differing strategies was in the pre-printed protest forms that each campaign prepared for use with the canvassing boards as they scrutinized each ballot envelope for legal defects.

The Gore instructions included one all-purpose protest form; the Bush instructions included two. The first Bush form protested defective ballots just as the Gore form did and listed many of the same potential flaws—

Originally published in *The New York Times*, July 15, 2001, p. A16. Reprinted by permission.

missing witnesses, late postmarks, domestic postmarks. In an accompanying "letter of instruction" the Bush lawyers were told that it was essential to check for defects and that there was to be no flexibility on the question of missing postmarks. To be valid, the letter said, ballots "must have" a military or foreign postmark.

The second form, which was used to protest the exclusion of military ballots, demanded that canvassing boards count military ballots that arrived without postmarks, or with illegible postmarks, or even in some cases with United States postmarks....

In addition, the Bush instructions contended repeatedly that civilian ballots were not entitled to the same leeway as military ballots—a distinction not found in either Florida election law or in the federal law that governs overseas voting. One example involved overseas ballots delivered by Fed-Ex or other commercial express mail services. "Late shipment by civilians through such channels raises reasonable questions about the legitimacy of the ballot," the instructions said....

Questioning Civilian Ballots, Defending Military Ballots

On Friday, Nov. 17, county officials across the state began counting the overseas votes, the only ballots not yet examined by man or machine.

By then Mr. Bush's unofficial 1,784-vote lead had been reduced to 300. That very day, the Florida Supreme Court had barred [Secretary] Harris from certifying any final results until the justices, all Democratic appointees, decided whether to allow hand recounts to proceed in South Florida.

The Bush lawyers involved in overseas ballots gave different responses to whether they approached that Friday with a two-tiered strategy. [Benjamin] Ginsburg acknowledged that they had fought for military ballots while opposing ballots from civilians. But [another Bush lawyer, David] Aufhauser said, "There was no such strategy to do something in Palm Beach that we did not do in the Panhandle."

But a review of the transcripts, minutes and recordings of canvassing board meetings shows otherwise. The records reveal example after example of Bush lawyers' employing one set of arguments in counties where Mr. Gore was strong and another in counties carried by Mr. Bush.

County by county, and sometimes ballot by ballot, they tailored their arguments in ways that maximized Mr. Bush's support among overseas voters. They frequently questioned civilian ballots, for example, while defending military ballots with the same legal defects.

In Bush strongholds they pleaded with election officials to ignore Florida's election rules. They ridiculed Gore lawyers for raising concerns about fraud, while making eloquent speeches about the voting rights of men and women defending the nation's interests in remote and dangerous locations.

"If they catch a bullet, or fragment from a terrorist bomb, that fragment does not have any postmark or registration of any kind," Fred Tarrant, a Republican City Council member from Naples, Fla., told the board in Collier County, a conservative outpost in southwest Florida.

Making frequent and effective use of the protest form they had developed to defend military ballots without postmarks, the Bush lawyers succeeded in persuading three counties in the western tip of the Panhandle, all of them Bush strongholds, to disregard Florida's postmark rules.

The three counties, Escambia, Okaloosa and Santa Rosa, counted 72 overseas ballots without postmarks, 63 from members of the military.

"We had never done it before," Pat Hollarn, the veteran Okaloosa County supervisor, said in an interview.

In Santa Rosa County, Doug Wilkes, the election supervisor, tried to argue that ballots without postmarks should be rejected. "The board always stuck to the rules, to the letter of the law of the State of Florida," he told his two fellow canvassing board members that Friday.

He was outvoted.

By contrast, in Democratic strongholds, Bush lawyers simultaneously worked to exclude as many likely Gore votes as possible.

There they spoke not of the right to vote but of the importance of following the letter of state election rules. The "fundamental" role of election officials is to detect "anything that could affect the honesty or integrity of the election," Craig Burkhardt, a Bush lawyer, told the Broward County canvassing board. At one point, Mr. Burkhardt grew so angry insisting on his right to scrutinize voter signatures that a board member told him, "Calm down, chill out."

In Broward and in other Gore strongholds, Bush lawyers questioned scores of ballots, almost always from civilian Democrats but occasionally from members of the military. They objected to the slightest of flaws, including partial addresses of witnesses, illegible witness signatures and slight variations in voter signatures. In at least six cases, the Bush lawyers relied on the Republican protest form that was barely distinguishable from the infamous protest form designed by Mr. Herron, the Gore election law specialist....

When ballots were defended, they were from military voters. "I cannot believe that our service boys, fighting hard overseas, that their ballots would be disqualified," Mr. McCown, the Bush lawyer, told the Palm Beach County canvassing board.

"All right," Judge Charles E. Burton, the board chairman, replied dryly. "We will file a protest and arrange for a violin."

Later, in their reports to senior Bush aides, the lawyers listed rejected ballots under two categories, "military" and "non-military," and their differing approaches to civilian and military ballots are reflected by this finding: While canvassing boards accepted 30 percent of the flawed civilian ballots, they counted 41 percent of the flawed military ballots, according to *The Times*'s database.

The duality of the Bush strategy was demonstrated in another way. In three South Florida counties, Miami-Dade, Broward and Palm Beach, boards rejected as illegal 362 of 572 overseas ballots that Friday. Most— including many military ballots—were thrown out without a word of protest from Mr. Bush's lawyers.

Some of their work was done by the Gore lawyers, who, true to their strategy, challenged hundreds of overseas ballots with little discrimination. They objected to ballots from Democrats, Republicans, civilians, military personnel—even in counties where Mr. Gore actually beat Mr. Bush among overseas voters....

The result was [also] unequal treatment of ballots with the same flaws. While Bush counties accepted 70 of 109 ballots that arrived without postmarks within two days of the election, Gore counties accepted 17 of 63 such ballots....

[W]hen the counting ended in the early hours of Nov. 18, Mr. Bush had gained 1,380 votes to Mr. Gore's 750 votes.

But Mr. Bush's strategists wanted even more [when they uncovered, in the meantime, a copy of the Herron memorandum].

Thanksgiving Reprieve for Rejected Votes

Hours after the last overseas absentee ballot was counted, the Bush campaign unleashed a full-scale legal and public relations offensive with a single aim: persuading selected Bush counties to reconsider hundreds of overseas military ballots rejected the night before.

The public relations campaign began when Gov. Marc Raciot of Montana, a Bush supporter, said that Democratic lawyers had "gone to war" against military voters. Gen. H. Norman Schwarzkopf called it "a very sad day in our country." Robert Novak, the conservative newspaper columnist, called the Herron memorandum a "quickie guide for tossing out the serviceman's vote."

The candidate himself took up the theme, calling on election officials to count more military ballots.

Almost immediately, the Democrats were in full retreat.

On Sunday, Nov. 19, Mr. Gore's running mate, Joseph I. Lieberman, appeared on the NBC program "Meet the Press." Faced with a barrage of aggressive questions, he called on Florida's canvassing boards to reconsider their rejection of military ballots. The next day, the attorney general of Florida, a Democrat, said that local officials should "immediately revisit this issue."

This extraordinary political reversal, combined that week with new Republican lawsuits that asked 14 counties to reconsider rejected ballots, helped open the door for Mr. Bush to win still more absentee votes. A Democratic lawyer, Mitchell Berger, later referred to the additional Bush votes as "the Thanksgiving stuffing," a label that stuck.

As a legal matter, the [state] lawsuits were a failure....

[But] [b]y the end of the week, canvassing boards in about a dozen Republican-leaning counties had reconvened for a second round of counting. In each place, longstanding election rules were bent and even ignored. Boards counted ballots postmarked as many as seven days after the election, including some from within the United States. They counted two ballots sent by fax. Officials in Santa Rosa County even counted five ballots that arrived after the Nov. 17 deadline. Again and again, election officials crossed out the words "REJECTED AS ILLEGAL" that had been stamped on ballot envelopes.

In all, over the Thanksgiving week, the counties accepted 288 ballots that they had rejected days earlier...[giving] Mr. Bush a net gain of 109 votes.

Lieberman Put Democrats in Retreat on Military Vote

Richard Berke

For many Democrats immersed in Florida's disputed presidential election, there was no worse moment than the one...when Senator...Lieberman appeared on national television....

"There was some gasping," recalled David Ginsberg, the research director for the Gore campaign, who watched it with other aides at Democratic headquarters in Washington. "People said: 'Wait a minute. That's really off. That's not what we're saying.' We could never effectively communicate why we were right because we got ourselves in a position where it looked like we were trying to throw out military ballots when we were trying to throw out illegal ballots."...

Mr. Herron, who was watching from Tallahassee, said Mr. Lieberman's comments had been devastating for both him and the campaign. "I got such a sinking feeling in my stomach that I walked outside," he said. "You don't like to see yourself barbecued on national television, especially by guys on your team. It was tough. I just don't think he was prepared for the question."...

[But] Mr. Lieberman, who was briefed in a conference call the night before the television appearance, said he was never urged to defend the memorandum.

"No one ever said to me, 'Senator, go out there and defend to the death what we are doing regarding military ballots, do not give an inch, we need you,'" Mr. Lieberman said. "That never happened. I was told there was a fuss about military ballots. Honestly, I never got a clear message on it. I can understand perhaps people on the ground who were under siege might have felt otherwise. But in this case there was no clarity, no clear conclusion to the telephone conference briefing."...

Originally published in *The New York Times,* July 15, 2001, p. A14. Reprinted by permission.

One member of the Democrats' legal team added that the Gore camp was hamstrung by their candidate's concerns about being unpatriotic.

"All of a sudden, he was Jimmy Stewart," he said. "Gore got very stuck on the notion that if he became president it was not in the national interest that he have a relationship characterized by his mistrust of the military."

PART 4

THE FIRST TRIP TO WASHINGTON

Even as George Bush was prevailing in the court-ordered recount, he was taking steps to void it. The day after the Florida Supreme Court's decision, his lawyers went to the United States Supreme Court, asking it to hear what was now *Bush v. Palm Beach County Canvassing Board*. They maintained that the misinterpretations of Florida law perpetrated by the state tribunal violated federal statutory and constitutional provisions.

Their argument in both areas was virtually identical. They claimed, first, that by transforming "may be ignored" in Section 102.112 to "could *not* ignore,"[1] by deviating from its own prior decisions giving deference to the judgments of the secretary of state, and by changing the deadline for submission of election returns from November 14 to November 26, the Florida court was "in flagrant violation"[2] of those words in Section 5 of the Electoral Count Act ordering the states to resolve controversies over the appointment of presidential electors "by laws enacted prior to" election day. (Shifting from their earlier defense of the Palm Beach County Canvassing Board, the Bush lawyers also saw a violation of Section 5 in the board's counting of occasional dimples, when the 1990 instructions said they shouldn't be counted.)

These contentions clearly assumed, as Secretary Harris's lawyers apparently assumed, that Section 5 laid down a strict federal mandate, imposed directly upon the states. The Bush lawyers also put forth another argument related to Section 5 that might have avoided this particular trip to Washington had Secretary Harris offered some version of it on November 15.

> [Florida law] clearly anticipates that results will be certified in a timely fashion, in order for the results to be contested in court. Pushing back the deadline for certification by judicial fiat thus runs headlong into the Florida Legislature's intent to allow a period of time for court challenges [before December 12].[3]

The pattern of judicial usurpation in Florida not only violated the electoral act. It "disregarded"[4] as well the part of Article II, Section 1, of the Constitution, providing that "each state shall appoint, in such Manner as the Legislature thereof may direct" its presidential electors. Florida's high court had "seen fit to revise the 'manner' in which Florida's electors are chosen by directing the Secretary of State to consider results from those counties that are conducting manual recounts, notwithstanding the fact that the statutory deadline has long since passed and no waiver of that deadline [was] granted. . . . The Constitution admits of no such *post hoc* alterations to the scheme of electoral appointments."[5]

Despite the short shrift everyone had given them in the Florida Supreme Court, Bush's certiorari brief also pursued his equal-protection arguments—arguments the justices were being asked to consider at the same time, on appeal from the Eleventh Circuit. The circuit court had set arguments in the injunction controversy for November 29, but the plaintiffs there were petitioning the United States Supreme Court to do something it virtually never did: take control of Judge Middlebrooks's decision denying an injunction against manual recounts before the court of appeals even heard the case.

To this end, petitioners relied largely on the record being compiled for the Eleventh Circuit hearing, which demonstrated in their view the immediacy of the threat posed "to the most fundamental of all constitutional rights—the right to vote"—by the use of "standardless and selective manual recounts," arbitrarily treating "voters differently based solely on where they happen to reside in Florida."[6] The circuit court record, some of it anecdotal, described instances of "Physical Manipulation and Degradation of Ballots." The cards had "been twisted, rumpled, creased, and dropped"; the multiple machine counts "dislodged large numbers of chads which littered the floors of the recount rooms."[7] The record also told of "irregularities in counting methods," and of "political pressure" exerted on vote counters, including the case of a Democratic assistant supervisor who supposedly "implied that a Republican President would endanger the economy and increase the chances of war."[8]

The certiorari brief in *Bush v. Palm Beach* stated its equal-protection claims without testimonial embellishments, relying on references to *Reynolds v. Sims*, and other path-breaking reapportionment cases such as *Roman v. Sincock* and *WMCA Inc. v. Lomenzo*. (It also mentioned that the "manual recount process has . . . undermined the physical integrity of the voters' ballots."[9]) Bush's lawyers asserted they had "expressly raised"[10] these claims in the Florida Supreme Court, making no mention of the footnote declaring that no one had broached "the constitutionality" of Florida election laws.

Gore's lawyers, headed by Harvard professor Laurence Tribe, scoffed at the Bush case for certiorari as a pack of "intemperate and insupportable mischaracterizations"[11] of the Florida decision. The justices of the state court had simply engaged in "an ordinary act of statutory interpretation of a law enacted prior to the election."[12] They found an obvious conflict between two sections of the Florida statute, and adjudicated it "by giving credence to the more specific, and the more recent, provision, a canon of construction certainly familiar to this Court."[13] Furthermore, Tribe maintained, because "of the unique circumstances of the case," the court properly used its "equitable powers" to set a deadline for submitting manual recounts that would give the canvassing boards a chance to perform their duties.[14] (He did not mention the court's lack of an explanation for why it could use its equity powers in this way.) "At bottom, [the Bush] contention is that the Florida Supreme Court committed an error of state law. [Their] argument does not describe post-election judicial legislation, so as to implicate 3 U.S.C. 5 or Article II § I."[15]

Tribe and his colleagues were especially scornful of the supposed "record" recited by the injunction brief to buttress an equal-protection grievance. It was in fact a "non-record," they argued, a series of "false. . . . partisan accusations" that "have not been tested in court through cross-examination, verification, or judicial fact-finding."[16]

The Supreme Court Acts—And Doesn't Act

The certiorari briefs came to the Supreme Court at a ticklish moment, since the Florida recounts were still ongoing, yet a court decision would surely issue only after they finished and contest proceedings were in progress. It was not absolutely certain at this point *who* would be bringing the contest, though it was most likely to be Gore. Many legal experts believed the Supreme Court would turn down the case, both on practical grounds, and because of its traditional disinclination to find constitutional error by second-guessing a state tribunal's interpretation of state law.[17]

The justices, however, aligned themselves 5-4 in favor of granting certiorari, and largely, it appears, because of the state law question. Shortly before they met in conference on Friday, November 24, a memorandum circulated, stating five of their number had decided to hear *Bush v. Palm Beach*. The five, not surprisingly, were Chief Justice Rehnquist, and Justices Scalia, O'Connor, Kennedy, and Thomas. (Four votes are required to grant certiorari.)[18]

That this memo was inspired in great part by the Florida Supreme Court treatment of Florida's election statute is indicated by the results of the November 24 conference. For while the Court accepted both the Article II and Section 5 issues, it turned down the equal-protection one. Its primary concern seemed to be with Article II, because on the Section 5 controversy the statement granting certiorari posed an inquiry that suggested considerable skepticism about the Bush position. "What would be the *consequences*," the justices asked, "of this Court's finding that the decision of the Supreme Court of Florida does not comply with 3 U.S.C. Sec. 5?"[19] They did not feel certain that Section 5 by itself could invalidate state actions.

According to later commentary, the majority justices were interested in the equal-protection issue, but finally put it aside in *Bush*, probably because of the nonexistent record on the issue in the lower courts. Certiorari before judgment in the injunction case was predictably denied, though "without prejudice," a term signaling the rejection might be largely procedural.[20]

Turning down these equal-protection submissions followed sound and established judicial procedures. Indeed, Gore's lawyers were quick to point out that in *Bush v. Palm Beach County*, "There is the greatest doubt . . . Petitioners' federal claims . . . are fairly presented . . . , given that [they] . . . raised the question before the state Supreme Court only in a few pages at the end of [the] brief."[21]

Yet there *was* warrant for the justices to reach out and clarify the equal-protection issue, at a time when introducing the maximum predictability and orderliness into the election crisis would serve the national interest. It was common knowledge, after all, by November 24 that Palm Beach and Broward Counties were using different standards in counting votes, and certainly everyone knew that only a few counties had agreed to hand recounts. The reply brief in the injunction case gave an uncontestably accurate general portrait of the situation in south Florida which had developed by Thanksgiving.

> The key facts supporting petitioners' case . . . are *undisputed*. These undisputed facts include: (1) manual recounts are proceeding only in selected Florida counties; (2) the recounts are being conducted under Florida statutes that do not provide uniform standards for the recounts; (3) canvassing boards have changed standards within counties during the course of the recounts, and the counties have been involved in post-election litigation to set standards or to change standards; (4) the selective recounts inevitably count purported "votes" in some counties that would not be counted in others.[22]

The Supreme Court's unwillingness to exercise its broad discretion and to take the equal-protection issue in *Bush v. Palm Beach County*, however much dictated by precedent, was certainly not in keeping with the hope expressed by some constitutional scholars that the justices would try "to calm the partisan storm with a finality . . . only they [can] bring."[23] It is unlikely, though, to have been part of a plot to later bring the Gore forces up against an equal-protection violation and a December 12 deadline, since the Court had yet to focus on Section 5's strictures and what they meant.

Continuing the Argument

The briefs on the merits in *Bush v. Palm Beach* continued to belabor the issue of whether Florida's high court had or hadn't made new law. But Tribe and his associates also pounced on the justices' query about the effect of breaching Section 5. This part of the Electoral Count Act, they now argued, could not possibly "preclude" or forbid the retroactive announcement "of a new rule of law,"[24] for it did not in fact *order* the states to do anything with regard to the choosing of presidential electors. It was not a federal mandate at all, but a choice states could make in designing their presidential election laws so as to avoid future trouble once their electoral certificates reached Congress. The section presented state authorities with a "safe harbor option."[25] They failed to cruise into this harbor at their own peril, but were not legally bound to do so. Section 5 "does not *require* the states to follow any procedure with respect to determining who its electors are, nor does it prohibit any such procedure."[26] Consequently, a finding by the justices "that the [Florida] decision did not 'comply' with . . . Section 5"[27] could never lead to its reversal. "At most, the consequence of such a determination . . . would be to render the safe-harbor provision inapplicable, so that Florida's selection of electors might not be 'conclusive' in the event of a dispute before Congress."[28]

This argument appeared to rely on the fact that there was no legislative proclamation by the Florida House or Senate indicating a desire to take advantage of the safe harbor, though Gore's brief does not bring up the matter. In defending the state supreme court decision, however, his lawyers agreed the December 12 cutoff date was a goal the secretary of state could properly strive for. The state opinion, they noted, properly found that Secretary Harris "lacked discretion to ignore supplemental certifications of returns . . . , *unless the returns are submitted too late for [the state] to make the federal December 12 deadline.*"[29]

The Bush brief on the merits sounded in places as if it had flopped over to the safe-harbor view. Any state action based on retroactive law, it noted at one point, "would fail to satisfy the requirements of [Section] 5 and would not receive the benefit Congress intended to confer."[30] The "plain language" of Section 5, it noted at another, indicated what states must do "if their decisions are to be given binding effect"[31]—causing the Gore lawyers to claim that "barely four days after this Court granted review in this case, petitioner has abandoned the principal ground on which his Petition For Certiorari rested."[32]

Actually, the Bush reply brief stuck to the position that Section 5 was binding. But this was now attributed, in stark contrast to Gore's brief, to a clear decision made by the State of Florida to enjoy safe-harbor protection, a decision the Bush lawyers found implicit in the entire structure of state election law. "Florida, through its legislature and consistent with Article II, has created a *system* whereby officers of Florida's executive branch are authorized to act to secure for Florida the advantages of section 5."[33] Furthermore, "Florida was in the process of resolving disputes and certifying its electors in accordance with § 5 when the Florida Supreme Court *sua sponte* issued an injunction to stop that process dead in its tracks ten days after the election and, four days later, rewrote the law that embodied Florida's attempt to comply with and gain the benefits of § 5."[34] If such intervention were "sustained, Florida and its voters face a risk that they will not obtain the benefits of § 5"; but if the Florida judicial action was properly declared a "nullity, . . . this Court can restore the order to Florida's election that its legislature endeavored to give it."[35] (The Bush lawyers to not cite an explicit legislative pronouncement on Section 5.)

The Legislators Enter the Picture

In the brief they filed amici curiae in *Bush v. Palm Beach County*, the Florida House and Senate agreed with Gore at least to the extend of assuming the Electoral Count Act set up more of a quid pro quo than a federal mandate. This assertion, though, was part of a larger, and from the Gore point of view, a more ominous whole.

The Florida lawmakers were generally quiet about the 2000 election until the Florida Supreme Court decision of November 21. But that decision unleashed a storm of denunciation against a body with which the Republican-dominated legislature was already at odds. The court's Democratic composition, as well as charges that it was thwarting legislative efforts to limit death penalty appeals and to make abortions more difficult to get, rendered relations between the two branches frosty, even before the court's election opinion. Several months before the election, Republican legislators endorsed a plan to pack the supreme court with appointees of Governor Jeb Bush.

In the wake of November 21, some house and senate members talked of a law flatly overruling *Harris v. Palm Beach County* by deciding that the secretary of state had correctly interpreted the intent of the legislature when she disallowed manual recounts. "What we have here," said a senior Republican senator named Daniel Webster, "is a court which has arbitrarily picked a new date and circumvented state law, and actually stomped on our constitutional rights as a Legislature."[36]

State senate president John McKay and Speaker Tom Feeney of the house of representatives took an ostensibly more measured course. Besides authorizing the amicus brief, they appointed a Select Joint Committee on the Manner of Appointment of Presidential Electors to "ensure that the fundamental right of Florida voters to participate in the 2000 presidential election is protected through the lawful selection of the electors to the electoral college."[37] The committee, composed of eight Republicans and six Democrats (including Senator Webster), was charged with reviewing "all relevant federal and state law and the manner in which that law was applied at the state and local levels in . . . 2000."[38]

The committee held hearings from November 28 to November 30 and heard from prominent constitutional lawyers of different persuasions. It is safe to say, however, that the majority found most congenial the views of the witnesses who had composed the supreme court brief (with the collaboration of a nonwitness, Professor Charles Fried of Harvard).[39]

They were Professor Einer Elhauge of Harvard Law School and Roger Magnuson, a prominent Minneapolis attorney and dean of Oakbrook College of Law and Government in Fresno. The two frankly warned the legislators that in the growing crisis they must be prepared to select their own slate of presidential electors, since there was a "significant risk"[40] Congress would not count the electors now being disputed.

One of the reasons for such a risk was the looming inability of the state to resolve all electoral controversies by December 12, thus depriving Florida of the conclusive presumption Congress must otherwise give to electors under Section 5. "In order to have conclusivity," said Dean Magnuson, "the Legislature . . . has to look very carefully at the issue. . . . Have all controversies stopped as of December 12?"[41]

To assert this, of course, was to differ with the proposition offered by Secretary Harris's lawyers, that an electoral slate in place "six days prior to the meeting of the electoral college" was "conclusive . . . whatever stage the contest proceeding" was in, and with Bush's suggestion that the legislature had specifically structured Florida law to meet the December 12 deadline.[42] Elhauge and Magnuson clearly believed that a slate of electors might indeed be chosen in a contest completed after December 12. "Are all those [contests] going to be fairly resolved in time?" asked Elhauge. "You could always resolve everything in time if you just dismiss everything . . . , but you have to have a process by which [contests] can be fairly tried."[43] It was precisely to counteract a slate of electors, chosen but lacking conclusive status, that the legislature must act. This was the opposite, however, of claiming that conclusivity required short-circuiting the contest process.

The other danger counseling action, according to the experts, stemmed from the fact that, regardless of timeliness, Congress might reject any Florida electors, including the ones certified on November 26, if they were suspected of being chosen by a process in which "preexisting rules were . . . modified or changed by the Supreme Court of Florida."[44]

But the legislators were scarcely helpless before these dangers. If they determined either was imminent, they had the power, under a provision now grouped in the same section of the United States Code as the Electoral Count Act —3 USC § 2—to conclude that Florida had "failed to make a choice [of electors] on the day prescribed by law [November 7]"; and they could exercise their own authority in accordance with this provision, and with the Constitution, to appoint electors "on a subsequent day in such a manner as the legislature . . . shall direct."[45] It was Magnuson's opinion "that if [such a] decision is made by the Florida Legislature prior to December 18, then in that case Florida can be assured that there is conclusivity" under Section 5.[46]

Gore's Supreme Court brief in *Bush v. Palm Beach* noted, however, that 3 USC § 2 dated back to 1845, and "simply . . . address[ed] the circumstance in which a winner failed to emerge, as when [in 1800 and 1824] a required majority of the votes was not secured by any candidate."[47] Besides, there was "no doubt that Florida *made* its choice" on November 7; state institutions were simply trying to figure out what that choice was. "Accordingly, any state legislative attempt . . . to appoint electors [in this situation] would appear to be federally preempted."[48]

Under the Florida House and Senate's view, however, *they* would decide this legal issue, not the courts, or even Congress. Elhauge maintained that the state legislature possessed plenary power to determine whether Section 5 requirements were satisfied, and whether, therefore, other aspects of federal law must come into play. Because appointing electors was "a constitutional power that is held by the state legislatures and not by Congress, . . . even Congress cannot restrict the power of [a] state legislature to appoint its presidential electors."[49] Hence, "the first body" capable of resolving the 2000 election was "the Florida Legislature." It could freely "make its own determination" that presidential electors were not chosen in a timely manner, or that "the election did not comply with preexisting rules and thus necessitates [legislative] appointment."[50] Only if the legislature did not exercise this responsibility before December 18 was Congress free to act on the matter. Otherwise, the Congress must use its power of counting electoral votes under the Twelfth Amendment to approve the legislatively chosen electors.

Consequently, the entire question "should be deemed nonjusticiable by the United States Supreme Court," or any other court.[51] Without going into this point in detail, Elhauge and his associates argued that the Bush-Gore controversy was a political question, one which either the text of the Constitution, or prudential considerations arising from our constitutional system of government, insulated from review by the judicial branch. "This is really a political dispute," Elhauge told the legislators, "and . . . political questions under Supreme Court precedent are generally resolved best by the political branches, not by the judicial branches."[52]

In actual fact, it was unthinkable that if Bush's electors prevailed in an election contest decided before December 18, even a divided Senate, with Vice President Gore in the chair, would reject those electors on Section 5 grounds. Proposed action by the Florida legislature was obviously meant to trump a Gore slate of electors produced by a victorious contest challenge.

Yet under the Electoral Count Act, Bush stood an excellent chance in late November of prevailing eventually, even if the state legislature never put forth its own slate. Governor Jeb Bush had stated by then that "no judicial power exist[ed]" which could compel him to certify a Gore slate, if such a slate won out in the contest.[53] And had the governor stuck to this position, legislative intervention would have been unnecessary. For if, in January 2001, a Republican House of Representatives refused to accept Gore's electors, and the Senate refused to accept the group approved on November 26, the Electoral Act decreed that Jeb Bush's certificate of ascertainment, sent to the National Archives on November 27, would be decisive, and Bush's original electors would prevail. "[I]f the two Houses shall disagree in respect of the counting of [the electoral] votes, . . . in that case, the votes of the electors whose appointment shall have been certified by the executive of the State . . . shall be counted."[54]

If under duress, however, Bush awarded Florida's electors to Gore following a contest, a legislative slate created in a bill signed by the governor could have assumed critical importance, confronting Congress with two slates of electors bearing the gubernatorial seal. The election would then have wound up in the House and the Senate respectively, with the prospect of Bush emerging as president and Democratic senator Joseph Lieberman as vice president. (For a presidential election, the House votes by state, and in January 2001, twenty-eight state delegations were majority Republican. In the 50-50 Senate, Vice President Gore had the power to elect his running mate.)[55]

The Florida legislature's preference was to act by resolution in appointing electors so as not to cast doubt on their plenary power, and to avoid embarrassing George Bush's brother. This is the course the senators and representatives would begin to pursue on December 11.[56] In the unlikely event Jeb Bush had given Florida's electors to Gore, however, the resolution would have done no good, at least under the Electoral Count Act.

Notes

1. *Bush v. Palm Beach County Canvassing Board*, "Petition for a Writ of Certiorari," pp. 14–15.
2. Ibid., p. 15.

3. Ibid.
4. Ibid., p. 12.
5. Ibid., pp. 19–20.
6. *Siegel v. LePore*, "Petition for a Writ of Certiorari," pp. 16, 18.
7. Ibid., p. 10.
8. Ibid., pp. 11, 13.
9. *Bush v. Palm Beach County Canvassing Board,* "Petition," pp. 21, 5.
10. Ibid., p. 9.
11. *Bush v. Palm Beach County Canvassing Board,* "Brief in Opposition of Respondents," p. 1.
12. Ibid., p. 17.
13. Ibid.
14. Ibid., p. 12.
15. Ibid., pp. 17–18.
16. Ibid., p. 1.
17. See Joan Biskupic, "Candidates' Legal Options Dwindle," *USA Today,* November 24, 2000, p. 1; William Glaberson, "Justices May See Task as Calming Storm," *New York Times*, November 25, 2000, p. A12; Charles Lane, "High Court Entering Area It Rarely Sees," *Washington Post*, November 25, 2000, p. A1.
18. See Linda Greenhouse, "Election Case and a Trauma for Justices," *New York Times*, February 20, 2001, p. A1.
19. *Bush v. Palm Beach County Canvassing Board*, 148 LEd 2d, 478 (italics added).
20. *Siegel v. LePore*, 148 LEd 2d, 478.
21. *Bush v. Palm Beach County Canvassing Board*, "Brief in Opposition of Respondents," p. 3, fn. 1.
22. *Siegel v. LePore*, "Reply Brief for Petitioners," p. 2.
23. Glaberson, "Justices May See Task."
24. *Bush v. Palm Beach County Canvassing Board,* "Petition," p. 17.
25. *Bush v. Palm Beach County Canvassing Board*, "Brief of Respondents," p. 22.
26. Ibid., p. 23.
27. Ibid., p. 31.
28. Ibid.
29. Ibid., p. 16 (italics added).
30. *Bush v. Palm Beach County Canvassing Board*, "Brief of Petitioner," p. 17.
31. Ibid., p. 29.
32. *Bush v. Palm Beach County Canvassing Board*, "Reply Brief of Respondents," p. 1.
33. *Bush v. Palm Beach County Canvassing Board,*" Reply Brief of Petitioner," p. 16 (italics added).
34. Ibid., p. 11.
35. Ibid.
36. David Barstow and Somini Sengupta, "Florida Legislators Consider Options to Aid Bush," November 23, 2000, Correspondents of *The New York Times, 36 Days* (New York: Times Books, 2001), p. 140.
37. Select Joint Committee on the Manner of Appointment of Presidential Electors, "Report and Recommendations," p. 2, Florida Division of Administrative Hearings.
38. Ibid.

39. *Bush v. Palm Beach County Canvassing Board*, "Brief of the Florida Senate and House *Amici Curiae* in Support of Neither Party."

40. Testimony of Professor Einer R. Elhauge before the Select Joint Committee, November 28, 2000, p. 14.

41. Testimony of Dean Roger Magnuson before the Select Joint Committee, November 28, 2000, p. 10.

42. *Palm Beach County Canvassing Board v. Harris*, Florida Supreme Court, "Answer Brief of the Secretary of State and the Elections Canvassing Commission," p. 24.

43. Testimony of Professor Elhauge, p. 14.

44. Testimony of Dean Magnuson, p. 7.

45. 3 USC § 2.

46. Testimony of Dean Magnuson, p. 11.

47. *Bush v. Palm Beach County Canvassing Board*, "Reply Brief of Respondents," p. 13.

48. Ibid., p. 14.

49. Testimony of Professor Elhauge, p. 6.

50. Ibid., p. 16.

51. Ibid., p. 17.

52. Ibid.

53. David Barstow and Somini Sengupta, "Jeb Bush Backs Plan for Legislature to Bypass Courts," November 30, 2000, in Correspondents of *The New York Times, 36 Days*, p. 195; David Kaplan, *The Accidental President* (New York: William Morrow, 2001), p. 230.

54. 3 USC § 15.

55. See Abner Greene, *Understanding the 2000 Election* (New York: New York University Press, 2001), part 5.

56. Dexter Filkins and Dana Canedy, "Legislature Prepares to Appoint Electors," December 12, 2000, in Correspondents of *The New York Times, 36 Days*, pp. 300–301.

14

Brief of the Florida House and Senate, *Amici Curiae*

The arguments made by Elhauge and Dean Magnuson were crystallized in a brief filed *amicus curiae* before the United States Supreme Court in *Bush v. Palm Beach County Canvassing Board*. Elhauge and Magnuson participated in the construction of the brief, and were joined by Professor Charles Fried of the Harvard Law School (who was listed as the brief's counsel of record). One of the nation's best-known "conservatives" among constitutional scholars, Fried served as solicitor general in the Reagan administration, where he argued, among other things, for the overturning of *Roe v. Wade*.

ARGUMENT

I. The State Legislature Has Plenary Authority to Appoint Electors and, When an Election Fails to Make a Timely Choice Pursuant to Pre-existing Rules, It Must Exercise that Authority to Assure Its Electors Are Counted By Congress....

[Article II, Section 1] confers "plenary power to the state legislatures in the matter of the appointment of electors." *McPherson v. Blacker*, 146 U.S. 1, 35 (1892). "The appointment of these electors is thus placed absolutely and wholly with the legislatures of the several states." *Id.* at 34 (quoting favorably Senate Rep. No. 395, 1st Sess. 43d Cong. [1874])....

Where, as in Florida, the Legislature has chosen to use an election to

---

From Brief of the Florida House and Senate, *Amici Curiae,* www.supremecourtus.gov, pp. 2–8.

determine which Electors to appoint, 3 U.S.C. § 5 provides that the results of that election shall be deemed conclusive by Congress when it counts electoral votes, provided controversies regarding that election are resolved in a manner that is both timely (here before December 12, 2000) and in conformance with rules and procedures adopted prior to the election. Timeliness is crucial because of, among other things, the importance of having a President and allowing preparations for an orderly transition. Even more crucial is the principle embodied in Section 5 that the rules of the election must be set before the election and cannot be changed after it becomes clear who would benefit from such a change. Otherwise the law would encourage post-election manipulations of election law to alter the outcome of a Presidential race.

If a State's election "has failed to make a choice" that is timely and conforms with pre-existing law, then 3 U.S.C. § 2 recognizes that appointment of Electors by the State Legislature is proper. In such a case, state legislative appointment would be necessary to assure the State will have Presidential Electors that will be counted by Congress....Indeed, the Florida Legislature would have an affirmative constitutional duty to appoint Presidential Electors before December 18 to assure Florida is represented in the Electoral College, because the Constitution dictates that each State "shall" appoint the requisite number of Presidential Electors "in such Manner as the Legislature thereof may direct".... Where purported Electors have been chosen by an election process that was not conducted in the manner that the State Legislature had directed, then it becomes necessary for the State Legislature to exercise that appointment authority directly.

2. The Question Whether a State Election of Presidential Electors Has Failed to Make a Timely Choice That Conforms to Pre-existing Rules Is a Matter to Be Decided by the Political Branches Rather Than by the Courts.

Although no single provision explicitly addresses which entity is responsible for deciding whether an election failed to make a choice that is timely and in conformance with pre-existing law under 3 U.S.C. § 5, a careful reading of the Constitution and the United States Code dictates the answer: the responsibility falls first to the State Legislature and, if it has not exercised that prerogative, then to Congress....

Because of the constitutional nature of a State Legislature's appointment authority, Title III of the United States Code cannot be understood as a limitation on the State Legislature's authority to appoint Presidential

Electors....Congress has no power to limit the exercise of a constitutional power granted [solely and] directly to the State Legislatures. As Charles Pinckney stated:

> Nothing was more clear...than that Congress had no right to meddle with [the electoral college] at all; as the whole was entrusted to the State Legislatures, they must make provisions for all questions arising on the occasion....

Where a State Legislature has directly appointed its Electors because there was no election or it was determined that (for reasons of timeliness or deviation from pre-existing rules) the election failed to make a choice, there can be no legitimate dispute in Congress whether the directly appointed Electors were appointed in the manner directed by the State Legislature and thus should be counted. The direct appointment removes any ambiguity about the exercise of the State Legislature's appointment authority. Thus, 3 U.S.C. § 2 provides that Congress will recognize those direct appointments when Congress exercises its own counting power. Congress has a constitutional obligation to count the votes of any qualified Elector who was indisputably appointed by the State Legislature.

Section 5 of Title III is meant to address the more complicated case where the State Legislature has not directly appointed its Electors but has instead directed that those Electors be chosen in an election conducted according to certain rules. Where the election process is conducted according to those pre-existing rules, then under Section 5 its results are conclusive on Congress when it counts the electoral votes....

The Florida Legislature respectfully submits that the [United States Supreme] Court should rule that questions regarding whether the electoral process has conformed with pre-existing law are not issues for this Court. Such questions should be determined by the State Legislature or, if it fails to act by December 18 when the Electors cast their votes, by Congress when it counts those electoral votes on January 6, 2000. Such a ruling that these are non-justiciable questions to be resolved by the political branches would recognize that the Constitution vests the State Legislatures with the power to appoint Electors, and Congress with the power to count their votes....The alternative would put this Court in the uncomfortable position of seeking to enjoin how Congress exercises its constitutional counting authority and how the State Legislatures exercise their constitutional appointment authority....

A ruling of non-justiciability would avoid involving this Court in a political dispute best resolved by the political process. It is neither surprising nor inappropriate that the law should lodge that authority in the State Legislatures and Congress. What is at stake here is after all a political determination of who shall be the next President. The issue to be determined is uniquely political. Nor is it likely to recur. Thus, in this rare circumstance, it is entirely appropriate to have it resolved by the branches of government that are most responsive to the will of the people. "The constitution...recognizes that the people act through their representatives in the legislature, and leaves it to the legislature exclusively to define the method of effecting the object." *McPherson*, 146 U.S. at 27. In any event, whether desirable or not, that is the constitutional scheme. *Id.* at 35 ("The question before us is not one of policy, but of power.")

15

Testimony of Professor Bruce Ackerman

Not all who testified before the joint committee of the Florida legislature endorsed the propriety of creating a legislative slate. Bruce Ackerman, Sterling Professor at the Yale Law School, expanded on the point made in Gore's Supreme Court brief, arguing that the whole legislative plan was based on a gross misreading of 3 U.S.C. § 2. Nor, he felt, were the courts precluded from intervening to prevent Florida's illegal course of action.

Professor Ackerman is not inaptly called one of the great constitutional "liberals" of our time. His seminal work, *We the People,* makes the powerful and controversial argument that our constitution is a document subject to tangible alteration, not only through formal amendment, but through sustained and decisive movements of public morality—constitutional "moments," as Ackerman calls them. These moments create a new constitutional order in the nation, an order ratified by our courts, as in the New Deal era, completely outside of Article V's amendment processes.

MR. ACKERMAN: [L]et's begin by focusing on the single most important provision of federal statutory law in this case. It is Section 2 of Title 3 of the United States Code. This provision has been self-consciously tailored for the case at hand and it's entitled, "Failure to Make a Choice on the Prescribed Day." This statute limits the powers of state legislatures once a presidential election is held.

After an election is held the statute...allows the state Legislature to intervene under one and only one condition and that is when, despite the

Hearings Before Select Joint Committee on the Manner of Appointment of Presidential Electors, pp. 20–26, 29–30.

election results, the State failed to make a choice. That is the quotation and that is the critical legal concept of its electors.

Florida has already made the legally relevant choice. This happened when Secretary Harris certified Florida's returns and Governor Jeb Bush signed the formal notification that was sent to the archives, that the State's 25...votes go to a slate of Republican electors who will vote for Governor George W. Bush on December 18th. Since Florida has not, quote, unquote, failed to choose, the federal statute bars the state legislature from further intervention. If the Florida Legislature were nevertheless to act in violation of Section 2, any federal court would be on solid ground in enjoining both Secretary Harris and Governor Jeb Bush from sending any further certificates of appointment to Washington, D.C.

But what if the Florida courts, next week, the week after, ultimately find that Al Gore deserves the state's electoral votes? Even if this were to occur, Florida will not, quote, unquote, fail to choose in the sense required by Section 2. Instead, it will simply replace one choice with another choice. The federal statute does not authorize further legislative intervention unless Florida has failed and it has not. But what if the Florida courts order the Secretary of State to change her certification and she refuses? So far as the federal statute is concerned, the earlier certification of Bush electors still sits in the national archives in Washington and so the State still has not failed to choose.

But what if the Florida courts hold Ms. Harris in contempt and order some other state official to file an amended certification? Even under this scenario Florida will not have failed to act but will have acted twice. This, quote, two-choice situation has also been foreseen in the federal statutes which have elaborate provisions for regulating the way in which the claims of rival slates should be assessed under the Constitution.

It is a bad mistake in short to suppose that we are on the frontier of a legal no-man's land. While our situation is unprecedented, the laws have in fact been carefully crafted to anticipate each and every possibility that may arise. It provides in Section 2 for the State's failure to make a choice and it provides in later sections for the possibility that the state makes one choice or that it makes more than one choice.

In short, the only scenario under which Florida's Legislature may legally intervene has already passed. Once Governor Bush sent a certificate to Washington earlier this week, Florida can no longer fail to make a choice....

The constitutional issue raised before your distinguished committee is far, far more important than whether George Bush or Al Gore gets to the White House. We are dealing here with a kind of precedent, we are setting the election of future presidents.

If the Florida Legislature proceeds to intervene at this late stage in violation of federal law, it will be setting a precedent for future state Legislatures to intervene in every close election. This is a recipe for continuing instability in the process of presidential selection. Such a precedent, once set, will gravely undermine the legitimacy of the presidential office on a permanent basis and severely damage the entire constitutional structure.

I earnestly request the members of this committee to consider this grim future as they determine their present course. Thank you very much....

REPRESENTATIVE [DUDLEY] GOODLETTE: Thank you. Professor Ackerman, this question: Does a sustainable objection in Congress constitute a failure to appoint?

MR. ACKERMAN:...[Under the Electoral Count Act] if a state certification arrives before the 12th of December of this year, and there is no further contest, then it tells Congress, the future Congress, that it should just count these votes....

[I]f another return arrived on the 18th from Florida, because the process doesn't finish by the 12th, then...subsequent provisions [of the act] tell Congress what to do, how to handle the fact that there are two certifications. It tells Congress that no longer is the one that is sent to Congress before the 12th to be given authoritative value and then it stipulates and specifies a procedure by which the two houses will resolve, which of these two returns should be counted in the overall count. However, in both the case in which one return, the one that Secretary Harris and Governor Bush have already sent to Congress, or a more complicated case in which two returns are ultimately sent to Congress, the state of Florida will have a vote counted. The state of Florida has made a decision....

SENATOR [JOHN] LAURENT:...I was a little perplexed. Basically what you are saying is that in the present situation if...Gore prevails and...the Florida Supreme Court directs the Secretary of State to certify his slate and that is sent to Washington, that as far as Congress is concerned, each slate has the same standing? Is that what you're implying?

MR. ACKERMAN: Absolutely correct. Under the subsequent proceeding, there is a very carefully crafted statutory scheme. If no decision—if no piece of paper is ever sent from Florida to Washington, D.C., then under Section 2, the Florida Legislature can act again. If one piece of paper is sent to Washington, D.C. before December 12th, then it shall be conclusive. If one piece of paper is sent to Washington after December 12th, then it won't be conclusive. If two pieces of paper are sent to Washington, D.C., one before and one after December 12th, then it won't be conclusive.

Before the U.S. Supreme Court:
The Oral Argument

Despite the arguments of Bush counsel Theodore Olson, the justices at oral argument inclined toward the safe-harbor view of Section 5, though, surprisingly, in light of their eventual decision, they did not probe the matter of whether Florida's legislature had sought to take advantage of it.

Some of Justice O'Connor's and Justice Scalia's comments during the argument indicate they agreed with the governor's main contention: that the Florida Supreme Court had altered state law after the voting in violation of Article II. Justice Kennedy also spoke of state law being altered, but he related the issue to Section 5 rather than to Article II, and, at least at one point, expressed some sympathy for the Florida courts. Those justices who did not want to hear the case in the first place sided with the state's judiciary.

More influential at oral argument than the question of altered state law was another Article II complaint voiced by Chief Justice Rehnquist and Justice Scalia. Rehnquist was especially concerned by those passages in the Florida decision indicating that the laws governing a secretary of state's discretion to reject late returns, even in a presidential election, must conform to the provisions of the state constitution. This position, the chief justice felt, trenched on the plenary power given to the state legislatures under Article II. He cited the case of 1892, *McPherson v. Blacker,* which specifically stated that the choosing of presidential electors "is conferred upon the legislatures of the States by the Constitution . . . , and cannot be taken from them or modified by their State constitutions" (though this statement was so-called dictum, not essential to resolution of the case).

From Before the Supreme Court: The Oral Argument, www.supremecourtus.gov, pp. 3–15, 18–20, 44–46, 49–52, 54–62, 60, 62–64.

Rehnquist did not say how far this doctrine theoretically might go, or how much independence Article II gave a legislature from its state constitution. Thus, if the Florida constitution had allowed citizens to vote at age eighteen, even before the Twenty-Sixth Amendment was added to the United States Constitution in 1971, could the legislature have raised the age to twenty-one for presidential elections?

In practice, though, the chief justice's focus in *Bush v. Palm Beach County* was fairly constricted, for at issue here were simply laws said to place greater limitations on uncovering voter intent than many democratic enthusiastics might like. It was the impact of these election laws, Rehnquist seemed to feel, which could not be mitigated based on principles embodied in a state constitution.

Such Article II concerns were plausible in light of some of the statements of the Florida Supreme Court, particularly its assertion that since the "right of suffrage" was "the preeminent right contained" in the state constitution, the legislature could enact only those election laws that "impose no 'unreasonable or unnecessary' restraints on . . . suffrage." But it is not clear the court relied wholly on the state constitution to make its point, as opposed to the spirit of the statutes it was interpreting.

> Because election laws are intended to facilitate the right of suffrage, such laws must be liberally construed in favor of the citizens' right to vote . . . .
> Courts must not lose sight of the fundamental purpose of election laws: The laws are intended to facilitate and safeguard the right of each voter to express his or her will in the context of our representative democracy. Technical statutory requirements must not be exalted over the substance of this right.

In any event, there was no doubt that, if commanded to, the Florida court could easily delete its references to the state constitution without loss of doctrinal coherence; reverence for the right to vote, like affection for motherhood and apple pie, was ascribable to any branch of government or to most any major state document.

In another area, Laurence Tribe found himself very much on the defensive with regard to the November 26 deadline.

Oral Argument of Theodore B. Olson
on Behalf of the Petitioners

MR. OLSON: And may it please the Court: Two weeks after the November 7 presidential election, the Florida Supreme Court overturned and materially rewrote portions of the carefully formulated set of laws enacted by Florida's legislature to govern the conduct of that election and the determination of controversies with respect to who prevailed on November 7th.... The election code that the Florida legislature developed conformed to Title 3, Section 5 of the United States Code. That provision invites states to devise rules in advance of an election, to govern the counting of votes and the settling of election controversy.

JUSTICE O'CONNOR: Well, Mr. Olson, isn't Section 5 sort of a safe harbor provision for states, and do you think that it gives some independent right of a candidate to overturn a Florida decision based on that section?

MR. OLSON: We do, Justice O'Connor. It is a safe harbor, but it's more than that. And Section 5 of Title 3 needs to be construed in connection with the history that brought it forth—

JUSTICE O'CONNOR: Yes. But I would have thought it was a section designed in the case of, some election contest ends up before the Congress, a factor that the Congress can look at in resolving such a dispute. I just don't quite understand how it would be independently enforceable.

MR. OLSON: That's why I've mentioned the context in which that section was adopted. In light of the extreme controversy that was faced by this country as a result of the 1876 election, and as this Court knows, that election was very close and led to controversy, contest, discord, Congress was very much concerned about the possibility of that happening again, and one of the reasons—

JUSTICE KENNEDY: Yeah, but what they did was [like a] typical…grant-in-aid program, they said if you run a clean shop down there, we'll give you a bonus, and if you don't, well, you take your chances with everybody else.

MR. OLSON: Justice Kennedy, I submit that it is much like a compact that Congress is offering in the form of Section 5…. If you do these things, certain things will happen. But among these things, what Congress wanted to accomplish with Section 5 was not only to provide the benefit to the states, but to provide the benefit to the United States of the states accepting that implicit proposal.

JUSTICE KENNEDY: But what is there in the opinion of the Supreme Court of Florida that indicates that it relied on this Federal statute in the reasoning for its decision and in its judgment?

MR. OLSON: Well, I think the fact is that it did not. What it did was it disregarded the compact….

JUSTICE SCALIA: Mr. Olson, suppose a less, a less controversial Federal benefit scheme, let's say the scheme that says states can get highway funds if, if they hold their highway speeds to a certain level, all right? And suppose you have a state supreme court that in your view unreasonably interprets a state statute as not holding highway speed to the level required in order to get the benefit of that safe harbor. Would you think that that raises a Federal question and that you could appeal the state court decision here because it deprived the state of the benefit of the highway funds?

MR. OLSON: No, I don't think so.

JUSTICE SCALIA: Why is this any different?

MR. OLSON: This is a great deal different because this is—first of all, Article II of the Constitution which vests authority to establish the rules exclusively in the legislatures of the state, ties in with Section 5. Secondly, as this Court has stated—

JUSTICE SCALIA: Well, let's just talk about Section 5. I mean, the constitutional question's another one. Why is Section 5 in that regard any different from the highway funding?

MR. OLSON: I think it—I think it can't be divorced from Article II of the Constitution because it's a part of a plan for the vesting in the legislatures of a state, and Section 5 implements Article II in the sense that it provides a benefit not just to the state but to the voters....

CHIEF JUSTICE REHNQUIST: Mr. Olson, do you think that Congress when it passed 3 U.S. Code, intended that there would be any judicial involvement? I mean, it seems to me it can just as easily be read as a direction to Congress, saying what we are going to do when these electoral votes are presented to us for counting....

JUSTICE STEVENS: Mr. Olson, your—your submission is based on the premise that the Florida court overturned something that the statute did not. Is it not arguable, at least, that all they did was fill gaps that had not been addressed before?

MR. OLSON: Justice Stevens, I don't think that in this case that's even remotely arguable. What the state supreme court did is take a set of timetables, a set of provisions...[and] [b]oth of those statutes, both of those provisions say that the returns must be, or shall be filed by a certain deadline. The shall and may provisions simply relate to the possible remedy. We submit that under either interpretation the Secretary of State of Florida either must or shall ignore those returns, or may set those aside in her discretion.

JUSTICE STEVENS: Does that mean if there were an act of God that prevented the returns from being filed that she would have discretion either to accept or reject the returns?

MR. OLSON: Yes, I believe—

JUSTICE STEVENS: She would have the discretion?

MR. OLSON: Yes.

JUSTICE STEVENS: Would she be compelled in that event to accept the returns?

MR. OLSON: I don't think so....

JUSTICE STEVENS: Is there any circumstance in which she would be compelled to accept a late return?

MR. OLSON: I don't know of any. I haven't thought of any, Justice Stevens.

JUSTICE STEVENS: Well, you are arguing in effect that it's a mandatory deadline....

MR. OLSON: Well, the Florida Supreme Court...said that it wasn't [mandatory]—and we'll accept this for purposes of this argument that it wasn't—

JUSTICE STEVENS: Yes, but one of the things that's of interest to me is the extent to which you say there was change in the law. It seems to me that in order to answer that question you have to know what your view of the law was before this all happened.

MR. OLSON: I think that we can answer that this way, is that whether it was shall ignore or may ignore. It was not must accept.

JUSTICE STEVENS: Under any circumstance it was not must?

MR. OLSON: No, under no circumstances was it must accept. Now—

JUSTICE STEVENS: Even in an act of God or fraud?

MR. OLSON: I don't believe so, Justice Stevens.

JUSTICE STEVENS: Okay.

JUSTICE BREYER: Isn't the law in Florida like as in most states, and in the Federal government, that when an official has discretion, may accept or may not accept, that has to be exercised within the limits of reason?

MR. OLSON: Yes.

JUSTICE BREYER: Well, then, isn't it possible that when the court says she must accept under certain circumstances, what they mean is outside those circumstances, given the circumstances here, it would be unreasonable to refuse?

MR. OLSON: Well, what the court did was so constrain those circumstances, virtually to make them nonexistent.

JUSTICE BREYER: All right. So then what you're arguing about is a determination by the state court of Florida as to what the circumstances are under state law where the action of a state official would or would not be reasonable.

MR. OLSON: [B]ut I think that it has to be looked at in the context in which that was done when the state supreme court so constrained and says in its opinion shall accept these late returns until 5 p.m. on November 26th, and in the context there was no discretion left for the Secretary of State at all.

JUSTICE GINSBURG: Mr. Olson, may I ask you, because you've been skipping over what I thought was a key piece of the Florida legislation. The Florida Supreme Court said, there's the deadline, and that conflicts with another provision of this law, the provision that says there shall be under certain circumstances recounts.... And it would be impossible in a populous county to do [by the deadline] what the statute instructs must be done when there's a recount. The Florida Supreme Court said...that there has to be a reconciliation between this, yes, there can be recounts and, yes, there's a deadline. So they are trying to reconcile two provisions.

MR. OLSON: ...Under any other kind of election, these things wouldn't be nearly as important, but we have very important timetables, and as this Court has said a presidential election is so important to the rest of the nation, and there is such high Federal interest in accomplishing these things in the right way, what the Florida legislature did is balance the protest period, the recount period with the contest period, and state that there shall be certain deadlines before which certain things need to be done,...so what those two statutes say is that there may be a recount, but that there shall be compliance with the time deadline....

JUSTICE GINSBURG: But that's something that one can certainly argue. My problem is, one could also argue what the Florida Supreme Court said, and I do not know of any case where we have impugned a state supreme court the way you are doing in this case. I mean, in case after case we have said we owe the highest respect to what the state says, state supreme court says, is the state's law.

MR. OLSON: This is a very unusual situation, Justice Ginsburg, because it is in the context of a presidential election, and it is in the context of Federal rights....

JUSTICE GINSBURG: [Still] Mr. Olson, would you agree that when we read a state court decision, we should read it in the light most favorable to the integrity of the state supreme court, that if there are two possible readings, one that would impute to that court injudicial behavior, lack of integrity, indeed dishonesty, and the other one that would read the opinion to say we think this court is attempting to construe the state law – it may have been wrong, we might have interpreted it differently, but we are not the arbiters, they are....

MR. OLSON: [U]nder almost any other circumstances, yes, Justice Ginsburg, but in this context, in this context, we are talking about a Federal right, a Federal constitutional right, and the rights of individual citizens under the Constitution and so therefore, this Court has a grave responsibility to look—

JUSTICE O'CONNOR: ...If it were purely a matter of state law, I suppose we normally would leave it alone where the state supreme court found it, and so you probably have to persuade us there is some issue of Federal law here. Otherwise, why are we acting?

MR. OLSON: Yes.

JUSTICE O'CONNOR: And are you relying in that regard on...Article II? Would you like to characterize the Federal issue that you think governs this?

MR. OLSON: Well, we are very definitely relying on Article II of the Constitution. The framers of the Constitution debated long and hard. It was one of the longest debates that took place during the formation of the Constitution. Where should this power be lodged, in the Federal legislature, in the state legislature, at the ballot booth or what. The one thing that was discussed and rejected by virtually everyone is that the power to select the manner in which electors would be appointed would be in the state judiciary.... That was rejected.

    The notion that it would be vested in the state judiciary was something that was rejected, and what the framers decided to do is to vest it in the state legislature and vested that authority under Article II, not just in the state, but the legislature....

Oral Argument of Laurence H. Tribe on Behalf of the Respondents

MR. TRIBE: Mr. Chief Justice, and may it please the Court:…[I]t is part of the popular culture to talk about how unfair it is to change the rules of the game. I think that misses the point when the game is over, and when it's over in a kind of photo finish that leaves people unsure who won, and then the question is, how do you develop great, sort of greater certainty, and a rather common technique is a recount, sometimes a manual recount, sometimes taking more time would be rather like looking more closely at the film of a photo finish….

JUSTICE KENNEDY: You're seeing no important policy in 3 U.S.C. Section 5.

MR. TRIBE: No, no.

JUSTICE KENNEDY: In fact, we can change the rules after—not important— the popular culture—

MR. TRIBE: Certainly not, Justice Kennedy, but I read… 3 U.S.C. Section 5 not as a requirement…. [A]nd I'll just read what I think are the key words, "if a state—"….

JUSTICE O'CONNOR: Well, I guess in the area, though, of presidential electors it could be that [the Florida] court… would…have to be informed, at least, by the provisions of Section 5 in reviewing the laws enacted by the legislature of the state. I mean, it had to register somehow with the Florida courts that that statute was there and that it might be in the state's best interest not to go around changing the law after the election…. [They had] to be aware of the consequences to the state of changing the rules.

MR. TRIBE: But, Justice O'Connor, under Article II, Section 1, Clause 2, the authority to regulate the manner of the choice of electors is vested in the state legislature. If the state legislature decides from the beginning to exercise that authority by instructing the various institutions…to exercise their roles in the process, with a specific view of—

JUSTICE O'CONNOR: Well, it certainly did by enacting that date. Here is the certification date. How could it have been clearer?…

MR. TRIBE: But it seems to me that the Federal question, which is really what brings us here, can only arise if 3 U.S.C. Section 5 is something other than…an invitation to the state.

CHIEF JUSTICE REHNQUIST: It can also arise under the section of the Constitution that was construed in Blacker. [Article II, Section 1] That's quite independent of 3 U.S. 5…. If one concluded that the Florida legislature had relied on the state constitution in a way that the Blacker case says it may not in construing the statute.

MR. TRIBE: I think that's possible, Mr. Chief Justice, but the judgment before you doesn't provide even an inkling, I think, of proof about those matters…. It seems to me that [the Florida Supreme Court used the state constitution] as a tiebreaker, as a way of shedding light on the provisions that are in conflict, [and] so long as it's not done in a way that conflicts with a Federal mandate, they are not violating any—

CHIEF JUSTICE REHNQUIST: Mr. Tribe, I don't—I don't agree with that. I don't—I don't think that the Florida Supreme Court used the Florida Constitution [just] as a tool of interpretation of this statute….

[The Court notes that the] text of our Florida Constitution begins with a declaration of rights. And it goes on to say that to the extent the legislature may enact laws regulating the electoral process, those laws are valid only if they impose no "unreasonable or unnecessary" restraint on the right of suffrage contained in the Constitution. In other words, I read the Florida court's opinion as quite clearly saying, having determined what the legislative intent was, we find that our state constitution trumps that legislative intent. I don't think there is any other way to read it, and that is, that is a real problem, it seems to me, under Article II, because in fact there is no right of suffrage under, under Article II. There is a right of suffrage in voting for the legislature but Article II makes it very clear that the legislature can itself appoint the electors….

JUSTICE SOUTER: Isn't there another way of looking at what the Florida court did,… that because the legislature intended one standard to cover both Federal and state recounts, it therefore is valid to consider the state constitution in order to derive a general meaning that will apply to a Federal, as well as a state election. Can you look at it that way?

MR. TRIBE: I fully accept that, Justice Souter....

JUSTICE BREYER: Professor... I think we would all agree that given that the legislature has to select the manner, a state can't say, our Constitution selects the electors. I suppose that's—

MR. TRIBE: That's right.

JUSTICE BREYER: All right, but thinking of this opinion, suppose the court had said, look, we reach our result based on the canons we found in Blackstone. Now, nobody is going to say they said Blackstone is selecting the electors, right?

MR. TRIBE: I think that makes sense.

JUSTICE BREYER: All right. Now,...suppose they said, we reached this decision based on the values found in the Constitution. That would be like Blackstone. But suppose they say, well, the legislature wants us to do X, but our Constitution requires us to do not-X. That might be different.

MR. TRIBE: It might be different.

JUSTICE BREYER: Now, what is it that they have done here?

MR. TRIBE: I certainly don't think they have done the [second]....

JUSTICE SCALIA: [There is] a separate section of the opinion, Professor Tribe, that is entitled the right to vote.... [I]t says categorically, to the extent the legislature may enact laws, they are invalid. And I suggest perhaps the reason that the court did it is that... they were almost constrained to use the constitution to override...the firm deadline....

I would feel much better about [your] resolution [of this matter] if you could give me one sentence in the opinion... that supports the proposition that the Florida Supreme Court...was using the constitutional right to vote provisions as an interpretive tool to determine what the statute meant. I can't find a single sentence for that.

MR. TRIBE: Justice Scalia, I can do a little better than find a sentence. The entire structure of the opinion...would be incoherent if the constitution was decisive. That is the highest law in Florida. Why bother with all the rest if that is anything more than an interpretive guide?

JUSTICE SCALIA: You would bother with it because having decided very clearly what the statute requires and finding no way to get around the firm dates set, you say the reason it's bad is because of the state constitution. That's how it's written.

MR. TRIBE: But, Justice Scalia—

JUSTICE SCALIA: They might have tried it another way, but it seems to me they didn't—....

JUSTICE GINSBURG: ...I suppose there would be a possibility for this Court to remand for clarification, but if there's two readings, one that's questionable, one that isn't, all of our decisions suggest that we read the one [that isn't].

JUSTICE KENNEDY: What is the November 26th date?...

MR. TRIBE: Well, it looks to me like an exercise of the chancellor's foot, as it were, in this particular case. When I saw the date, November 26th, I couldn't come up with an algorithm or a formula that would generate it, but the court was confronted with the task of drawing, as this Court has recognized, what are sometimes inevitably arbitrary lines; that is, it said it was not consistent with the overall scheme of the statute to require these recounts, which had just begun, to terminate. That truly would be a promise to the ear to be broken to the hope, like a munificent bequest, Justice Jackson said – in the pauper's will. Why tell people to count if you won't count it?

JUSTICE KENNEDY: And if the legislature had jumped into the breach and said this same thing, would that be a new statute or new enactment under 5 U.S.C.?

MR. TRIBE: I – honestly, Justice Kennedy, I'm not sure because the language that I quoted from 3 U.S.C. Section 5 focuses on the institutional dispute resolution arrangement that is in place....

JUSTICE KENNEDY: [A]re you saying you can't tell us whether [the legislature], in the hypothetical, supposed that it would be a new enactment?

MR. TRIBE: Well, there are certainly no cases on the subject. The language gives me very little guidance. Since the section is addressed to Congress, neither my opinion about it nor the Court's opinion is necessarily –

JUSTICE KENNEDY: You don't think you could tell us what you might advise the Congress if you were the counsel for the Judiciary Committee?

MR. TRIBE: I think I would advise the Congress that it is not a new enactment.

Bush v. Palm Beach County Canvassing Board

By the time the United States Supreme Court heard oral arguments in *Bush v. Palm Beach County Canvassing Board,* the recount challenged in it was over, with Palm Beach and Miami-Dade Counties not reporting, and with Governor Bush certified as the winner in Florida. Hence, overturning the Florida Supreme Court decision, and setting the clock back to November 14, would have affected only the results in Broward County (and those results could then easily be wound by Gore into a contest appeal).

This explains, most likely, the Court's indefinite disposal of the case. Certainly, its action meant that the original and controversial decision to hear the controversy did not turn out to be terribly consequential. Except, perhaps, in one respect. The members of the Florida Supreme Court were on notice not to do anything that remotely hinted of altering the state's election law, even if they thought it a legitimate exercise of their interpretive function.

About one thing, the justices were definite. They did not even take note of the possibility, raised by the branch of government they were protecting, that *Bush v. Palm Beach County* presented nonjusticable political questions, even though the very case cited so prominently in their decision was apposite to the issue. *McPherson v. Blacker* had explicitly rejected the premise "that all questions connected with the election of a presidential elector are political in their nature [and] that the court has no power . . . to dispose of them"(146, US 1, 23). Blacker concerned an earlier phase of the presidential election process than did *Bush v. Palm Beach County,* but the majority was uninterested, apparently, in the whole matter.

From *Bush v. Palm Beach County Canvassing Board,* 148 LEd 2d 366, 371–372.

Per Curiam

As a general rule, this Court defers to a state court's interpretation of a state statute. But in the case of a law enacted by a state legislature applicable not only to elections to state offices, but also to the selection of Presidential electors, the legislature is not acting solely under the authority given it by the people of the State, but by virtue of a direct grant of authority made under Art. II, § 1, cl. 2, of the United States Constitution....

There are expressions in the opinion of the Supreme Court of Florida that may be read to indicate that it construed the Florida Election Code without regard to the extent to which the Florida Constitution could, consistent with Art. II, §1, cl. 2, "circumscribe the legislative power." [*McPherson v. Blacker*, 146 US 1, 25]. The opinion states, for example, that "[t]o the extent that the Legislature may enact laws regulating the electoral process, those laws are valid only if they impose no 'unreasonable or unnecessary' restraints on the right of the suffrage" guaranteed by the state constitution. The opinion also states that "[b]ecause election laws are intended to facilitate the right of suffrage, such laws must be liberally construed in favor of the citizens' right to vote...."

In addition,...[t]he parties before us agree that whatever else may be the effect of [3 USC Section 5], it creates a "safe harbor" for a State insofar as congressional consideration of its electoral votes is concerned. If the state legislature has provided for final determination of contests or controversies by a law made prior to election day, that determination shall be conclusive if made at least six days prior to said time of meeting of the electors. The Florida Supreme Court cited 3 U.S.C. §§ 1-10 in a footnote of its opinion, but did not discuss § 5. Since § 5 contains a principle of federal law that would assure finality of the State's determination if made pursuant to a state law in effect before the election, a legislative wish to take advantage of the "safe harbor" would counsel against any construction of the Election Code that Congress might deem to be a change in the law.

After reviewing the opinion of the Florida Supreme Court, we find "that there is considerable uncertainty as to the precise grounds for the decision." *Minnesota v. National Tea Co.*, 309 U.S. 551, 555 (1940). This is sufficient reason for us to decline at this time to review the federal questions asserted to be present....

Specifically, we are unclear as to the extent to which the Florida Supreme Court saw the Florida Constitution as circumscribing the legislature's authority under Art. II, § 1, cl. 2. We are also unclear as to the consideration the Florida Supreme Court accorded to 3 U.S.C. § 5. The judgment of the Supreme Court of Florida is therefore vacated, and the case is remanded for further proceedings not inconsistent with this opinion.

It is so ordered.

Reactions to *Bush v. Palm Beach County Canvassing Board*

Cass Sunstein thought the Supreme Court intervention in *Bush v. Palm Beach County* was both legally justified and wise. He found the decision appropriate, even statesmanlike, under the circumstances. (By the same criteria, he would feel very differently about *Bush v. Gore*.)

However, Stuart Taylor, columnist for the *National Journal* and a frequent commentator on public television, felt judicial participation in this whole matter was constitutionally impermissible. He was convinced the Court should have rendered no substantive decision at all. Casting himself as a "volunteer clerk" to the justices, Taylor offered a draft opinion contending that *Bush v. Palm Beach County* did not present a justiciable controversy. He invoked the Florida brief on his behalf, though not agreeing with its limitations on the power of Congress.

The Broad Virtue in a Modest Ruling

Cass R. Sunstein

This United States Supreme Court proceeds in small steps. Most of the time, the court says no more than it must. It leaves the most fundamental issues for other institutions and for another day.

Its ruling yesterday on the Florida Supreme Court's decision to continue vote counting is entirely characteristic of its minimalist nature. Neither George W. Bush nor Al Gore won a clear victory; the court refused to give what either of them sought. In the most important sentence in its little opinion, the court announced that it will "decline at this time to review the federal questions asserted to be present."

In so saying, the court allowed the Florida courts a great deal of room to resolve the continuing controversy....

The inconclusiveness of the United States Supreme Court's decision is bound to be a disappointment to those hoping for a final resolution in federal court. But because of its very modesty and narrowness, and because of its unanimity, the court's decision can be counted as a triumph for good sense and even for the rule of law.

Mr. Bush challenged the decision of the Florida Supreme Court on two different grounds. First, he argued that the Florida court, by changing state law, had violated Article II of the United States Constitution, which provides that states shall appoint electors "in such manner as the Legislature," and not any court, may direct.

Second, Mr. Bush invoked a federal law saying that a state's appointment of electors is "conclusive" if a state provides for the appointment of electors "by laws enacted prior to the day fixed" for the election. According to Mr. Bush, the Florida court did not follow, but instead changed, the law "enacted prior" to Election Day.

Originally published in *The New York Times*, December 5, 2000, p. A31. Reprinted by permission.

Mr. Bush wanted the nation's highest court to say that because the State Supreme Court had violated the federal Constitution and federal law, Katherine Harris, Florida's secretary of state, had the authority to certify the vote as of Nov. 14. For his part, Mr. Gore wanted the court to affirm the Florida Supreme Court on the ground that that court had merely interpreted the law, without changing it at all.

The United States Supreme Court refused these invitations. It took a much smaller step, asking the State Supreme Court to clarify the basis for its decision. Did the state court use the Florida Constitution to override the will of the Legislature? That would be a serious problem, because the United States Constitution requires state legislatures, not state constitutions, to determine the manner of appointing electors. And the nation's highest court asked the state court to address the federal law requiring electors to be appointed under state law enacted "prior to" Election Day. In its own opinion, the Florida Supreme Court had said nothing about that law.

With these exceedingly narrow requests for clarification, the court did not settle the dispute over the meaning of the constitutional and statutory provisions at issue in the case. Maybe it refused to do so on principle, thinking that the judiciary should insert itself as little as possible into the continuing electoral struggle. Or maybe the court sought unanimity and found, as groups often do, that unanimity is possible only if as little as possible is decided. Certainly, the court was aware that it might not be necessary to resolve the federal issues, because Mr. Gore might lose other challenges in the state courts.

Should the court be criticized for leaving so much undecided? In some circles, the court is being castigated for failing to produce clarity and certainty. But a narrow decision has large virtues, not least in an era in which "activist judges" are so often reviled. A court that takes small steps is likely to stick closely to the legal texts, without taking sides in partisan struggles. A court that proceeds incrementally is more likely to proceed unanimously, and unanimity can go a long way toward deflecting political passions. Such a court helps to ensure that the federal judiciary will not take an excessive role in American democracy.

Taken by itself, the United States Supreme Court decision does not determine the identity of our next president. But in its own quiet way, it was a great moment for the rule of law.

A First Draft for the Justices to Consider

Stuart Taylor Jr.

Dear Mr. Chief Justice: I offer below a first draft of an opinion for your consideration. It stresses that no court has the constitutional power to pass final judgment on a dispute over who won a presidential election and that the Florida Supreme Court's decision of Nov. 21—which concocted new vote-counting rules after the election—is binding neither on the Florida Legislature nor on Congress. The bottom line is that this virtual tie between Bush and Gore presents a political question on which the Constitution gives the last word to the people's elected representatives, not to judges seeking to divine "the will of the people" by squinting to see almost-invisible dimples....

—Volunteer Clerk

In this case, we consider whether the winner of the extraordinarily close presidential election is to be authoritatively identified by Florida judges, by this Court, or by elected representatives of the people.

Petitioner, Gov. George W. Bush, asks us to hold that the Florida Supreme Court violated federal law in the decision below by "usurp[ing]" the power of the Florida Legislature to specify procedures for choosing presidential electors. That Nov. 21 decision eschewed "hypertechnical reliance" upon the Legislature's deadline (Nov. 14) for submission of county election returns, including any new votes found in manual recounts. Instead, the court created its own deadline (5 p.m. on Sunday, Nov. 26) to allow more time for manual recounts. The court effectively ordered that Vice President Al Gore be certified as winner of Florida's electoral votes if the recounts in three heavily Democratic counties erased Bush's existing lead. This, said the Florida court, was the best way to divine the "will of the people."

National Journal, December 2, 2000, pp. 3715–3716. Reprinted by permission.

Bush claims that the Florida court disregarded the Florida Election Code's carefully crafted plan for resolving disputes over vote counts and chose instead to invent new rules in the guise of statutory interpretation. This post-election rule change, Bush submits, was contrary to the federal Electoral Count Act of 1887.

Respondents, including Gore, urge that we affirm the Florida Supreme Court on the ground that it simply "applied garden-variety principles of statutory interpretation to resolve ambiguities and reconcile conflicting provisions" in the Florida Election Code. Noting our usual deference to state courts as final expositors of state law, Gore concludes that we have no power to question the Florida court's interpretation, even if we find it logically unpersuasive.

The Florida Legislature, in a thoughtful amicus brief in support of neither party (signed by former Solicitor General Charles Fried), argues principally that the dispute at the heart of this case is not justiciable because it is a political matter to be decided by Congress. This brief also asserts that competing claims by presidential candidates about having their electors' votes counted are "to be decided in the first instance by the state Legislature," not state courts, and thus seems to imply that Congress should count the electors (if any) approved by the Legislature....

Bush says (as does the Legislature arguing in the alternative) that the Florida Supreme Court's ruling was contrary to the 1887 act because that court made up new rules rather than applying "laws enacted prior to" Election Day. Gore denies this, asserting that Florida Supreme Court decisions are conclusive as to the meaning of Florida laws and that there was thus no post-election rule change. Gore thereby suggests that this Court lacks power to review either the Nov. 21 decision or any future interpretations of Florida law, even if the Florida courts purport to pick the next President.

We decline the invitations from both Bush and Gore to decide whether the Florida court departed from pre-existing state law, and whether any such departure would in these unique circumstances violate federal law. We need not consider those issues, because we rule instead that (as the Florida Legislature contends) this case involves a nonjusticiable political matter to be resolved by elected representatives: Congress has the judicially unreviewable power to determine the meaning of both Article II, Section 1 and the 1887 act, and thus to resolve any dispute between Florida's Legislature and its courts over appointment of electors.

This is implicit in the 12th Amendment's exclusive assignment to Congress of the authority to "count" electoral votes. It is consistent with the 1887 act's design to discourage retroactive judicial (or other) manipulations of election law to change the outcome of a presidential election. And it is in keeping with our decision in *McPherson vs. Blacker* (1892), which held: "The appointment of these electors is thus placed absolutely and wholly with the legislatures of the several states."

We express no view on the Florida Legislature's further [argument]... that any electors approved by it should be the ones counted by Congress in the event of a dispute.

We are aware of suggestions that we alone can somehow legitimize the outcome of this election in the eyes of the public and the losing side. But we are judges, not magicians. Any process that we could choose at this date would be seen as favoring either Bush or Gore. (So would a dismissal of *certiorari* as improvidently granted.) Indeed, some might even see today's decision as favoring Bush, by implicitly encouraging the Florida Legislature to challenge any and all Florida court decisions won by Gore— or perhaps as favoring Gore, by allowing the Florida Supreme Court's much-criticized November 21 decision to stand. It is far from clear to us, however, whether or not the Florida courts will ultimately rule that Gore has won Florida's electors; whether or not the Legislature will decide to intervene; and how Congress would resolve any dispute between Florida's Legislature and its courts.

More important, it is the Constitution, as construed by the people's elected representatives in Congress—and not (in this unusual instance) by any court—that apportions power between state legislatures and courts in the choice of presidential electors. If, in the end, people on the losing side believe that Congress or the Florida Legislature has flouted the will of the people, their remedy must lie at the polls, not in any courtroom.

More Supreme Than Court?
The Fall of the Political Question Doctrine and the Rise of Judicial Supremacy

Rachel E. Barkow

The visible anger directed at the Florida Supreme Court by most of the justices who voted to hear *Bush v. Palm Beach County* could explain why they ignored the political question doctrine. But the reasons for this omission may be more principled and, for some, more ominous.

Rachel Barkow, a John M. Olin Fellow at the Georgetown University Law Center in 2001, believes a good case can be made that disputes arising under Article II are nonjusticable political questions. And the contemporary Supreme Court's apparent disinterest in this matter, she maintains, stems above all from a conception of judicial supremacy that largely doubts the existence of political questions because it sees the relation among the branches of the national government as "decidedly more hierarchical than coordinate." This is part of a pattern which has led the justices to use their undoubted jurisdiction over provisions of the Constitution such as the so-called Commerce Clause to sharply restrict the powers traditionally exercised by Congress and the executive.

The whole point of the political question doctrine...is that some issues are for the political branches, not the federal judiciary, to confront and resolve. And the Article II question in the Bush cases presented a strong candidate for application of the political question doctrine. The text and structure of Article II, the original understanding,...and prudential factors all make a strong case for congressional resolution. Yet the Court did not even consider that possibility.

Columbia Law Review 102 (2002), pp. 237, 300–309, 311–314, 317–319. Reprinted by permission.

III. The Decline of the Political Question
Doctrine and the Trend Toward Judicial Supremacy

The Supreme Court's failure even to consider the political question doctrine reflects a broader trend in which the Court overestimates its own powers and prowess vis-à-vis the political branches. The political question doctrine itself cannot coexist with the current Court's views of how
interpretive power is allocated under the constitution....

III-A. Judicial Immodesty and the Decline of Deference

One reading of *Marbury v. Madison* is that it endorses the judiciary as the
final, independent arbiter of the meaning of all constitutional language.
But, as [Professor] Henry Monaghan has pointed out, "the judicial duty 'to
say what the law is' does not demand an independent judgment rule; it is in
fact quite consistent with a clear-mistake standard." That is, the
Constitution itself can be read to vest interpretive authority with the other
branches of government—and the Court's obligation to say what the law is
might require recognition that some interpretive power has been allocated
elsewhere.

The Constitution's vesting of interpretive power with the other branches on some constitutional questions reflects the institutional differences
among the branches. In particular, the judiciary's independence and isolation from popular pressures and sentiment make it a poor policymaker.
Indeed, it is because of the judiciary's institutional limitations that a prominent theory of judicial review at the time *Marbury* was decided, even when
a case was properly within the Court's jurisdiction, was one of great deference to the political branches. Courts consistently stated that Congress's
constitutional judgments would be overturned only if plainly in error....

In the past few decades, however, the Supreme Court has become
increasingly blind to its limitations as an institution—and, concomitantly,
to the strengths of the political branches—and has focused on *Marbury's*
grand proclamation of its power without taking that statement in context.
The modern Supreme Court—beginning with the Warren Court, continuing
through the Burger Court, and exponentially gaining strength with the
Rehnquist Court—acknowledges few limits on its power to say what the
law is. While the Warren and Burger Courts used the supremacy rhetoric of
Marbury to advance the Court's position vis-à-vis the states, the Rehnquist
Court has used that language to assert a superior place in the constitutional
order vis-à-vis the other federal branches.

The current Court increasingly displaces Congress's view with its own
without much more than a passing nod to Congress's factual findings or
policy judgments.... [T]he unmistakable trend is toward a view that all

constitutional questions are matters for independent judicial interpretation and that Congress has no special institutional advantage in answering aspects of particular questions. The Court rarely engages in a threshold determination of whether the constitutional provision at issue contemplates that the political branches receive some deference in their interpretation. The Court has therefore become increasingly immodest when it comes to deciding how constitutional interpretive power should be allocated.

[T]his trend [is certainly evident] in...areas in which the Court has [undoubted] jurisdiction....

III-A-1. Section 5 of the Fourteenth Amendment. Section 5 of the Fourteenth Amendment gives Congress the "power to enforce, by appropriate legislation, the provisions of this article." This language appears to contemplate a unique interpretive role for Congress based on Congress's special position in the federal scheme. Indeed, the Court itself held as much in *Katzenbach v. Morgan*, stating that it would defer to congressional judgments about how to enforce this provision. The Court concluded that "it was for Congress...to assess and weigh the various conflicting considerations.... It is not for us to review the congressional resolution of these factors. It is enough that we be able to perceive a basis upon which the Congress might resolve the conflict as it did."...

The Rehnquist Court however, has all but abandoned this view. In a series of recent cases—*City of Boerne v. Flores, Florida Prepaid Postsecondary Education Expense Board v. College Savings Bank, Kimel v. Florida Board of Regents,* and *Board of Trustees of the University of Alabama v. Garrett*—the Court has indicated that it will, in practice, accord essentially no deference to Congress's remedial judgment, even insofar as that interpretation rests on congressional findings and policy judgments.

Boerne involved Congress's efforts to provide greater protection under the Free Exercise Clause of the First Amendment [imposed upon the states under the Fourteenth] than the Court had recognized. Congress passed the Religious Freedom Restoration Act in 1994 essentially to overrule the Supreme Court's decision [four years earlier] in *Employment Division v. Smith* and to reinstate the previous [more rigorous] standard that had applied to Free Exercise Clause claims. The Court rebuffed Congress's attempts and stated unequivocally its view that it is supreme in its interpretation of the Constitution....

The Court emphasized that Congress's power under Section 5 was solely an enforcement power, "not the power to determine what constitutes a constitutional violation." Although the Court conceded that "the line between measures that remedy or prevent unconstitutional actions and measures that make a substantial change in the governing law is not easy to discern" and that "Congress must have wide latitude in determining where it lies," its rejection of Congress's decision in *Boerne* [began] to make clear that the Court alone will determine where the line is drawn and accord Congress no deference. The Court's decision reflects its view that its capacity for enforcing the Fourteenth Amendment is greater than Congress's ability.

Although *Boerne's* holding could have been prompted by the fact that Congress passed RFRA specifically to undercut *Smith*, subsequent cases made clear that the Court's strict scrutiny of Congress's Section 5 legislation applies even in the absence of a Supreme Court decision on the matter. In *Florida Prepaid*, the Court reviewed legislation that subjected states to suit in federal court for patent infringement. Unlike in *Boerne*, no Supreme Court case had addressed the substantive issue. Although the Court did not disagree that a patent was property for purposes of the Fourteenth Amendment, the Court nevertheless struck down the statute on the grounds that Congress failed to show that there was a "pattern of patent infringement by the States." As Justice Stevens argued in dissent, it was "quite unfair" to demand a showing of a "pattern of patent infringement" when the Court had never articulated such a requirement. "This Court has never mandated that Congress must find 'widespread and persisting deprivation of constitutional rights'…in order to employ its 5 authority." Moreover, there was evidence in the congressional record that state remedies were inadequate for patent infringement, and that infringement was likely to increase. The Court, however, gave no deference to these findings. "Rather, the Court placed the onus for establishing the necessary factual predicate on Congress and found that Congress had not met its burden."

In *Kimel*, the Court held that Congress lacked the authority under Section 5 to abrogate the states' sovereign immunity [against suit] in the Age Discrimination in Employment Act of 1967. The Court in *Kimel* made clear that "the ultimate interpretation and determination of the Fourteenth Amendment's substantive meaning remains the province of the Judicial Branch." By ultimate, the Supreme Court appeared to mean that its view was not merely final, but also that it would pay little attention to Congress's factual findings and policy judgments.

The Court's view that Congress possesses no special ability to analyze the weight of its findings is most striking in *Garrett*, in which the Court concluded that Congress lacked the authority under Section 5 to abrogate states' immunity [against suit] under the Americans with Disabilities Act. In so doing, the Court rejected a substantial congressional record of discrimination as failing to show a "history and pattern" of discrimination. Nevertheless, the Court seemed persuaded by the fact that these numbers paled in comparison to the overall number of individuals with disabilities. "It is telling, we think, that given these large numbers, Congress assembled only such minimal evidence of unconstitutional state discrimination…."

Apparently, the Court has in mind some ratio, and Congress failed to satisfy it....[Thus] the Court replaced its constitutional opinion for that of Congress, without acknowledging or conceding that Congress might have a better vantage point insofar as the question involved factual findings and policy predictions....

It seems clear that an animating force behind the Court's Section 5 decisions is its view that Congress possesses no special institutional advantages in enforcing the Constitution. If anything, the Court believes the opposite: that it has the superior ability to make such decisions....

III-A-2. The Commerce Clause. Commerce Clause interpretation is perhaps the area in which the Court's displacement of Congress's constitutional judgment for its own is most evident. The Court's Commerce Clause decisions were once cited, along with the political question cases, as examples of the Supreme Court's deference to congressional constitutional judgments. Indeed, the Court's treatment of the Commerce Clause tracks the rise and fall of the political question doctrine. At the same time that Chief Justice Marshall recognized the existence of political questions, he expressed his belief that Congress has broad—though not unlimited—power to regulate commerce. Similarly, just as the political question doctrine began to expand with the New Deal Court..., so too, did the Court's deference to Congress under the Commerce Clause. Now, just as the political question doctrine has fallen out of favor, the Commerce Clause seems to be fertile ground for reversing congressional interpretations....

The Court's theory of institutional competency is [most] evident in the Court's scrutiny of Congress's judgment as to whether something will have a substantial effect on interstate commerce. Determining what has an effect on interstate commerce involves the same type of factfinding expertise at issue in the social and economic legislation that the Court reviews under the Due Process and Equal Protection Clauses. Indeed, the...era [up to 1937] saw the Court strike down various acts as outside Congress's commerce power. In *A.L.A. Schechter Poultry Corp v. United States*, for example, the Court struck down regulations fixing wages and hours in intrastate businesses, and emphasized that the line between direct and indirect effects of intrastate transactions on commerce was fundamental. Later, after it became apparent that "no court was capable of drawing such a line in terms appropriate for continuing judicial administration," the Court rejected the distinction between "indirect" and "direct," and held that Congress's Commerce Clause power extends to activities having a "substantial relation" to interstate commerce. This test is similar to the Necessary and Proper Clause standard, under which the Court gives wide latitude to Congress. It is therefore not surprising that from 1937 to 1995, the Court deferred to Congress in all of its Commerce Clause cases.

[T]hat deference seemed to come to a halt in [*United States v. Lopez*, in 1995, when the Court denied Congress authority under the Commerce Clause to pass a law forbidding possession of firearms within 1,000 feet of a public or private school. But the decision] could be explained by the fact that Congress failed to amass any evidence to support its conclusion that the behavior it was regulating has a substantial effect on interstate commerce. The government conceded in *Lopez* that "neither the statute nor its legislative history contains express congressional findings regarding the effects upon interstate commerce of gun possession in a school zone." The Court noted that it "would have to pile inference upon inference" to defer to Congress. Some thought that the result would be different if Congress provided a more explicit record of reasoning—because then the Court would clearly be substituting its judgment for that of Congress. Thus, although Justice Breyer's dissent compiled a great deal of information to support Congress's judgment as rational, the Court may have been persuaded by the fact that Congress had not undertaken such an effort itself, so its expertise in factfinding was not a factor in the decision.

This limited view of *Lopez* could no longer be maintained after the Court held in *United States v. Morrison* that Congress lacked the authority under the Commerce Clause to pass the Violence Against Women Act. Congress held four years of hearings, received reports from task forces on gender bias in twenty-one states, and issued eight reports with specific factual findings. Congress relied on evidence that violence against women resulted in annual costs of between $5 and $10 billion in 1993 and that gender-based violence prevents women from participating fully in the national economy. The record, in fact, was "far more voluminous than the record compiled by Congress and found sufficient in two prior cases upholding Title II of the Civil Rights Act of 1964 against Commerce Clause Challenges." Indeed, the Court conceded that "in contrast with the lack of congressional findings that we faced in *Lopez*, [the Violence Against Women Act] is supported by numerous findings regarding the serious impact that gender-motivated violence has on victims and their families."

The Court nevertheless held that these findings were insufficient. The Court stated that it would scrutinize congressional findings to determine whether the regulated activity itself was of an economic nature, regardless of the cumulative effect of the activity on commerce. The Court therefore reformulated the substantial effects test to limit the facts Congress may consider to those that are economic in nature, regardless of whether Congress believes the aggregation of those facts has an effect on commerce. The Court's rationale was that, without such a restriction, Congress would be able to regulate any crime or activity, no matter how local, as long as its aggregated impact has substantial effects on employment, production, transit, or consumption. This result would make the "enumerated" commerce power meaningless.

The Court's opinion reveals that animating its decision was a potent reading of *Marbury's* judicial supremacy rhetoric, without regard for *Marbury's* recognition of the judiciary's limits. The Court quoted the familiar supremacy rhetoric from *Cooper v. Aaron* that "the federal judiciary is supreme in the exposition of the law of the Constitution" and noted that "ever since *Marbury* this Court has remained the ultimate expositor of the constitutional text." The Court then stated that "the Constitution's separation of federal power and the creation of the Judicial Branch indicate that disputes regarding the extent of congressional power are largely subject to judicial review."

But this raw claim to "ultimate" power says nothing about whether the Supreme Court should defer to Congress's judgment because of its superior competence at making the types of judgments necessary under the Court's "substantial effects" test. In a more deferential mood, the Court itself has noted that it "is institutionally unsuited to gather the facts upon which economic predictions can be made, and professionally untrained to make them." But whether the Court will leave to itself or Congress the authority to determine whether a cause is "economic" remains to be seen; given the piercing judicial supremacy rhetoric in *Morrison*, it seems likely that Congress will receive little deference....

IV. The Political Question Doctrine and the New Judicial Supremacy

The demise of the political question doctrine is part and parcel of this larger trend of refusing to accord interpretive deference to the political branches. The political question doctrine cannot coexist with the current Court's view of the judiciary's place in the constitutional structure. The doctrine requires the Court to acknowledge that the other branches "may make constitutional law—i.e., make judgments about the scope and meaning of its constitutionally authorized...functions—subject to change only if [the branch] later changes its mind or by a constitutional amendment."... [But] the Rehnquist Court [does] not trust the political branches to make these determinations.... That is why the Court no longer seems interested in analyzing as a threshold matter whether the Constitution gives an interpretive role to another branch.

If "[a] strong view of judicial supremacy implies an absence of judicial deference," a fortiori it demands the demise of the political question doctrine. If the Court does not trust the political branches enough to give their decisions deference in cases over which the Court has jurisdiction, it would be anomalous for the Court to conclude that the political branches possess institutional advantages that justify giving them complete control over some constitutional questions....

The most expedient way to remove the intellectual tension between the Court's theory of judicial superiority and the political question doctrine is to eliminate one or the other. And so the Court has ushered out the doctrine—allowing its supremacy theory to flower and its confidence in its own constitutional abilities to grow.

PART 5

THE CONTEST

On November 27, 2000, Vice President Gore filed a contest complaint in Leon County Circuit Court under Section 102.168 of the Florida election code.

The legislature had substantially rewritten 168, and parts of 102.166, just a year earlier. Until that time, complainants could not only ask a canvassing board for a manual recount in the protest phase of an election, they could also file a suit in circuit court if they believed there was "fraud in the way the votes were tabulated."[1] After certification, they might institute a contest under 102.168, though the possible bases for such a suit were not spelled out in the statute.

The 1999 amendments ended court actions under 102.166, and enumerated specific grounds for a contest.

(3) The complaint shall set forth the grounds on which the contestant intends to establish his or her right to such office or set aside the result of the election on a submitted referendum. The grounds for contesting an election under this section are:

(a) Misconduct, fraud, or corruption on the part of any election official or any member of the canvassing board sufficient to change or place in doubt the result of the election.

(b) Ineligibility of the successful candidate for the nomination or office in dispute.

(c) Receipt of a number of illegal votes or rejection of a number of legal votes sufficient to change or place in doubt the result of the election.

(d) Proof that any elector, election official, or canvassing board member was given or offered a bribe or reward in money, property, or any other thing of value for the purpose of procuring the successful candidate's nomination or election or determining the result on any question submitted by referendum.

(e) Any other cause or allegation which, if sustained, would show that a person other than the successful candidate was the person duly nominated or elected to the office in question or that the outcome of the election on a question submitted by referendum was contrary to the result declared by the canvassing board or election board.[2]

It was the third of these grounds on which the Gore lawyers (headed by David Boies) buttressed their complaint: the failure of the secretary of state to count the 215 (or 176) additional Gore votes found in the Palm Beach recount, and the unwillingness of the Palm Beach board itself to count as votes 3,300 dimpled ballots; the failure of the Miami-Dade canvassing board to ask for certification of 388 votes recovered during its partial recount (showing a gain of 160 for Gore), and its leaving of 9,000 under-votes untouched. This all constituted "rejection of a number of legal votes sufficient to change or place in doubt the result of the election"—"legal votes" being the ballots of "voters who intended to vote for a presidential candidate."[3] Consequently, the circuit court should order Harris and the Florida Elections Canvassing Commission to include in the certified totals the Palm Beach and Miami ballots already reviewed by hand. Furthermore, it should "cause the uncounted ballots cast in Miami Dade County . . . to be manually counted," and "cause the . . . disputed ballots cast in Palm Beach County" to be reviewed.[4] Following the Miami canvassing board's lead, Gore did not demand the counting of any overvotes.

The vice president's grievances took the form of suits against the offending county canvassing boards, as stipulated in 102.168, and against Secretary Harris and the Florida Elections Canvassing Commission. But Governor Bush was named as a defendant as well, and the Bush lawyers actually handled the litigation. Since the secretary of state's name led the pleadings, the case took the name *Gore v. Harris.* (One of the canvassing boards sued was the Nassau County board, which, Gore's lawyers maintained, counted 51 votes illegally for Bush, when it decided to use the original machine count in its final certification, instead of the automatic machine recount; the recount showed Bush losing 124 votes and Gore only 73 from the original count.[5] But since this grievance was rejected without comment by both the trial court and by the Florida Supreme Court, we will leave it aside for the sake of clarity.)

In making their claims, the Gore forces were actually using the words "rejection of a number of legal votes" in two different ways. Applied to the additional 375 votes for the vice president in Palm Beach and Miami-Dade Counties, and the 9,000 undervotes, rejection of legal votes meant ballots still not recounted, or if they had been, not included in the Gore totals. In relation to the dimpled ballots in Palm Beach, the words of 3(c) meant votes improperly rejected because the board counted them under a legally deficient standard.

With regard to the latter, Boies and his colleagues made the rather startling claim that prior events demonstrated the *Delahunt* standard to be the only legally appropriate one for recounting ballots in Florida. Judge LaBarga, they asserted, "relied in part upon *Delahunt v. Johnston*"[6] for his November 22 order (though this was actually in a footnote saying *Delahunt* "*may be* of assistance to the [canvassing] board").[7] The Palm Beach officials, therefore, "did not follow the correct legal standard, endorsed by Judge LaBarga," in using a criterion "that failed to count ballots with indentations or dimples for a presidential candidate unless the ballot also revealed similar indentations" in other races.[8] Miami-Dade, too, should presumably use the "correct standard."

The plaintiffs not only wanted their contest adjudicated as quickly as possible. They wanted the trial judge assigned to the case, Judge N. Sanders Sauls, to begin reviewing immediately the uncounted ballots in Miami-Dade, and the 3,300 disputed ones in Palm Beach. The unprecedented closeness of the presidential race was enough to make out "a *prima facie* case" that those ballots raised "substantial issues about whether there has been . . . 'rejection of a number of legal votes sufficient to change or place in doubt the outcome of the election.'"[9]

Bush Answers

The Bush defendants rejoined that the standard for hand counting ballots in Florida was anything but clear. Only a trial, in their view, could clarify it, with particular reference to Palm Beach. But a trial was also necessary, they believed, to decide if there should be any counting at all. For since much of Gore's contest ran against the county canvassing boards, the only way further recounts were possible would be if the canvassing boards had acted arbitrarily and unfairly in doing what they did, not merely because some votes happened to go uncounted. "In a contest case challenging a county . . . board's actions during a protest under 102.166, this Court reviews the canvassing board's decisions for *abuse of discretion*."[10] The defendants cited the "leading case" on this matter, the Fourth District Court of Appeals decision in *Broward County Canvassing Board v. Hogan* (1992), which stated, with regard to a recount, "Although section 102.168 grants the right of contest, it does not change the discretionary aspect of the review procedures outlined in section 102.166."[11]

This discretionary standard applied to other state officials as well under law and practice in Florida. Hence, the determinative issue in the Gore contest boiled down to whether the appropriate authorities behaved in a reasonably sensible manner, whether in deciding to count or not count votes, or in setting standards to evaluate them.

There was no doubt those officials had behaved reasonably, Bush asserted. Thus a canvassing board, such as Miami-Dade, "that acts in compliance with the Supreme Court of Florida's deadline for manual recounts" could not be liable for refusing to extend the recount so as to "violate that deadline."[12] Florida law gave the Palm Beach County Canvassing Board, or any other board, "broad discretion to determine the standard to apply when evaluating voter intent, and Plaintiffs are not entitled to second-guess that standard to effect a desired result."[13] Similarly, the "Election Canvassing Commission properly excluded the totals of the manual recount [in Palm Beach] which was concluded after the 5:00 P.M. deadline" on November 26.[14]

Bush and his allies in the Florida House and Senate believed, then, that only official misconduct in the rejection of votes was actionable under Section 168.3(c), as indicated by its legislative history and its logical import. Ballots not counted in the first place by a properly functioning machine were recorded legally as "no votes," and "cannot be said to have been rejected. In such a case, all the votes are accepted."[15] Furthermore, votes not counted because they had missed, or would miss, a properly constituted deadline, or because of a canvassing board's reasonably promulgated standards, were votes "rejected legally, not illegally," in accordance with the "proper exercise" of official discretion. "Thus [they] do not represent the rejection of legal votes."[16] If election officials were acting in a legally justified or principled manner, they could *not be* rejecting legal votes. Or as Professor Abner Greene puts it in his brilliant study of the 2000 election, "Bush argued. . . . [that] votes are not legal ones if they have been rejected according to law. . . . It is possible [therefore] that a vote is not a legal one, even if . . . there is a clear indication of the intent of the voter, if, for some other, valid reason, the ballot was not counted."[17] Whatever the merits of this position (which we will examine later), it presents an interesting contrast to the insistence by the Bush forces at the protest phase that Gore could fully adjudicate his claims in a contest.

The governor's lawyers put forth a third reason why a trial was necessary. There was "no reason in law or logic," they argued, "to limit" a recount, even if ordered, "to the undervotes . . . 'cherry-picked' by Plaintiffs."[18] Sauls was required by subsection 8 of 168 to provide "relief appropriate under [the] circumstances,"[19] so he must ponder, based on the evidence, whether proper relief in the form of a recount did not mean reviewing all the ballots in the state, or, at the least, all the undervotes. Part of the equal-protection claim ignored in the protest phase now became a demand for what the defendants regarded as proper remedial action, if the court (wrongly) decreed any action. (They did not mention overvotes, however, at this point.)

Judge Sauls Acts—And So Does David Boies

Judge Sauls ruled a trial was necessary to decide whether he should assess the disputed ballots, though he ordered all the Miami-Dade and Palm Beach ballots sent to Tallahassee.[20]

David Boies responded by filing an emergency motion in the Florida Supreme Court, attacking the "legally erroneous"[21] premises on which he felt Sauls's refusal to start counting, and the entire Bush case, rested. Boies continued to insist the "standard of determining the voter's intent" was "well established" in Florida: "Only the *impossibility* of determining the voter's choice justifies rejecting a ballot."[22] He also scoffed at the notion that the contest needed to involve statewide recounts. Gore's complaint clearly identified the "ballots to be counted," and "no other votes or ballots cast"[23] were in dispute. "The suggestion that all ballots must be reviewed— whether contested or not—is nothing less than a defense delay tactic," not sanctioned by previous contest cases.[24] (Those cases, however, did not concern a type of ballot error common to all precincts in the state.)

Most important, Boies felt, Judge Sauls had misconceived the standard of review governing an election contest. It was not an abuse of discretion standard, a criterion tilted almost irretrievably toward the official actions contested. Rather, it was a *de novo* standard, which viewed the plaintiffs' contentions afresh. Under Florida law, after all, a complainant did not need to have filed a protest before bringing a contest suit. "In [such] an original action [therefore] the Court must decide *in the first instance* what intent of the voter [a] ballot manifests."[25]

This standard, if accepted, would get the plaintiffs a brand-new look at the dimpled Palm Beach ballots. But with respect to the rest of the Palm Beach complaint, and the Miami one, Boies went a step further. The very language of 168.3(c), he contended, actually made standard of review *irrelevant* to these matters. "The statute authorizes a challenge based on . . . 'rejection of . . . legal votes.' . . . By its terms, this provision requires proof *merely* that a potentially decisive number of valid votes were not counted, and focuses *solely on the votes themselves*; it [does not] call for 'review' of the Canvassing Board's decisions."[26]

Gore's lawyers repeatedly reminded the state supreme court that time was of the essence. Indeed, they now implied, in contrast to their earlier position, that the contest must end by December 12, not only for Florida to achieve conclusivity, but because any ongoing contest process could be rendered null and void on that date. "The state effectively faces a deadline of December 12th for resolution of this contest. . . . Any efforts to resolve [it] that stretch beyond that date are likely to be futile. As a practical matter, Florida's electors will be determined by that date."[27] At another point, the

lawyers noted, "A victory . . . in circuit court (or on later appeal from a circuit court decision) will be meaningless if it comes too late for counting the
unlawfully rejected ballots before the December 12th deadline."[28]

Notwithstanding these pleas, the Florida Supreme Court unanimously
rejected the Gore motion to force an immediate manual recount.[29] The
decision came down on Friday, December 1, with the contest trial scheduled to begin the next day.

The Seminole-Martin Factor

The vice president's attorneys originally considered adding some other
counts to their contest complaint. These related to the curious situation that
had developed in Seminole and Martin Counties. In both counties, suspicions emerged over the handling by the Republicans and by local officials
of applications for absentee ballots.

It was common practice in Florida, and in many other states, for both
parties to send preprinted applications for such ballots to their faithful. The
application came with much of the information the voter needed to get a
ballot already supplied. In Florida, this included something voters were
especially unlikely to know, the voter identification number assigned to
them by state election officials. Under Section 101.62 of the election code,
the "VID" must appear on an absentee application, along with such things
as the voter's name, address, signature, and the last four digits of his or her
social security number.[30]

The form sent out by the Republican committees of Seminole and
Martin Counties, however, did not contain the preprinted voter identification numbers. (The Democrats did not have any problem.) Thus, more than
two thousand applications in Seminole, and close to a thousand in Martin,
came back to the canvassing boards with no number indicated. In each
county, officials made it clear that they would not send absentee ballots to
those whose applications lacked the VIDs, and that the number could only
be supplied by directly contacting the voter. Board of Supervisor employ-
ees were not permitted to check files or computers and supply the number
themselves.[31]

Yet Republican political operatives *were* allowed to do it. In Seminole
County, a paid worker for the party named Michael Leach came in with a
laptop computer, looked up the missing voter identification numbers, and
put the numbers on the Republican-generated ballot applications. Leach,
and some volunteers who helped him, put numbers on 2,126 applications;
1,932 of this number sent in valid absentee ballots on election day.[32] In
Martin County, Supervisor Peggy Robbins let two Republican officials,
including state committee member Charles T. Kane, actually remove appli-

cations from the supervisor's office. They corrected 766 ballots, with 673 of them validly submitted on November 7.[33]

Democrats in both counties filed contest actions charging "intentional wrongdoing" by election officials, one of the factors cited in the landmark case of *Boardman v. Esteva* as sufficient to disqualify absentee ballots. The preferred remedy for these illegalities, the plaintiffs argued, was to throw out all the absentee ballots in the two counties, more than fifteen thousand in Seminole, over ten thousand in Martin.[34] Bush had won the absentee vote in the former by 4,700, in the latter by 2,815. Plaintiffs suggested less radical remedial alternatives as well, subtracting just the 1,932 tainted votes in Seminole County, and the 763 in Martin, from the Republican totals, or even allocating the subtracted votes between the candidates based on a statistical analysis of how they would have gone. This last suggestion figured to cost Bush 612 votes in Martin County and as many as 1,779 in Seminole.[35] Obviously, any decision for the plaintiffs "would hit the election like a neutron bomb."[36]

On November 26 and 27, Gore's lawyers were tempted to join these suits and effectively take them over as their own. But as with the military ballots, the vice president feared giving away his advantage as the champion of voter intent, the candidate who "condemned 'hypertechnical' reliance on rules"; after all, "in neither Seminole County nor Martin County was there any suggestion that the voters themselves had done anything wrong."[37] As in the butterfly case, William Daley and Warren Christopher urged Gore to desist, noting that to "the extent . . . he had public support for contesting the [election], that support rested on the foundation of count every vote."[38]

David Boies, joined by Ron Klain, felt Gore should embrace the absentee suits, in order to expose what he saw as Republican hypocrisy. "In Miami and Palm Beach, the Republicans are saying you have to observe the letter of the law. . . . But in Seminole and Martin, they say they want to respect the intent of the voter, even if they break some rules along the way. But they can't have it both ways."[39] Including the absentee issue in the contest suit, Boies felt, would "flush them out": a hardline decision on ballot requests would ruin the Republicans, but a soft one might "get us our votes in Miami and Palm Beach."[40]

Gore, however, felt Boies's approach "too clever by half"; the public would see only "that the Democrats were trying to get thousands of ballots thrown out."[41] He decided to let the Seminole and Martin cases go forward on their own, though, again, allies in the labor movement and financial supporters of the vice president aided the plaintiffs.

Actually, the innocence of the voters in Seminole and Martin Counties would be no guarantee of legal victory for the Republicans if the collusion between the county officials and the political operatives was as incriminating as the rule forbidding public officials to supply the VIDs made it seem. Surely, if the Republican preprinted application had left off the place for the voter's signature, and party workers had forged those signatures, with official knowledge, the voter's lack of complicity would not save the ballots.

The decisive fact in this instance, however, was that under Florida law, the voter identification number was almost certainly not needed to make the application valid. *Boardman v. Esteva* stated as a general proposition that "unless the absentee voting laws which have been violated . . . expressly declare that [a] particular act is essential to the validity of the ballot, . . . the statute should be treated as directory, not mandatory, *provided such irregularity is not calculated to affect the integrity of the ballot or election.*"[42] The First District Court of Appeals later found that 101.62 did not stipulate failure to include all the information it asked for would void an absentee request. "We are unable to glean from the provision of that section a legislative intent that [not] follow[ing] the letter of its provisions should result in the invalidation of absentee ballots cast by qualified voters who are also qualified to vote absentee."[43] Instead of colluding with county officials in Seminole and Martin, Republicans could profitably have sued them over their policy of disqualifying absentee ballot applications just because the voter identification never appeared. They might have pointed out that other counties in Florida honored absentee ballot requests without VIDs.[44]

Gore's (Forlorn) Trial Strategy

The Gore team did not expect much from Judge Sauls, even before his rulings on the instant recount. "He was probably the worst of the judges we could draw," David Boies later commented. "We're gonna lose" was the instant appraisal of Gore's chief Florida counsel, Dexter Douglass.[45]

A conservative Democrat from a well-connected north Florida family, Sauls was known as a literalist in interpreting the law; the Florida Supreme Court had overruled him in 61 of 198 prior cases. The supreme court also chastised him in 1998 for the allegedly autocratic way he was running the Leon County Circuit Court as chief judge, especially in his firing of the court administrator. This led Sauls to submit an indignant letter of resignation.[46] The judge's wife remains convinced the real issue between Sauls and the justices concerned judicial philosophy. "It [all] has to do with them doing whatever they feel is in the interest of their own political agenda and promoting their own pet projects. They're over there legislating from the bench."[47]

Under the circumstances, the Gore lawyers limited their effort at trial. Expanding on evidence presented to Judge LaBarga, they offered testimony by a prominent statistician, Professor Nicholas Hengartner, confirming that there were five times as many undervotes in punch-card counties as in counties using optical scanners (the *Miami Herald* survey showed over eight times as many), and that votes rescued in a recount could be expected to break as machine counts had broken.[48] The attorneys also sought to account for the fact that so many voters in Palm Beach County dimpled the presidential column, while punching through the other races. But most basically, they wanted to get the contest trial over with as quickly as possible.

Notes

1. Florida House of Representatives Committee on Election Reform Analysis, Report on H.B. 281, February 3, 1999, p. 5.

2. *The 2000 Florida Statutes*, 102. 168 (3) (c), www.flcourts.org.

3. *Gore v. Harris*, 2nd Judicial Circuit, "Complaint to Contest Election," p. 17.

4. Ibid., pp. 19, 20.

5. Ibid., pp. 10–13.

6. Ibid., p. 18.

7. *Florida Democratic Party v. Palm Beach County Canvassing Board*, 15th Judicial Circuit, "Order on Plaintiff's Emergency Motion to Clarify Declaratory Order of November 15, 2000," p. 5, fn. 1 (italics added).

8. *Gore v. Harris*, "Complaint to Contest Election," p. 18.

9. *Gore v. Harris*, "Motion to Appoint Special Master for the Limited Function of Immediate Counting of Palm Beach Ballots," p. 4.

10. *Gore v. Harris*, "Motion and Memorandum in Support of Defendants George W. Bush and Dick Cheney's Motion to Dismiss," p. 8 (italics added).

11. Ibid. See *Broward County Canvassing Board v. Hogan*, 607 So. 2d 508, 510 (Fla. 4th DCA 1992).

12. Ibid., p. 25.

13. Ibid., p. 33.

14. Ibid., p. 32.

15. *Gore v. Harris*, Florida Supreme Court "Amended Brief of Appellees George W. Bush and Dick Cheney," p. 24, fn. 10.

16. *Bush v. Gore*, "Brief of the Florida House of Representatives and Florida Senate as *Amici Curiae* in Support of Neither Party and Seeking Reversal," pp. 10, 9.

17. Abner Greene, *Understanding the 2000 Election* (New York: New York University Press, 2001), pp. 61, 66.

18. *Gore v. Harris*, "Motion . . . to Dismiss," p. 19.

19. *The 2000 Florida Statutes*, 102.168 (8).

20. *Gore v. Harris*, "Order Requiring the Delivery of Certain Ballots from Palm Beach and Miami-Dade Counties."

21. *Gore v. Harris*, "Petition for Writ of Mandamus or Other Writ or, in the Alternative, Review of Trial Court Rulings and Brief of Appellants," p. iii.

22. Ibid., pp. 33, 35.

23. Ibid., p. 38.

24. Ibid., pp. 38–39.

25. Ibid., p. 42 (italics added).

26. Ibid., p. 43 (italics added).

27. Ibid., p. 4.

28. Ibid., p. 23.

29. *Gore v. Harris*, "Order Requiring the Delivery of Certain Ballots," Friday, December 1, 2000.

30. *The 2000 Florida Statutes*, 101.62.

31. *Jacobs v. Seminole County Canvassing Board*, 2nd Judicial Circuit, "Brief of Appellant," pp. 11–12; *Taylor v. Martin County Canvassing Board*, 2nd Judicial Circuit, "Initial Brief of Appellants," pp. 2–7.

32. *Jacobs v. Seminole County Canvassing Board*, "Brief of Appellant," p. 15.

33. *Taylor v. Martin County Canvassing Board*, "Initial Brief of Appellants," p. 8.

34. *Jacobs v. Seminole County Canvassing Board*, "Brief of Appellant," part III; *Taylor v. Martin County Canvassing Board*, "Initial Brief of Appellants," part 3.

35. *Jacobs v. Seminole County Canvassing Board*, "Brief of Appellant," p. 42, fn. 19; *Taylor v. Martin County Canvassing Board*, "Initial Brief of Appellants," p. 30.

36. The Political Staff of *The Washington Post, Deadlock: The Inside Story of America's Closest Election* (New York: Public Affairs, 2001), p. 160.

37. Ibid.

38. Ibid.

39. Jeffrey Toobin, *Too Close to Call* (New York: Random House, 2001), p. 200.

40. Ibid.

41. Ibid.

42. *Boardman v. Esteva*, 323 So. 2d 259, 265 (1976).

43. *McLean v. Bellamy*, 437 So. 2d 737, 742 (Fla. 1st DCA 1983).

44. See Robert Zelnick, *Winning Florida* (Stanford: Hoover Institution Press, 2001), pp. 94–95.

45. The Political Staff of *The Washington Post, Deadlock*, p. 166; David Kaplan, *The Accidental President* (New York: William Morrow, 2001), p. 197.

46. David Barstow and Somini Sengupta, "Saul's Difficult History with Florida High Court," December 8, 2000, in Correspondents of *The New York Times*, *36 Days* (New York: Times Books, 2001), p. 259.

47. The Political Staff of *The Washington Post, Deadlock*, p. 166.

48. "Contest Trial Before Judge Sauls," pp. 183–184, www.flcourts.org; Martin Merzer and the Staff of *The Miami Herald, The Miami Herald Report, Democracy Held Hostage* (New York: St. Martin's Press, 2001), pp. 231–232.

The Trial Testimony

It was critical that the Gore team explain the dimpled voting patterns in Palm Beach County. Yet in the frenzied atmosphere of the trial, they could put forward only one witness on this subject, Kimball Brace, an election consultant from Fairfax, Virginia. Since he had been in Florida for only three days before trial, Brace's testimony, as elicited by Gore attorney Stephen Zack, was necessarily quite general. The defendants' crack litigator, Phil Beck, had little trouble picking it apart.

Professor Hengartner also ran afoul of the hasty and sometimes slapdash preparation for the trial. In an affidavit submitted to the court, he, like Brace, hypothesized that there might be something about the first column (the presidential column) of punch-card voting machines that thwarted voters trying to register their choices, and explained in part the degree of undervotes. Hengartner offered some pre-2000 empirical proof for this, supplied to him by the Gore attorneys. In the 1998 statewide elections, he claimed, there were 3.5 percent more votes in Palm Beach County for governor, recorded in the second column of the ballot, than for United States senator, "recorded in the first column." Phil Beck confronted Hengartner with an interesting revelation.

John Ahmann was one of the inventors of the Votomatic, and staunchly defended its reliability. He testified about experiments showing the resiliency of the rubber strips in the machines. Ahmann also scoffed at the notion that an ordinary voter could not punch out a chad properly, and argued it was almost a mathematical impossibility for the receptacles at the bottom of the Votomatic to overflow with chad particles.

Gore attorney Stephen Zack got Ahmann to backtrack on some of his assertions about chad buildup, and to admit that punching out the chads might be harder than he had let on. In any event, Ahmann's testi-mony, like Brace's, was almost exclusively second-hand.

The Bush forces called Thomas Spencer, a Coral Gables attorney and Republican election monitor, to rebut the notion that Gore would gain anything of consequence by having the remaining 9,000 under-votes in Miami-Dade manually perused, Spencer showing that the Democratic strongholds in the county were in the 20 percent already counted. The Democrats replied with additional testimony by Professor Hengartner, which attempted to show (again contradictorily) that there were generally likely to be more undervotes in precincts carried by Gore, even in the areas of the county Bush had won. (The *Miami Herald* survey came out on Spencer's side. It showed that even if dim-pled and pinpricked ballots counted, Gore would have harvested only 49 votes in Miami-Dade; counting just two- and three-corner hangers, and fully punched ballots, Bush would have gained 16.)

Prodded by Judge Sauls, however, Spencer gave probably the most important testimony in the trial. He sketched a portrait of the Miami canvassing board at work that would have later reverberations.

Testimony of Kimball Brace

Direct Examination by Stephen Zack

Q   I wanted...to [ask you] specifically [about] the ways that an indentation [on a ballot] can be made, from your own personal observations.

A   Yes, from my own personal observations, there's actually four ways
that an indentation could be made....[O]ne of them [is] when the ballot
is placed on top of the machine [instead of inside the voting device].
[I]t is also possible that an indentation is made if, in fact, the machines
are not cleaned out on a regular basis, and there's chad buildup, and,
therefore, the voter may not be able to push down as firmly. The third
reason is that those rubber strips, if they're not properly maintained
may become old, brittle, hard, and keep a voter –

MR. BECK: Your Honor, may I [question the witness] on his expertise?...

THE COURT: Well, let him testify about his own experience....

THE WITNESS: Yes, sir. And so the rubber strips could cause an indentation
by not—by being too hard, and you're not being able to push through
the chad.
　　And then, finally, the throat on that template is like a funnel, and
I've observed that if you put that stylus in on a slight angle, instead of
straight up and down, then that will actually create a dimple, an indentation in the card, but you're kind of caught partway into that throat,
and you can't create the full vote by pushing out the chad....

From Hearing Contest Before Judge Sauls, www.flcourts.org, pp. 76–78, 83–84,
109–110, 113, 117, 120–122, 125–128.

Q [Now] I'd like you to go back to Palm Beach, and tell me, sir, when you looked at the [voting machines you were allowed to inspect], did you look at the plastic sheet or face that you referred to earlier?

A Yes, the template itself.

Q Could you tell anything from that template at all, from your personal observations?

A Yes, from my personal observation, I was noticing that there was more extensive wear of that template on the left-hand side than on the right-hand side, which would be understandable and normal in the course of business, in terms of the use of the voting equipment.

 The left-hand side of these machines get more use because when an election administrator sets up the ballot, he generally starts from the left-hand side and moves to the right-hand side as the ballot is filled out as more contests are listed....

Q And is that indication that you saw and that you described to the Court, would that in any way affect the voter's abilities to have an indentation in the left-hand column, and not have any others in the other column?...

A Well, clearly, if, in fact, the left-hand side is getting more use,...as indicated by the scars on the template,... there's more heavier use of the rubber strips on the left-hand side than on the right-hand side generally, because the ballot is utilized that way....

Cross Examination by Phil Beck

Q In all your years of study and observation around the country, did you find that a lot of people take these ballots and put them on top, and vote on top instead of following the instructions, and put them in that, what's that called?

A Into the throat.

Q Do a lot of people vote on top instead of doing what they're told and putting it into the throat?

A I would hope they don't, and I hope maybe in this demonstration, now, people will pay attention and vote the proper way the next time.

THE COURT: He just asked you if you know or not, if you don't, say, yes, or no.

Q   Now, if somebody, in fact does what you're hypothesizing they do, put it on top of the machine and vote, and they continued voting that way, what you'd be left with is a ballot that, for every office, or almost every office, had a dimple or some kind of an indentation, right?

A   That is correct....

Q   Now, let's get back to your theory about how there could be dimples on a ballot, but your theory that they're going to be on the left side of the ballot where the presidential race is, and not on the middle and the right, okay?

A   Okay.

Q   Now, I think you said that one basis for your theory is that, rubber, on the left side of this machine, somehow gets harder, faster, than rubber in the middle, and the right side of the machine; is that right?...

A   Yes, that's correct.

Q   Now, have you ever tested that in any way, sir?

A   No, I have not tested that. It would be something that would be worthwhile testing with a real machine that had been subject to a lot of use.

Q   Do you know the name of the instrument that you would use to test that?

A   During a deposition, yes, it was mentioned, and I don't remember precisely what it is.

Q   Before you heard our witness testify about how you can actually measure hardness of rubber, in your whole life, have you ever heard of the name of the machine that's used by experts in the field to see whether rubber at one place is as hard as rubber in another place?

A   I'm pretty sure that I have heard it. I don't keep the name of that machine in my memory from that standpoint. But, certainly, in my observations, and use of the machines, and talking with people all around the country, sure, that's been—

THE COURT: If you'd just answer, yes, or, no,...if we could follow that format.

MR. BECK: I've forgotten the question, so I don't know whether it was a yes or no.

BY MR. BECK:

Q   Do you know the difference between synthetic rubber, and natural rubber?

A   Just roughly, not to any big degree, no.

Q   Do you know whether the rubber strips that are used in this voting machine are synthetic rubber or natural rubber?

A   I've been told that they are mostly more a combination of the two. But I don't know that, I haven't—I'm not an engineer, I haven't tested that.

Q   Do you know whether natural rubber over time tends to get harder or softer as it ages?

A   I'm not a rubber expert. I didn't—

THE COURT: Just answer yes or no. If you don't know, say you don't know.

A   I don't know.

Q   Do you know whether synthetic rubber over time tends to get harder or softer?

A   I don't know.

Q   Do you know whether natural rubber, when it's impacted repeatedly, tends to get harder or softer?

A   I don't know entirely.

Q   You don't know entirely?

A   No, I don't know.

Q   Tell us what you do know about that.

A   I don't know. I mean, all I can tell you is my observations of rubber strips in heavily used machines, it looks to me that they are more heavily used, and that's what the basis of my observations were....

Q   Let's move on to your other theory how it is that dimples could occur on the left side of the card, and more frequently than in the middle, and on the right.

A   Okay.

Q   And I think you had a theory, that you called chad buildup, right?

A   Yes.

Q   And the chad, of course, are the little rectangles, or paper that get dislodged by the stylus, right?

A   That's correct.

Q   And the theory is that there's a bunch of people voting for the President of the United States, and all these little chads fall down, and they kind of stack up on one another, and then they stop somebody from pushing the stylus through the hole, right?...[Now] [d]o you know how many people, on average, use one of these machines in a Presidential election?...

A   No, I don't. But I was—if I had had more time, and we weren't doing this three days after I came here—

THE COURT: Just say, yes, or, no.

Q   I'm not blaming you, I just asked if you do know.

A   I don't. It would be a good number to know.

Q   Yeah, because before you came in and testified under oath...that you thought that the chads built up on the left side, and stopped people from voting,...it would be kind of important to know how many people on average, actually used these machines, wouldn't it?

A   Well, if you—I study election returns all the time.

Q   Would it be important to know this, sir?

A   That would be important, but I know from the election returns that that top of the ticket gets more votes....

Q   But if only 500 people use the machine on an average election day for the presidential election, and all 500 might vote for the President, but we know...there's only 500 of these little chads falling through the hole, right?

A   That's correct.
      So, therefore, one of my inquiries, in my questions to both Palm Beach and Miami, was how frequently do you clean out the machines?

Q   Please, sir. Try to stick with my questions.... Do you know how many times people would actually have to vote to fill up the bottom of that machine?

A   No, I have not done that calculation, yet.

Q   Yet, you think you're going to do that calculation?

A   I would like to do that calculation, certainly.

Q   Do you know whether it would be in the thousands, and thousands, and thousands of chads that you'd have to punch through, under the Presidential holes, in order to build up a pile enough that it would even be possible for this to take place?

A   I don't know. That's what I would—that's what I was attempting to determine.

Q   Well, in fact, what you were doing was swearing under oath that it happens. You weren't attempting to determine it, were you sir?

A   No, I was swearing....

Q   Is this [something] you're imagining might happening?

A   I'm not imagining. It's based on long experience and observations of election results and how ballots are constructed is the basis of my observation....

Q   Now, this [voting] machine [you brought with you] is your machine, right?

A   Yes, that's correct.

Q   And you've had it for 20 years, right?

A   Something like that.

Q   Would you stick the ballot in the machine, please?

A   Certainly.

Q   It's 20 years old. Have you ever changed the rubber strips in your machine?

A   No, I haven't.

Q   Would you now vote for President, please, without trying to make a dimple?

A   Sure.

Q   Did it work?

A   Yeah, I voted for number five.

THE COURT: You don't have to say who you voted for. (*LAUGHTER.*)

Q   And if somebody actually puts the card in the machine like they're instructed to, and attempts to vote, rather than attempts to make a dimple, it's not all that hard to knock out the little chad, is it, sir?

A   Well, it depends on the template in there.... [T]he template can be a slight prohibitive. Remember, you're going into a funnel, and people start into that funnel to get to the hole down below to then go into the card.
    I imagine that people could hit the funnel.

Q   You imagine this?

A   And think that they're voting.

Q   You imagine this?

Testimony of Nicholas Hengartner

MR BECK: Read, please, for the Court...what is the race here up at the top of column one [of the Palm Beach ballot]?

PROFESSOR HENGARTNER: This is the congressional United States Senator.

Q And then what's right underneath the United States Senator in Column 1?

A State Governor and Lieutenant Governor.

Q So what you said in your sworn affidavit was in Column 2 was actually in Column 1, right?

A It was the second race.

Q Was it in Column 1 on that ballot or not?

A My understanding, it was the second race, and it should have been in Column [2], a mistake, it was the second race, and that's what I meant.

Q Well, in your affidavit, you didn't say it was the fact that it was—the second race is what's important. You said that the fact that the Senate was Column 1, and the Governor was in Column 2, why, that seemed to suggest that the voting machine wasn't recording all the votes cast in Column 1, because the guys in Column 2 were getting more votes? Do you remember that?

From Testimony of Nicholas Hengartner, www.flcourts.org, pp. 228–229.

A   I said that this was possible, yes.

Q   And you can see here that that sworn affidavit of yours,…that just wasn't true, was it?

A   It contained a mistake.

Q   And …you never even looked at the ballot, right?

A   I've looked at the order in which the races were run, sir.

Q   And when you signed that sworn statement, you were relying on the Gore legal team to give you the straight facts, weren't you?

A   Well, I relied on the facts that I received, yes.

MR. BECK: That's all that I have, Judge.

Testimony of John Ahmann

Direct Examination by Phil Beck

Q Now, in your years of working with this—these cards, the actual ballots, and the voting machines, have you come to any conclusions about how likely it is that someone who is actually following the instructions, and putting the ballot in like they're supposed to, and attempting to vote would, instead, end up leaving a dimple instead of punching a chad through?...

A ...If [the voter] goes in and [just] taps it, it's quite possible you can dimple the ballot and have no intention of actually voting. Conversely.... It takes [only] three-quarters of a pound to punch down, which if you take the weight of your hand, it punches real easy....

Q [So] the fact that there is, let's say, a particular chad that we're confident the imperfection did come from the stylus, does that mean that the person intended to vote, but was unable to push that chad through?

A I seriously doubt that the voter would be unable to push the chad through on a normal voting device....

Q Okay. I want to turn now, to, back to your days at IBM. And in the 1960s, did you participate in a test at IBM, concerning the effect on the T-strips of extended use by—extended impacts by a stylus?

Testimony of John Ahmann, www.flcourts.org, pp. 402–403, 405, 412–416, 419, 439–440, 440–442, 442–445.

A   Yes, sir, I did.

Q   Would you please describe [this] for the Court....

A   ...We had two men punching out the cards, every card was punched, all
    228 positions [on the cards].
        We punched out 15,000 cards per voting device. We wore out
    many templates. We broke many styluses.
        But we proved that you did not get any degradation of the T-strips,
    until it was beyond 10,000 punches in every position, and still punch-
    ing reliably up to 15,000 punches....

Q   [Well] someone could do the math, and I haven't, but that would be
    15,000 times 228. In all those times, when some[one] was putting the
    stylus through, was there ever an occasion where they made a dimple
    instead of a fully dislodged chad or the occasional hanging chad?

A   Not that I recall.

Q   Now, the last subject that I want to deal with is this supposed phenom-
    enon called chad buildup. Were you here in Court the other day when
    the political scientist called by Vice President Gore's legal team talked
    about his hypothesis that piles of chad build up underneath the ballot
    and that might keep somebody from casting an effective vote? You
    were here for that testimony?

A   Yes, sir....

Q   [I]s it even remotely possible that little mountains of chad go to build
    up underneath Al Gore's name, and somebody is going to try to vote
    for him, and they're going to be thwarted and they're going to leave a
    dimple instead of punching through that chad?

A   ...I do not believe it's possible....

Q   Let's say somebody didn't clean it out any more often than ten years,
    would that be a problem in terms of chad buildup under... Al Gore's
    name, versus everybody else on the ballot?

A   I would first say, no, but then that would also depend on whether you
    had an election every week, or if you only had an average of two or
    three elections a year.

JUDGE SAULS: I believe you testified at one point, 38,000,000 pieces of chad could be accumulated in one, so however many elections it would take for [that].

A   In order to fully fill it up, you could go 50 years, but eight to ten years, it might not cause you any problem, depending on how many elections, how many votes cast on that unit.

Cross Examination by Stephen Zack

Q   Now, sir, it is true that these [voting] machines need to be maintained properly; is that not so?...

Q   And you [have] told [election officials] to remove the chads after each election; is that correct?

A   That's correct.

Q   And, sir, are you aware that the voting machines in Dade County are used for other elections, such as union elections, in addition to elections for public office holders, are you aware of that, sir?

A   Yes.

Q   You heard that?

A   I heard that.

Q   Are you aware, sir, that there had been eight—it's been eight years since Dade County has cleaned the chads from their machines, are you aware of that, sir?

A   I heard that yesterday.

Q   You and me both....

Q   [Y]ou indicated that you...have [a] patent where you invented a stylus that had more—it was a more flexible stylus, correct....
      And the reason for creating that is you found that people do not do what you would ideally like and that is to vertically press down, and they come in at an angle, and that that patented rubber stylus that you have created allows them to... [vote properly], correct?

A   It is designed to allow the voter, because they do roll in, to straighten out that punch,...so that when it goes all the way through it punches out reliably, more reliably.

Q   And when they roll in, using your terminology, if they don't have your more flexible stylus, they can end up leaving an indentation, a hanging chad, or some other form of chad.... [So] what you did do is offer an alternative to people who use this machine that would allow a voter who comes in at an angle to actually have a clean punch, that was the idea behind it?

A   Yes, sir.

Q   You offered that to Palm Beach, and they went with another manufacturer, other than yourself; isn't that correct?...

A   I believe you're referring to Dade County.

Q   Oh, you know what, I stand corrected. So Dade County rejected it, and that's where we're talking about 9,000-plus ballots that have not been counted, yet; is that correct?...

A   Everybody keeps saying all of those ballots haven't been counted. All of those have been counted.

Q   They haven't been manually counted.

A   They haven't been manually counted.

Q   You and I are on the same page....

A   That's correct.

Q   What I'm saying to you is, there are 9,000-plus ballots in Dade County that had not been hand counted as far as you know, correct?

A   I have no firsthand knowledge of that, but that's the number.

Q   And that is the county that rejected this new stylus that you invented to make sure that people's votes counted because you were concerned about the old stylus being used in a way that would keep people's votes...from being counted, yes, or, no?

A   Partially, yes, partially, no. The yes part is that the flexible body does align better so that the votes are counted. But, at the same time, a major ingredient in that was that we wanted to reduce template wear, which will keep the stylus on the chad so that they have clean punches, rather than gouges, or pinholes, or hanging chad.

Q   I'm glad you brought that up, because I wouldn't have brought it up had you not mentioned it. Template wear is important in making sure that you've got a clean vote; isn't that correct?

A   Yes, sir.

Q   And you tried to get Dade County to buy this stylus, but they refused to, and you would assume from that, that the old styluses are causing more template wear; isn't that correct?

A   I don't know that for a fact....

Q   I want to ask you, sir, you, personally, have...sat in on hand recounts of ballots in elections, correct?

A   Yes sir.

Q   And you are aware that that hand recount, en masse, caused a different individual to be elected, you're aware of that, are you not?

A   I have heard that, yes.

Q   And, sir, you also believe that—and as you told me [at deposition], in close elections, you should have a hand recount; is that correct?

MR. BECK: Your Honor, I'm going to object, both on relevance, and also beyond the scope of Direct Examination.

THE COURT: Overruled.

BY MR. ZACK:

Q   Isn't that what you told me just the day before yesterday, sir?

A   This is normally—yes, however, normally it's in small elections, not nationwide elections.

And when you have one candidate who is off by one vote or two votes, which has happened,... you know, it's a good idea to have a recount, you betcha....

Q You made no qualifications when you answered my [earlier] question and I said: In close elections a hand recount is advisable, correct?

A In very close elections, yes.

Q Well, we'll let the Court decide whether this is a close election.

Testimony of Thomas Spencer

JUDGE SAULS: Well, if you don't mind, let me ask one question. You made reference to difficulties down there in the manner in which they were implementing, I suppose, the hand count when it started, is that correct?

MR. SPENCER: Yes, sir.

THE COURT: Well, were you able to…tell what kind of system…or standards that the board was using when they were—when they began counting and counted the approximately 15 or 20 percent of the first numbered precincts?

THE WITNESS: Yes, sir.

THE COURT: What was it?

THE WITNESS: I should explain, I was behind the Canvassing Board watching them, about as close as I am to the computer screen here. And essentially what happened is that there were different variations of decisions that I observed.

For example, my observation of Judge King was if there was simply a dimple or a pregnant chad of any kind, he would determine that that was a vote, regardless of whether or not there were indentations or clear punches on the rest of the card.

On the other hand, I observed that Supervisor Leahy, on the full manual recount, used a different approach. I observed that he would take the ballot and hold it up to the light, like I'm indicating here, and look to see

---

From Testimony of Thomas Spencer, www.flcourts.org, pp. 496–498.

whether there was some separation on the top of the ballot, light separation of some type. And if there were,… and there were some other indication on the ballot, he would determine that that was a vote.

Judge Lehr used a different approach, and she would take the ballot and hold it to the front, and also turn it over on the back, to see whether or not there was some paper separation.

This was different than the process they used on the first go-round, on the three precincts. And I saw all kinds of different variations….

And I reached the conclusion that there was no standard that was being used, but that there were different approaches being used by each of the three of them.

THE COURT: Well, even if that was the case, when they decided after they reviewed it to place one in the stack that would count as a vote, were they unanimous when they did that?

THE WITNESS: No, Your Honor…. Most of the time, it was a two-to-one vote…. And I would say that the vast majority of the judgments I saw, they were by majority vote, not by unanimous decision.

THE COURT: The same majority, or did the majority vary?

THE WITNESS: The majority varied. It was, in certain circumstances, Judge King would use sort of a dimple test, and one of the other, Leahy, or Lehr, would go along with him. . . . . [T]he one consistency . . . that I recall was that Judge King seemed to see a vote in every dimple.

Judge Sanders Sauls Decides *Gore v. Harris*

Judge Sanders Sauls's decision in *Gore v. Harris* came down on December 4, just a few hours after the United States Supreme Court decision. To no one's surprise, he ruled for the defendants on all points. There was no provision in Florida law, Sauls held, for de novo review of canvassing board actions. And neither the Miami nor the Palm Beach boards abused their discretion, though the judge admitted there had traditionally been problems with the voting machines in both counties. He also agreed that Gore's entire contest plea was fundamentally flawed from the outset, because it dealt with only a few jurisdictions. (The vice president's lawyers understood him to say that in a statewide contest all ballots must be counted, but Sauls may have meant only all no votes.)

This was enough to carry the defendants' case, but Judge Sauls asserted another reason for the propriety of his decision, which seemed to constitute legal error. Under a First District Court of Appeals decision of 1982, he claimed, a plaintiff seeking a recount in a contest proceeding must show, aside from anything else, that but for the irregularity alleged, he or she would have won the election. Such an analysis clashed with the language of 102.168, which spoke of votes "sufficient to change or place in doubt the result of [an] election."

The judge's hurried opinion lacked a bit in grammatical fluency.

From Proceedings *Gore v. Harris*, www.flcourts.org, pp. 2–5.

Gore v. Harris

The Court...finds and concludes the evidence does not establish any illegality, dishonesty, gross negligence, improper influence, coercion, or fraud in the balloting and counting processes.

Secondly, there is no authority under Florida law for certification of an incomplete manual recount of a portion of...less than all ballots from any county by the state elections canvassing commission, nor authority to include any returns submitted past the deadline established by the Florida Supreme Court in this election.

Thirdly, although the record shows voter error, and/or, less than total accuracy, in regard to the punch-card voting devices utilized in Dade and Palm Beach Counties, which these counties have been aware of for many years, these balloting and counting problems cannot support or effect any recounting necessity with respect to these counties....

The Court further finds the Dade Canvassing Board did not abuse its discretion in any of its decisions in its review in recounting processes.

Fourthly, with respect to the approximate 3,300 Palm Beach County ballots of which Plaintiffs seek review, the Palm Beach Board properly exercised its discretion in its counting process, and has judged those ballots which Plaintiff wish this Court to, again, judge de novo....

The local boards have been given broad discretion which no Court may overrule, absent a clear abuse of discretion.

The Palm Beach County Board did not abuse its discretion in its review and recounting process.

Further, it acted in full compliance with the order of the Circuit Court in and for Palm Beach County.

Having done so, Plaintiffs are estopped from further challenge of this process and standards. It should be noted, however, that such process and standards were changed from the prior 1990 standards, perhaps contrary to Title III, Section (5) of the United States Code....

The Court finds further that the Nassau County Canvassing Board did not abuse its discretion in its certification of Nassau County's voting results....

Further, this Court would further conclude and find that the properly stated cause of action under Section 102.168 of the Florida Statutes to contest a statewide federal election, the Plaintiff would necessarily have to place at issue and seek as a remedy with the attendant burden of proof, a review and recount on all ballots, and of all the counties in this state with respect to the particular alleged irregularities or inaccuracies in the balloting or counting processes alleged to have occurred....

There is in this type of election, one statewide election, and one certification. Palm Beach County did not elect any person as a presidential elector, but, rather, the election with the winner-take-all proposition, dependent on the statewide vote....

Further, it is well-established and reflected in the opinion of Judge Joanas and *Smith v. Tine* [*Smith v. Tynes*, 412 So. 2d 925], that in order to contest election results under Section 102.168 of the Florida statutes, the Plaintiff must show that, but for the irregularity, or inaccuracy claimed, the result of the election would have been different, and he or she would have been the winner.

It is not enough to show a reasonable possibility that election results could have been altered by such irregularities or inaccuracies, rather, a reasonable probability that the results of the election would have been changed must be shown.

In this case, there is no credible statistical evidence, and no other competent substantial evidence to establish by a preponderance of a reasonable probability that the results of the statewide election in the State of Florida would be different from the result which has been certified by the State Elections Canvassing Commission....

In conclusion, the Court finds that the Plaintiff failed to carry the requisite burden of proof, and judgment shall be hereby entered, and that Plaintiffs will take nothing by this action.

Four Justices Reverse Judge Sauls

In the early afternoon of December 8, the circuit court decisions in the Seminole and Martin County cases came down. Inevitably, the Republican defendants won (judgments unanimously upheld by the Florida Supreme Court four days later).

Then the tide turned yet one more time. At 3:50 p.m. on December 8, spokesman Craig Waters announced that by a 4-3 vote the Florida Supreme Court had reversed Judge Sauls on the issues of the Miami-Dade undervotes, and of whether the Miami and Palm Beach certifications were final. The split decision, it is significant to note, represented the initial time any court in the state had tackled the language of the 1999 contest revisions. *Gore v. Harris* was genuinely a case of "first impression."

The majority was quick to pounce upon the trial judge's misinterpretation of Florida law in demanding plaintiffs show the votes denied them would have changed the outcome of the election. But more basically, they agreed with Gore's analysis of the entire contest process. This process, they held, called for de novo review of canvassing board decisions, primarily because a contest could properly be a search for votes reflecting the intent of the voter, which the machines had missed. This being so, however, the search must encompass all undervotes in the state of Florida. Like Gore and the Miami-Dade canvassing board, the court ignored the Florida overvotes.

Chief Justice Wells's dissent sharply called attention to this bifurcated approach. The chief justice now believed as well that Section 5614 (5) of the Florida code meant what it said, and referred only to ballots that were actually damaged or defective. Neither Wells nor the majority justices looked to the analysis of 5614 found in their own *Beckstrom* decision two years earlier—an analysis favorable in fact to

195

the majority. "We construe 'defective ballot' to include a ballot which is marked in a manner such that it cannot be read by a scanner" (at 722, fn. 4).

Justices Major Harding and Leander Shaw also dissented, agreeing with Judge Sauls on the significance of Gore's failure to demand contest recounts in more than four counties. However, they largely accepted the majority's view of the Florida contest process.

Since, by any measure, time was running "desperately short" in the Florida election dispute, the justices had decided to tackle *Gore v. Harris* before replying to the United States Supreme Court remand.

Gore v. Harris, Per Curiam

III. Order on Review

A. The Trial Court's Standard of Review

The Florida Election Code sets forth a two-pronged system for challenging vote returns and election procedures. The "protest" and "contest" provisions are distinct proceedings. A protest proceeding is filed with the County Canvassing Board and addresses the validity of the vote returns. The relief that may be granted includes a manual recount. The Canvassing Board is a neutral ministerial body.... A contest proceeding, on the other hand, is filed in circuit court and addresses the validity of the election itself. Relief that may be granted is varied and can be extensive. No appellate relationship exists between a "protest" and a "contest"; a protest is not a prerequisite for a contest. Cf. *Flack v. Carter*, 392 So. 2d 37 (Fla. 1st DCA 1980) (holding that an election protest under section 102.166 was not a condition precedent to an election contest under section 102.168). Moreover, the trial court in the contest action does not sit as an appellate court over the decisions of the Canvassing Board. Accordingly, while the Board's actions concerning the elections process may constitute evidence in a contest proceeding, the Board's decisions are not to be accorded the highly deferential "abuse of discretion" standard of review during a contest proceeding.

In the present case, the trial court erroneously applied an appellate abuse of discretion standard to the Boards' decisions.... In applying the abuse of discretion standard of review to the Boards' actions, the trial court relinquished an improper degree of its own authority to the Boards. This was an error.

From *Gore v. Harris, Per Curiam*, 772 So. 2d 1243, 1252–1262.

III-B. Must All the Ballots be Counted Statewide?

Appellees contend that even if a count of the undervotes in Miami-Dade were appropriate, section 102.168, Florida Statutes (2000), requires a count of all votes in Miami-Dade County and the entire state as opposed to a selected number of votes challenged. However, the plain language of section 102.168 refutes Appellees' argument....

[S]ection 102.168 (3) (c) explicitly contemplates contests based upon a "rejection of a number of legal votes sufficient to change the outcome of an election." Logic dictates that to bring a challenge based upon the rejection of a specific number of legal votes under section 102.168 (3) (c), the contestant must establish the "number of legal votes" which the county canvassing board failed to count. This number, therefore, under the plain language of the statute, is limited to the votes identified and challenged under section 102.168 (3) (c), rather than the entire county. Moreover, counting uncontested votes in a contest would be irrelevant to a determination of whether certain uncounted votes constitute legal votes that have been rejected. On the other hand, a consideration of "legal votes" contained in the category of "undervotes" identified statewide may be properly considered as evidence in the contest proceedings and, more importantly, in fashioning any relief.

We do agree [therefore] that it is absolutely essential in this proceeding and to any final decision, that a manual recount be conducted for all legal votes in this State, not only in Miami-Dade County, but in all Florida counties where there was an undervote, and, hence a concern that not every citizen's vote was counted. This election should be determined by a careful examination of the votes of Florida's citizens and not by strategies extraneous to the voting process. This essential principle, that the outcome of elections be determined by the will of the voters, forms the foundation of the election code enacted by the Florida Legislature and has been consistently applied by this Court in resolving elections disputes....

The clear message from this legislative policy is that every citizen's vote be counted whenever possible, whether in an election for a local commissioner or an election for President of the United States.

The demonstrated problem of not counting legal votes inures to any county utilizing a counting system which results in undervotes and "no registered vote" ballots. In a countywide election, one would not simply examine such categories of ballots from a single precinct to insure the reliability and integrity of the countywide vote. Similarly, in this statewide election, review should not be limited to less than all counties whose tabulation has resulted in such categories of ballots. Relief would not be "appropriate under [the] circumstances" if it failed to address the "otherwise valid exercise of the right of a citizen to vote" of all those citizens of this State who, being similarly situated, have had their legal votes rejected. This is particularly important in a Presidential election, which implicates both State and uniquely important national interests. The contestant here satisfied the threshold requirement by demonstrating that, upon consideration of the thousands of undervotes or "no registered vote" ballots presented, the number of legal votes therein were sufficient to at least place in doubt the result of the election. However, a final decision as to the result of the statewide election should only be determined upon consideration of the legal votes contained within the undervote or "no registered vote" ballots of all Florida counties, as well as the legal votes already tabulated....

III-C. Plaintiff's Burden of Truth....

Legal votes. Having...identified the proper standard of review, we turn now to the allegations of the complaint filed in this election contest. To test the sufficiency of those allegations and the proof, it is essential to understand what, under Florida law, may constitute a "legal vote," and what constitutes rejection of such vote.

Section 101.5614 (5), Florida Statutes (2000), provides that "[n]o vote shall be declared invalid or void if there is a clear indication of the intent of the voter as determined by the canvassing board." Section 101.5614 (6) provides, conversely, that any vote in which the board cannot discern the intent of the voter must be discarded. Lastly, section 102.166 (7) (b) provides that, "[I]f a counting team is unable to determine a voter's intent in casting a ballot, the ballot shall be presented to the county canvassing board for it to determine the voter's intent." This legislative emphasis on discerning the voter's intent is mirrored in the case law of this State, and in that of other states.

This Court has repeatedly held, in accordance with the statutory law of this State, that so long as the voter's intent may be discerned from the ballot, the vote constitutes a "legal vote" that should be counted.... As the State has moved toward electronic voting, nothing in this evolution has diminished the longstanding case law and statutory law that the intent of the voter is of paramount concern and should always be given effect *if* the intent can be determined....

Accordingly, we conclude that a legal vote is one in which there is a "clear indication of the intent of the voter." We next address whether the term "rejection" used in section 102.168 (3) (c) includes instances where the County Canvassing Board has not counted legal votes. Looking at the statutory scheme as a whole, it appears that the term "rejected" does encompass votes that may exist but have not been counted. As explained above, in 1999, the Legislature substantially revised the contest provision of the Election Code.... The House Bill noted that one of the grounds for

contesting an election at common law was the "Receipt of a number of illegal votes or rejection of a number of legal votes sufficient to change or
place in doubt the result of the election." As noted above, the contest
statute ultimately contained this ground for contesting the results of an
election.

To further determine the meaning of the term "rejection", as used by
the Legislature, we may also look to Florida case law. In *State ex rel. Clark
v. Klingensmith*, 163 So. 704 (1935), an individual who lost an election
brought an action...challenging his opponent's right to hold office. The
challenger challenged twenty-two ballots, which he divided into four
groups. One of these groups included three ballots that the challenger
claimed had not been counted. *See* 121 Fla. at 298, 163 So. at 705. This
Court concluded that "the *rejection* of votes from legal voters, not brought
about by fraud, and not of such magnitude as to demonstrate that a free
expression of the popular will has been suppressed," is insufficient to void
an election, "at least unless it be shown that the votes rejected would have
changed the result." 121 Fla. at 300, 163 So. at 705. Therefore, the Court
appears to have equated a "rejection" of legal votes with the failure to
count legal votes, while at the same time recognizing that a sufficient number of such votes must have been rejected to merit relief....

This also comports with cases from other jurisdictions that suggest that
a legal vote will be deemed to have been "rejected" where a voting
machine fails to count a ballot, which has been executed in substantial
compliance with applicable voting requirements and reflects the clear
intent of the voter to express a definite choice. See *In re Matter of the
Petition of Katy Gray-Sadler*, 753 A. 2d 1101, 1105-06 (N.J. 2000); *Moffat
v. Blaiman*, 361 A. 2d 74, 77 (N.J. 1976).

Here, then, it is apparent that there have been sufficient allegations
made which, if analyzed pursuant to the proper standard, compel the conclusion that legal votes sufficient to place in doubt the election results have
been rejected in this case.

This case.   We must review the instances in which appellants claim that
they established that legal votes were rejected or illegal votes were included in the certifications.

*The refusal to review approximately 9,000 additional Miami-Dade Ballots,
which the counting machine registered as non-votes and which have never
been manually reviewed....*   Specifically as to Miami-Dade County, the
trial court found:...

> that the Dade Canvassing Board did not abuse its discretion in any of its
> decisions in its review in recounting processes.

This statement is incorrect as a matter of law. In fact, as the Third District determined in *Miami-Dade County Democratic Party v. Miami-Dade County Canvassing Board,*...the results of the sample manual recount and the actual commencement of the full manual recount triggered the Canvassing Board's "mandatory obligation to recount all of the ballots in the county." In addition, the circuit court was bound at the time it ruled to follow this appellate decision. This Court has determined the decisions of the district courts of appeal represent the law of this State unless and until they are overruled by this Court, and therefore, in the absence of interdistrict conflict, district court decisions bind all Florida trial courts....

However, regardless of this error, we again note the focus of the trial court's inquiry in an election contest authorized by the Legislature pursuant to the express statutory provisions of section 102.168 is not by appellate review to determine whether the Board properly or improperly failed to complete the manual recount. Rather, as expressly set out in section 102.168, the court's responsibility is to determine whether "legal votes" were rejected sufficient to change or place in doubt the results of the election. Without ever examining or investigating the ballots that the machine failed to register as a vote, the trial court in this case concluded that there was no probability of a different result.... Appellants have...been denied the very evidence that they have relied on to establish their ultimate entitlement to relief. The trial court has presented the plaintiffs with the ultimate Catch-22, acceptance of the only evidence that will resolve the issue but a refusal to examine such evidence. We also note that whether or not the Board could have completed the manual recount by November 26, 2000, or whether the Board should have fulfilled its responsibility and completed the full manual recount it commenced, the fact remains that the manual recount was not completed through no fault of the Appellant.

3300 votes in Palm Beach County. Appellants also contend that the trial court erred in finding that they failed to satisfy their burden of proof with respect to the 3,300 votes that the Palm Beach County Canvassing Board reviewed and concluded did not constitute "legal votes" pursuant to section 102.168 (3) (c). However, unlike the approximately 9,000 ballots in Miami-Dade that the County Canvassing Board did not manually recount, the Palm Beach County Canvassing Board *did* complete a manual recount of these 3,300 votes and concluded that, because the intent of the voter in these 3,300 ballots was not discernable, these ballots did not constitute "legal votes."...

We find no error in the trial court's determination that appellants did not establish a preliminary basis for relief as to the 3300 Palm Beach County votes because the appellants have failed to make a threshold showing that "legal votes" were rejected. Although the protest and contest proceedings are separate statutory provisions, when a manual count of ballots has been conducted by the Canvassing Board pursuant to section 102.166, the circuit court in a contest proceeding does not have the obligation de novo to simply repeat an otherwise-proper manual count of the ballots. As stated above, although the trial court does not review a Canvassing Board's actions under an abuse of discretion standard, the Canvassing Board's actions may constitute evidence that a ballot does or does not qualify as a legal vote. Because the appellants have failed to introduce any evidence to refute the Canvassing Board's determination that the 3300 ballots did not constitute "legal votes," we affirm the trial court's holding as to this issue....

Whether the vote totals must be revised to include the legal votes actually identified in the Palm Beach County and Miami-Dade County manual recounts?... The circuit court concluded as to Palm Beach County that there was not any "authority to include any returns submitted past the deadline established by the Florida Supreme Court in this election." This conclusion was erroneous as a matter of law. The deadline of November 26, 2000, at 5 p.m. was established in order to allow maximum time for contests pursuant to section 102.168. The deadline was never intended to prohibit legal votes identified after that date through ongoing manual recounts to be excluded from the statewide official results in the Election Canvassing Commission's certification of the results of a recount of less than all of a county's ballots....

As to Miami-Dade County, in light of our holding that the circuit court should have counted the undervote, we agree with appellants that the partial recount results should also be included in the total legal votes for this election. Because the county canvassing boards identified legal votes and these votes could change the outcome of the election, we hold that the trial court erred in rejecting the legal votes identified in the Miami-Dade County and Palm Beach County manual recounts. These votes must be included in the certified vote totals. We find that appellants did not establish that the Nassau County Canvassing Board acted improperly.

Conclusion

Through no fault of appellants, a lawfully commenced manual recount in Dade County was never completed and recounts that were completed were not counted. Without examining or investigating the ballots that were not counted by the machines, the trial court concluded there was no reasonable probability of a different result. However, the proper standard required by section 102.168 was whether the results of the election were placed in doubt. On this record there can be no question that there are legal votes within the 9,000 uncounted votes sufficient to place the results of this election in doubt. We know this *not* only by evidence of statistical analysis but also by the actual experience of recounts conducted. The votes for each candidate that have been counted are separated by no more than approximately 500 votes and may be separated by as little as approximately 100 votes. Thousands of uncounted votes could obviously make a difference....

However, the need for accuracy must be weighed against the need for finality. The need for prompt resolution and finality is especially critical in presidential elections where there is an outside deadline established by federal law. Notwithstanding, consistent with the legislative mandate and our precedent, although the time constraints are limited, we must do everything required by law to ensure that legal votes that have not been counted are included in the final election results....

While we recognize that time is desperately short, we cannot in good faith ignore both the appellant's right to relief as to their claims concerning the uncounted votes in Miami-Dade County nor can we ignore the correctness of the assertions that any analysis and ultimate remedy should be made on a statewide basis....

Because time is of the essence, the circuit court shall commence the tabulation of the Miami-Dade ballots immediately. The circuit court is authorized, in accordance with the provisions of section 102.168 (8), to be assisted by the Leon County Supervisor of Elections or its sworn designees. Moreover, since time is also of the essence in any statewide relief that the circuit court must consider, any further statewide relief should also be ordered forthwith and simultaneously with the manual tabulation of the Miami-Dade undervotes.

In tabulating the ballots and in making a determination of what is a "legal" vote, the standard to be employed is that established by the Legislature in our Election Code which is that the vote shall be counted as a "legal" vote if there is "clear indication of the intent of the voter." Section 101.5614(5), Florida Statutes (2000).

It is so ordered.

Dissent of Chief Justice Charles Wells

I want to make it clear at the outset of my separate opinion that I do not question the good faith or honorable intentions of my colleagues in the majority. However, I could not more strongly disagree with their decision to reverse the trial court and prolong this judicial process. I also believe that the majority's decision cannot withstand the scrutiny which will certainly immediately follow under the United States Constitution.

My succinct conclusion is that the majority's decision to return this case to the circuit court for a count of the under-votes from either Miami-Dade County or all counties has no foundation in the law of Florida as it existed on November 7, 2000, or at any time until the issuance of this opinion. The majority returns the case to the circuit court for this partial recount of under-votes on the basis of unknown or, at best, ambiguous standards with authority to obtain help from others, the credentials, qualifications, and objectivity of whom are totally unknown. That is but a first glance at the imponderable problems the majority creates.

Importantly to me, I have a deep and abiding concern that the prolonging of judicial process in this counting contest propels this country and this state into an unprecedented and unnecessary constitutional crisis. I have to conclude that there is a real and present likelihood that this constitutional crisis will do substantial damage to our country, our state, and to this Court as an institution.

On the basis of my analysis of Florida law as it existed on November 7, 2000, I conclude that the trial court's decision can and should be affirmed....

At the outset, I note that, after an evidentiary hearing, the trial court expressly found no dishonesty, gross negligence, improper influence, coer-

From Dissent of Chief Justice Charles Wells, 772 So. 2d 1243, 1263–1270.

cion, or fraud in the balloting and counting processes based upon the evidence presented. I conclude this finding should curtail this Court's involvement in this election through this case and is a substantial basis for affirming the trial court. Historically, this Court has only been involved in elections when there have been substantial allegations of fraud and then only upon a high threshold because of the chill that a hovering judicial involvement can put on elections. This to me is the import of this Court's decision in *Boardman v. Esteva*, 323 So. 2d 259 (Fla. 1976). We lowered that threshold somewhat in *Beckstrom v. Volusia County Canvassing Board*, 707 So. 2d 720 (Fla. 1998), but we continued to require a substantial noncompliance with election laws. That must be the very lowest threshold for a court's involvement.

Otherwise, we run a great risk that every election will result in judicial testing. Judicial restraint in respect to elections is absolutely necessary because the health of our democracy depends on elections being decided by voters—not by judges. We must have the self-discipline not to become embroiled in political contests whenever a judicial majority subjectively concludes to do so because the majority perceives it is "the right thing to do." Elections involve the other branches of government. A lack of self-discipline in being involved in elections, especially by a court of last resort, always has the potential of leading to a crisis with the other branches of government and raises serious separation-of-powers concerns.

I find that the trial judge correctly concluded that plaintiffs were not entitled to a manual recount. Appellants filed this current election contest after protests in Palm Beach and Miami-Dade Counties. Section 102.168, Florida Statutes, in its present form is a new statute adopted by the Legislature in 1999. I conclude that the present statutory scheme contemplates that protests of returns and requests for manual recounts are first to be presented to the county canvassing boards. *See* § 102.166, Fla. Stat. This naturally follows from the fact that, even with the adoption of the 1999 amendments to section 102.168, the only procedures for manual recounts are in the protest statute. [An accompanying footnote states:

Also problematic with the majority's analysis is that the majority only *requires* that the "under-votes" are to be counted. How about the "over-votes?" Section 101.5614 (6) provides that a ballot should not be counted "[i]f an elector marks more names than there are persons to be elected to an office," meaning the voter voted for more than one person for president. The underlying premise of the majority's rationale is that in such a close race a manual review of ballots rejected by the machines is necessary to ensure that all legal votes cast are counted. The majority, however, ignores the over-votes. Could it be said, without reviewing the over-votes, that the machine did not err in not counting them?

It seems patently erroneous to me to assume that the vote-counting machines can err when reading under-votes but not err when reading over-votes. Can the majority say, without having the over-votes looked at, that there are no legal votes among the over-votes?]...

I conclude in the case at bar that sections 102.166 and 102.168 must be read in pari materia. My analysis in this regard is bolstered in situations, as here, where there was an initial protest filed in a county pursuant to section 102.166 and a subsequent contest of that same county's return pursuant to section 102.168. It appears logical to me that a circuit judge in a section 102.168 contest should review a county canvassing board's determinations in a section 102.166 protest under an abuse-of-discretion standard. I see no other reason why the county canvassing board would be a party defendant if the circuit court is not intended to evaluate the canvassing board's decisions with respect to manual recount decisions made in a section 102.166 protest....

I do not believe there is any sound reason to conclude that the Legislature's adoption of a revised section 102.168 in 1999 intended to change this and provide for a duplicative recount by an individual circuit judge....

The majority quotes section 101.5614(5) for the proposition of settling how a county canvassing board should count a vote. The majority states that "[n]o vote shall be declared invalid or void if there is a clear indication of the intent of the voter as determined by the canvassing board." § 101.5614(5), Fla. Stat. (2000). Section 101.5614(5), however, is a statute that authorizes the creation of a duplicate ballot where a "ballot card…is damaged or defective so that it cannot properly be counted by the automatic tabulating equipment." There is no basis in this record that suggests that the approximately 9000 ballots from Miami-Dade County were damaged or defective.

Laying aside this problem and assuming the majority is correct that section 101.5614(5) correctly annunciates the standard by which a county canvassing board should judge a questionable ballot, section 101.5614(5) utterly fails to provide any meaningful standard. There is no doubt that every vote should be counted where there is a "clear indication of the intent of the voter." The problem is how a county canvassing board translates that directive to these punch cards. Should a county canvassing board count or not count a "dimpled chad" where the voter is able to successfully dislodge the chad in every other contest on that ballot? Here, the county canvassing boards disagree. Apparently, some do and some do not. Continuation of this system of county-by-county decisions regarding how a dimpled chad is counted is fraught with equal protection concerns which will eventually cause the election results in Florida to be stricken by the federal courts or Congress.

Based upon this analysis and adhering to the interpretation of the 1992

Hogan case, I conclude the circuit court properly looked at what the county canvassing boards have done and found that they did not abuse their discretion....

Laying aside the constitutional [and statutory] infirmities of this Court's action today, what the majority actually creates is an overflowing basket of practical problems. Assuming the majority recognizes a need to protect the votes of Florida's presidential electors, the entire contest must be completed "at least six days before" December 18, 2000, the date the presidential electors meet to vote. *See* 3 U.S.C. § 5 (1994). The safe harbor deadline day is December 12, 2000. Today is Friday, December 8, 2000. Thus, under the majority's time line, all manual recounts must be completed in five days, assuming the counting begins today.

In that time frame, all questionable ballots must be reviewed by the judicial officer appointed to discern the intent of the voter in a process open to the public. Fairness dictates that a provision be made for either party to object to how a particular ballot is counted. Additionally, this short time period must allow for judicial review. I respectfully submit this cannot be completed without taking Florida's presidential electors outside the safe harbor provision, creating the very real possibility of disenfranchising those nearly six million voters who were able to correctly cast their ballots on election day....

This case has reached the point where finality must take precedence over continued judicial process. I agree with a quote from John Allen Paulos, a professor of mathematics at Temple University, when he wrote that, "[t]he margin of error in this election is far greater than the margin of victory, no matter who wins." Further judicial process will not change this self-evident fact and will only result in confusion and disorder.

Dissent of Justice Major Harding
(Joined by Justice Leander Shaw)

I would affirm Judge Sauls' order because I agree with his ultimate conclusion in this case, namely that the Appellants failed to carry their requisite burden of proof and thus are not entitled to relief. However, in reaching his conclusion, Judge Sauls applied erroneous standards in two instances.... While abuse of discretion is the proper standard for assessing a canvassing board's actions in a section 102.166 protest proceeding, it is not applicable to this section 102.168 contest proceeding. Judge Sauls improperly intertwined these two proceedings and the standards applicable to each....

Where a contestant alleges that the canvassing board has rejected a number of legal votes "sufficient to change or place in doubt the result of the election" due to the board's decision to curtail or deny a manual recount, the circuit judge should examine this issue de novo and not under an abuse of discretion standard. § 102.168(3) (c), Fla. Stat. (2000).

Second, Judge Sauls erred in concluding that a contestant under section 102.168 (3) (c) must show a "reasonable probability that the results of the election would have been changed."...

I conclude [however] that the application of the erroneous standards is not determinative in this case. I agree with Judge Sauls that the Appellants have not carried their burden of showing that the number of legal votes rejected by the canvassing boards is sufficient to change or place in doubt the result of this *statewide* election. That failure of proof controls the outcome here....

The basis for Appellant's claim for relief under section 102.168 is that there is a "no-vote" problem, i.e., ballots which, although counted by machines at least once, allegedly have not been counted in the presidential election. The evidence showed that this no-vote problem, to the extent it

---

From Dissent of Justice Major Harding, 772 So. 2d 1243, 1270–1273.

exists, is a statewide problem. Appellants ask that only a subset of these no-votes be counted....

However, in this contest proceeding, Appellants had an obligation to show, by a preponderance of the evidence, that the outcome of the statewide election would likely be changed by the relief they sought.

Appellants failed, however, to provide any meaningful statistical evidence that the outcome of the Florida election would be different if the "no-vote" in other counties had been counted; their proof that the outcome of the vote in two counties would likely change the results of the election was insufficient. It would be improper to permit Appellants to carry their burden in a statewide election by merely demonstrating that there were a sufficient number of no-votes that could have changed the returns in isolated counties. Recounting a subset of counties selected by the Appellants does not answer the ultimate question of whether a sufficient number of uncounted legal votes could be recovered from the statewide "no-votes" to change the result of the statewide election. At most, such a procedure only demonstrates that the losing candidate would have had greater success in the subset of counties most favorable to that candidate....

Any other remedy [than a statewide one] would disenfranchise tens of thousands of other Florida voters, as I have serious concerns that Appellant's interpretation of 102.168 would violate other voters' rights to due process and equal protection of the law under the Fifth and Fourteenth Amendments to the United States Constitution.

As such, I would find that the selective recounting requested by Appellant is not available under the election contest provisions of section 102.168. Such an application does not provide for a more accurate reflection of the will of the voters but, rather, allows for an unfair distortion of the statewide vote. It is patently unlawful to permit the recount of "no-votes" in a single county to determine the outcome of the November 7, 2000, election for the next President of the United States. We are a nation of laws, and we have survived and prospered as a free nation because we have adhered to the rule of law. Fairness is achieved by following the rules....

Clearly, the only remedy authorized by law would be a statewide recount of more than 170,000 "no-vote" ballots by December 12. Even if such a recount were possible, speed would come at the expense of accuracy, and it would be difficult to put any faith or credibility in a vote total achieved under such chaotic conditions....

The circumstances of this election call to mind a quote from football coaching legend Vince Lombardi: "We didn't lose the game, we just ran out of time."

23

Comment:
Were Gore's Contest Claims Justified?

Mark Whitman

The Florida judges who examined the state's contest statute split 4-4 on the critical question of whether it justified the litigation brought by Vice President Gore. A change of one vote on the supreme court would have terminated the election controversy.

Consequently, as with the protest provisions of Florida law, we need to look more closely at the contest section—102.168—to see if its language and structure definitively validate the claims of either Gore or Bush.

Again, there is no simple answer. Taken by themselves, the words "rejection of . . . legal votes" can support the vice president's position: that is, they can bear what is called a "plain language defense"[1] of the import given to them by Gore's lawyers and narrowly affirmed by the Florida Supreme Court. Ballots counted wholly with machines, as virtually all the ballots cast on election day are counted, can properly be "rejected" only by those machines (assuming the machines display no malfunction). Thus fully punched ballots, and ones with hanging and dangling chads, that pass through a machine unrecorded for any candidate, are quite literally "legal votes" rejected, according to the standard for legal votes widely accepted in Florida in 2000. They are in their essence ballots displaying the intent of the voter "that may exist but have not been counted." They remain present even after a machine count is done, capable of being discovered, no matter how reasonable a canvassing board's action in suspending a recount at the protest stage, or a secretary of state's action in enforcing a deadline.

As Professor Jack Balkin of Yale Law School points out,

> The [Florida Supreme Court] held that the best way to make sense of the statutory scheme was to hold that "legal votes" are "rejected" under section 102.168 (3) (c) when they are not read by a machine count. Otherwise the court would have to hold that legal votes sufficient to change the outcome of the election might exist but that failure of machines to count

them could not be raised in an election contest because the votes were not "rejected," which seems to be a perverse result.[2]

Indeed, Professor Richard Friedman of the University of Michigan Law School sees a critical linguistic parallel between the protest and the contest statutes. "[I]t would appear," he notes, "that . . . 'an error [in the vote tabulation]' is [in fact] the counting of illegal votes or the failure to count legal votes."[3]

Function Questions Form

But looked at from another angle, reading 168.3 (c) to perform the ambitious functions assigned to it by *Gore v. Harris* creates its own possible perversities, starting when the words of 3 (c) are taken from isolation and placed in the context of the entire contest statute—even in the full context of 168.3. That section lists all the other specific grievances triggering a contest suit, and all of these other causes involve illegalities or irregularities that would fundamentally corrupt the election process: "Misconduct, fraud, or corruption on the part of any election official"; "Ineligibility of the successful candidate"; "Proof that any elector, election official, or canvassing board member was given or offered a bribe."

Viewed from this angle, "rejection of legal votes," which is paired, remember, with the words "receipt of a number of illegal votes," seems to be aimed less at voter intent than at "cases of misconduct [by] election officials," as Professor Richard Epstein points out. For "if the Florida legislature wanted to make the *failure to ascertain the intention of the voter* the [basis] for triggering a contest [as opposed to using an improper standard for ascertaining intent], it could have done so in just those words."[4] (A section of Florida law dealing with the canvass of absentee ballots, 101.68, states that if election officials find a ballot they believe to contain irremediable defects, they are to write on the ballot, "rejected as illegal," suggesting it is an irregular or improper action on their part which produces "rejection of [a] *legal* vote.")

Furthermore, reading 3 (c) to cover any search for genuine votes entails significant practical consequences. It means contests could easily become the venue of choice for recounts in close elections, and judges the operative authorities on chads and dimples, since a protest does not need to precede a contest under Florida law. As Judge Richard Posner notes, "Even though they lack staff and experience for counting and interpreting ballots . . . the courts become the primary vote tabulators, rather than the election officials. . . . This is all upside down."[5]

Indeed, there would seem to be virtually no incentive under this regimen to follow the deadlines for submitting returns in a tight election, since deadlines signal only the end of the certification period and the beginning of a contest phase where courts will most likely count the rest of the votes anyway. Whether a secretary of state "must ignore" or "may ignore" late returns would scarcely be a question worth debating, and Judge Burton need not have been so frantic on the afternoon of November 26.

The certification itself, in a close race, would become a meaningless provisional document, even if it was considered final as far as it went. The Florida Supreme Court decision did not even concede that. By ordering that the 388 votes recovered in Miami-Dade's partial recount be added immediately to the "certified vote totals," even though there was no absolute assurance this recount would ever be completed, the court seemed to view certification as a continuous, ongoing process, rather than as two clearly defined stages of an election—one certification at the end of the protest period, a revised document after a completed contest. It candidly stated of its own November 26 cutoff date, "[It] was never intended to prohibit legal votes identified after that date" from being included in the "Elections Canvassing Commission's *certification* of the results of a recount of *less than all of a county's ballots.*"[6] This meant, as Michael McConnell argues, that in their November 21 decision the Florida justices "added twelve days to a [protest period] that had no real legal significance, while shortening the time for obtaining genuine legal relief."[7]

State Precedent

Florida case law reflects a limited view of contests. *Boardman v. Esteva*, though dealing specifically with absentee ballots, summarizes the sorts of concerns that had traditionally driven contest challenges in the state:

(a) the presence or absence of fraud, gross negligence, or intentional wrongdoing;
(b) whether there has been substantial compliance with the essential requirements of the . . . law; and
(c) whether the irregularities complained of adversely affect the sanctity of the ballot and the integrity of the election.[8]

A landmark case of 1998, *Beckstrom v. Volusia County Canvassing Board* (also concerning absentee ballots), modified *Boardman*, holding that a trial court could "sustain a certified election result," even after finding "substantial noncompliance with the election statutes," if it "also found that [the election] result reflects the will of the people."[9]

But *Beckstrom* still dealt with alleged irregularities by election officials, as did the leading cases cited by the vice president's lawyers in their contest brief for the proposition that there was "no discretion" under Section 168 to let "legal votes" go uncounted. None of these cases concern a demand for a recount solely because such votes will probably be uncovered thereby, even though election equipment functioned properly and the authorities were diligent.[10]

Possibly, the 1999 amendments to the contest law were designed to change the system in the way the Florida Supreme Court suggested, unwieldly as the system then created would have been. But such legislative background as we have on these 1999 efforts indicates they were not meant to alter Florida's basic election system. A house of representatives report on the bill [H.B. 281] that, with minor changes, became the new Section 168, states, "HB 281 *codifies* the grounds for contesting an election,"[11] suggesting that it had not "dropped the substantial noncompliance requirement . . . long . . . necessary to bring a contest under Florida law."[12]

The majority justices in *Gore v. Harris* relied primarily on cases from New Jersey to support their view of 102.168. New Jersey law, which permits recounts, also contains a provision like Florida's allowing the contest of "legal votes rejected,"[13] and *Gore* found this provision consistent with the idea "that a legal vote will be deemed to have been 'rejected' where a voting machine fails to count a ballot . . . which . . . reflects . . . the clear intent of the voter to express a definite choice."[14] In fact, the seminal New Jersey decision on this matter ruled that "rejected" was "properly read to include any situation in which qualified voters are *denied access to the polls* including a denial because of *shutdown of a voting machine*."[15] New Jersey courts later deemed the term to include "inability to cast [a] vote because of a partially malfunctioning voting machine,"[16] and "write-in votes placed on the wrong line due to insufficient and *unintelligible* instructions."[17]

The lone Florida case cited in *Gore v. Harris,* from 1935, concerned a situation in which the plaintiff, having lost an election by five votes, alleged among other things, that three votes were lawfully cast for him, "but not counted."[18] The trial court referred to these ballots as "the rejection of votes from legal voters,"[19] thereby "equat[ing]," said the majority in *Gore v. Harris,* "a 'rejection' of legal votes with the failure to count legal votes."[20] But no dispute is mentioned in this case over the standards used in assessing ballots. And the flat omission of supposedly valid votes from a certification, as apparently happened here, would represent "substantial noncompliance" with state election laws, something not involved in the 2000 contest trial.

What Might Have Been

The circumstantial evidence points, then, toward the view that 168.3 (c) was meant to deal only with such things as wrongdoing, gross negligence, or abuse of discretion by election officials. (Neither was it written to adapt to the special timetable of choosing a president.) If the statute is thus limited, there could be no satisfactory solution to Gore's problem under it, since a contest action has to rest on the quality of official action, not on whether votes are there waiting to be credited or counted.[21]

All of which leads one to speculate on what might have happened had Gore followed out from the beginning the proper implication of his "count every vote" mantra, and insisted that *only* a statewide recount in Florida was appropriate. Bush's (and Baker's) certain refusal to join forces in urging such a count would have left Gore with the task of making requests to sixty-seven counties, something he could have dramatized as patently chaotic and absurd (which is why the Florida legislature amended 102.166 in 2001 to read, "For federal, statewide, . . . and multicounty races . . . requests for a manual recount shall be made . . . to the State Elections Canvassing Commission").[22] In any event, with many of the canvassing boards under Republican control, and likely to endorse Secretary Harris's blockade against hand counts, it is hard to imagine the vice president not having seen fairly early the necessity of a court-ordered and controlled process.

Thus, as his shrewd Florida counsel, Dexter Douglass, suggested, Gore's best hope would probably have rested on withholding any challenge to Harris's certification deadline.[23] Then, on November 15, he could have brought a contest suit based on the claimed violations of law that kept a recount from taking place, a contest aimed at getting a manual count of all of Florida's votes, or at least of all undervotes and overvotes, under uniform standards. The public might well have been as patient with Gore during this process as it was with the legal maneuvers he did pursue, particularly since here he would truly be seeking an honest assessment of the Florida vote, not just trying to jump ahead.

The Conundrums of *Gore v. Harris*

In sending *Gore v. Harris* back to Judge Sauls, the majority justices again refused to set a specific standard for the recounting they demanded, whether the *Delahunt* approach or any other. They contented themselves with the familiar bromide about divining the intent of the voter as "established by *the Legislature* in our Election Code."[24]

Though we cannot be certain, it is possible to ascribe this reticence about setting standards to what must have been the court's heightened fear, after the December 4 per curiam, of doing anything that could be construed as tampering with state law. If so, the justices were heading into a trap on the equal-protection issue. In Alan Dershowitz's view, "The Florida Supreme Court . . . followed the advice implicit in the unanimous per curiam opinion: It applied the Florida legislative standard without trying to narrow it further so as to eliminate . . . equal-protection concerns. Little did it know that *Bush v. Gore* would turn out to be a "catch-22.""25

The practical implications of laying down a definite standard, however, may have been enough to deter the justices from doing so. A requirement of uniformity would mean extending the undervote count to yet another perusal of the ballots in Palm Beach, Broward, and Volusia Counties (and of the ones already counted in Miami-Dade). This would further devalue the recounting process in the public mind, particularly since there was no telling what might happen when authorities ran the voting machines in Palm Beach and Broward Counties again to isolate the undervotes and count them. When Broward officials resegregated and reassessed these ballots for the *Miami Herald* survey, the new tally showed that before counting any dimpled or pinpricked ballots at all, Gore had gained 646 votes, as opposed to 567 total in the official recount.26

If inhibited on one front, perhaps, by the United States Supreme Court decision, *Gore v. Harris* took action on another. Without saying so explicitly, the majority justices responded to the Supreme Court's second concern in its December 4 per curiam, about the relation between state law and Section 5. *Gore* obediently noted that "[the election] statutes established by the Legislature govern our decision today." And, it went on, "We consider these statutes *cognizant of the federal grant of authority* derived from the United States Constitution and *derived from 3 U.S.C. § 5.*"27 The opinion later states that "the need for prompt resolution and finality is especially critical in presidential elections where there is an outside deadline established by federal law," and "that practical difficulties may well end up controlling the outcome of the election."28 Though certainly not decisive on the point, *Gore v. Harris* creates the impression that December 12 marked the automatic termination of all adjudication over the 2000 election, because the Florida legislature had embraced that deadline.

Whatever its legal strengths, or weaknesses, the Florida decision kept the vice president's hopes alive, but as many of his advisors suspected, even on December 8, "Gore's favorite court in the land"29 had probably sealed his electoral doom by refusing to sanction a reassessment of the dimpled ballots in Palm Beach County. The court had also sown trouble with the justices in Washington because of its perilous, if understandable, decision, in light of the electoral deadlines, to place the contest decision above its response to the United States Supreme Court's December 4 per curiam.

The End of the Butterfly

With such tumultuous events unfolding in the first week of December, few paid attention to the fact that on December 1, the Florida Supreme Court brought the once-heralded butterfly controversy to a close. In a unanimous opinion running barely three pages, the justices upheld a lower-court decision by Judge LaBarga, and ruled there would be no revote in Palm Beach County.[30]

The legal issues were simple. Under the landmark *Beckstrom* decision, a court could not even consider voiding an election unless "[it] finds *substantial noncompliance* with statutory election procedures and *also* makes a factual determination that reasonable doubt exists as to whether a certified election expressed the will of the voters."[31] Whatever the relevance to Palm Beach of the second criterion in *Beckstrom*, the Florida justices did not see placing some candidates' names to the left of their punch hole, with an arrow pointed toward it, as meeting the threshold requirement. "In the present case, even accepting [the] allegations [presented], we conclude as a matter of law that the Palm Beach County ballot does not constitute substantial noncompliance."[32]

The supreme court cited, as had the canvassing board's lawyers, a Second District Court of Appeals decision from 1974, which seemed directly on point.[33] It concerned a ballot conceded to be highly misleading in a Pinellas County election. The trial judge, though ruling the ballot was in "substantial compliance" with state election law, set the election aside anyway, because he found the "alignment and location" of the defendants' names "'confusing,'" and "'prejudicial'" to their election chances.[34] The court of appeals reversed, however, ruling that "*mere confusion* does not amount to an impediment to the voters' free choice if *reasonable time and study will sort it out.* . . . If a candidate appears on the ballot in such a position that he can be found by the voters upon a responsible study of the ballot, then such voters have been afforded a full, free and open opportunity to make their choice."[35]

Notes

1. David A. Strauss, "*Bush v. Gore*: What Were They Thinking?" in Cass Sunstein and Richard Epstein (eds.), *The Vote: Bush, Gore and the Supreme Court* (Chicago: Chicago University Press, 2001), p. 201.

2. Jack Balkin, "*Bush v. Gore* and the Boundary Between Law and Politics," 110 *Yale Law Journal* (2001), pp. 1407, 1418.

3. Richard Friedman, "Trying to Make Peace with *Bush v. Gore*," 29 *Florida State University Law Review* (2001), pp. 811, 843.

4. Richard Epstein, "'In Such Manner as the Legislature May Direct': The Outcome in *Bush v. Gore* Defended," in Sunstein and Epstein (eds.), *The Vote*, p. 33 (italics added).

5. Richard Posner, *Breaking the Deadlock* (Princeton, N.J.: Princeton University Press, 2001), p. 119.

6. *Gore v. Harris*, 772 So. 2d 1243, 1260 (italics added).

7. Michael McConnell, "Two-and-a-Half Cheers for *Bush v. Gore*," in Sunstein and Epstein (eds.), *The Vote*, p. 110 (italics added).

8. *Boardman v. Esteva*, 323 So. 2d 259, 269 (1976).

9. *Beckstrom v. Volusia County Canvassing Board*, 707 So. 2d 720, 725 (1998).

10. See *Nuccio v. Williams*, 120 So. 310 (1929); *Wiggins v. State*, 144 So. 62 (1932); *State v. Smith*, 144 So. 333 (1932); *Carpenter v. Barber*, 198 So. 49 (1940); see also *Darby v. State*, 75 So. 411 (1917).

11. Florida House of Representatives, Report on H.B. 281, p. 7 (italics added), www.leg.state.fl.us.

12. *Bush v. Gore*, "Brief of Florida House of Representatives and Florida Senate as *Amici Curiae* in Support of Neither Party and Seeking Reversal," p. 11.

13. *New Jersey Statutes*, 19: 29-1 (e).

14. *Gore v. Harris*, p. 1257.

15. *Magura v. Smith*, 330 A. 2d 52, 54 (1974) (italics added).

16. *Application of Moffat*, 361 A. 2d 74, 77 (1976).

17. *In Re Gray-Sadler*, 753 A. 2d 1101, 1105 (2000) (italics added).

18. *State ex. rel. Clark v. Klingensmith*, 163 So. 704, 705.

19. Ibid.

20. *Gore v. Harris*, p. 1257.

21. Balkin, "*Bush v. Gore* and the Boundary," p. 1419, puts forth a contrary view.

22. *The 2002 Florida Statutes*, 102.166 (2) (b), www.flcourts.org.

23. In this connection, see The Political Staff of *The Washington Post*, *Deadlock* (New York: Public Affairs, 2001), p. 157. See Douglass's own account, "A Look Back—One Lawyer's View," 13 *Florida Journal of Law and Public Policy* (2001), p. 15.

24. *Gore v. Harris*, p. 1262 (italics added).

25. Alan Dershowitz, *Supreme Injustice* (New York: Oxford University Press, 2001), p. 45.

26. Martin Merzer and the Staff of *The Miami Herald*, *The Miami Herald Report: Democracy Held Hostage* (New York: St. Martin's Press, 2001), p. 239.

27. *Gore v. Harris*, p. 1248 (italics added).

28. Ibid., pp. 1261, 1261–1262, fn. 21.

29. The Political Staff of *The Washington Post*, *Deadlock*, p. 157.

30. *Fladell v. Palm Beach County Canvassing Board* (slip opinion); the published version is barely over a page, 772 So. 2d 1240 (2000).

31. *Beckstrom v. Volusia County Canvassing Board*, 725 (italics added).

32. *Fladell v. Palm Beach County Canvassing Board*, 772 So. 2d 1240, 1242 (2000).

33. *Nelson v. Robinson*, 301 So. 2d 508 (1974).

34. Ibid., p. 510.

35. Ibid., pp. 511, 512 (italics added).

PART 6

DENOUEMENT—RETURN TO THE U.S. SUPREME COURT

The Leon County Circuit Court wasted no time in dealing with the Florida justices' remand of *Gore v. Harris*. It convened at 8:35 on the evening of December 8, less than five hours after announcement of the supreme court action.

Judge Sauls was no longer presiding, however. Angry and hurt, he had recused himself from further participation in the case. Judge Terry Lewis took his place. Barry Richard was also absent from the Bush counsel table. He was sorely disappointed by the contest decision, and temporarily exhausted. Phil Beck argued for Governor Bush.

With an eye on the appeal his colleagues were even then rushing to the United States Supreme Court, Beck dwelled on the importance of doing something he felt almost certain Judge Lewis would not feel empowered to do: set a consistent standard for the counting of the under-votes. And from both "a legal point of view as well as a factual point of view,"[1] Beck argued, this standard must not countenance the inclusion of dimpled ballots. "If this Court now articulates a standard that allows dimples and indentations to be counted, that will be a new and different approach than was in place . . . and therefore, would violate 3 US Code Section 5."[2]

The possibility that dimples might nonetheless be considered allowed Beck to continue praising and condemning the Palm Beach County Canvassing Board at the same time. "We believe that if you're going to be looking at dimples, which you should not do, that you should only count the dimples where there is a pattern of clear attempts, but failures to punch the chad through."[3] That was the kind of standard used "in Palm Beach County," and represented "a fair indication of voter intent," as opposed to "what happened in Broward County, [which] was just awful."[4] Yet Beck also reminded Judge Lewis that the only written regulation on counting standards in Florida came from Palm Beach, and it reflected, "we believe, a statewide standard in practice, . . . which was to count . . . dislodged chads only."[5]

The next morning, Bush's lawyers filed a brief with Lewis that enlarged upon the "degradation" theory they had mentioned several times earlier. The lawyers sought to have the 9,000 remaining undervotes in Miami-Dade County invalidated, because "these ballots have degraded to the point that they are not the same ballots that were counted and recounted on November 7 and 8, 2000."[6] The brief quoted some testimony from the contest trial, in which a Bush lawyer maintained that when county election officials were machine-sorting the undervotes on November 19 and 20 for the abortive manual recount, he saw lying on the floor "at least 1,000 new pieces of chad . . . that [were] being generated in that process."[7] (In no way were such leavings incriminating evidence, however, according to Miami-Dade election supervisor David Leahy, who told reporters during the sorting process that only hanging or dangling chads fell off during machine runs, and they were already considered valid votes. A chad that "wasn't punched at all" would not fall out, he claimed.[8] Judge Burton also testified, with regard to Palm Beach, that the machine readers "don't destroy or degrade the cards"; only "dangling chads that are hanging" detached during machine runs, and they would be counted "as an indication of the voter's intent to begin with."[9])

The degradation theory was debatable. But the Bush lawyers were unquestionably correct in citing a related problem in Miami that affected all punch-card recounts. When the Miami canvassing board segregated its undervotes by machine on November 19 and 20, they pointed out, officials failed to tally them and compare the totals to the number of undervotes generated in the November 8 machine run—this despite the fact that by their own analysis chads could fall off during machine runs (or, conversely, could fail to open up to the light though having done so before). Hence, in preparing to send the ballots to Judge Sauls on November 29, they inevitably found discrepancies between the number of undervotes they had at this point, and the earlier machine count of such ballots. One hundred and twenty precincts had less undervotes, thirty-four had more—granted that the biggest variation was 6 votes, and most were of 1 or 2.

More important, the submission to Judge Sauls contained no new totals of the number of *valid* votes for each candidate, totals which would surely vary from earlier runs, not only because of the different number of undervotes, but because no one could be certain that the overvotes would come out exactly as before, or that a different number of ballots had not stuck together during this run than during previous ones. The only way to deal with Miami-Dade's ballots now, the Bush brief argued, "would be to conduct a full manual recount of *all* ballots," or "to run the *entire* set of ballots through the tabulation machine [again], simultaneously (a) counting the 'clear' votes and (b) identifying undervotes and overvotes rejected by the machine."[10] Furthermore, those counties separating undervotes for the first time must be very careful to secure new totals for Bush, Gore, and the others as they tackled the spoiled ballots. If there were more spoiled or stuck ballots than before, and no new totals supplied, there would be double counting of votes in the recount; if there were less, candidates could lose votes.

Judge Lewis Disposes, Florida Begins to Count

Not surprisingly, Judge Lewis refused to lay down any standard for the recounts beyond the intent of the voter, since the "Florida Supreme Court has been asked at least twice recently to do so and has specifically declined."[11] The judge also refused Beck's invitation to count all the ballots himself, ordering the canvassing boards in each of sixty-three counties to get the undervotes together and devise a scheme for assessing them. The Miami-Dade ballots would be counted in Tallahassee, with the Leon County supervisor of elections and judges of the second circuit helping out. The other counties were "urged—but not required—" to follow the pattern in the capitol and "enlist the services of [their] judges."[12]

Observers for Bush and Gore could monitor the counting process, but, contrary to Beck's wishes, "may not make a verbal objection or challenge to any particular ballot determination nor in any way disrupt . . . the counting process. Any objections or challenges shall be in writing and filed with the Clerk of Court."[13] Ballots disputed by the counters would be saved as well for Judge Lewis's review. It was not likely to be a capacious one. In discussing the recount on Friday night with some of his judicial colleagues who had volunteered for the Miami project, Lewis said, "Don't forget that first word, *clear* intent. . . . I've got my Johnnie Cochran sound bite for you. 'If in doubt, throw it out.'"[14]

While the judge pondered Bush's Miami-Dade brief on Saturday morning, along with a list of thirty-one objections to the recounts filed by Joe Klock,[15] the counting moved ahead quickly for Miami, in the Leon County Public Library. Numerous other jurisdictions were recounting votes by late morning. An early Associated Press report on the unofficial tally showed Gore gaining just 16 votes statewide, though Gore's lead attorney in the recount, Ron Klain, asserted at a press conference that of thirteen counties that had completely or partially finished their recounts, five of them solidly Republican, the vice president had gained 58 votes.[16]

Some counties were having trouble getting off the mark, though. Duval County, a GOP stronghold, informed Judge Lewis it could not begin counting until Sunday. Officials there cited the need to elaborately reprogram their election equipment so it could "run all 291,000 [punch-card] ballots through the machine readers . . . another time," yet "stop . . . the machine . . . whenever a no vote is recorded for a ballot in the Presidential race."[17]

Bush Takes a Flyer

Duval County never got a chance to start its recount, nor Miami-Dade to finish its, and have Judge Lewis pass on the count's legality. This was because of the action taken by the U.S. Supreme Court on the plea that accompanied George Bush's notice that he was seeking a writ of certiorari in *Gore v. Harris*. For while advising the justices on Friday night of their client's intention to file such a request the next day, based on updated Article II and equal-protection claims (and further evidence of supposed ballot degradation), Bush lawyers also requested a stay of enforcement of the Florida Supreme Court's judgment—a halt, in other words, to the state's recount until Washington reviewed the *Gore* decision.

The attorneys did not think their prospects for securing a stay were very good.[18] Whatever the chances of ultimately prevailing on the merits, they must show in addition, of course, that Governor Bush would suffer "irreparable harm" if the stay was not granted. Their various efforts to do so illustrated why they were not optimistic.

The governor's lawyers initially maintained he would "suffer irreparable injury unless a stay issues in this case," because a continuing recount raised "a reasonable possibility that the November 26 certification of Governor Bush as the winner of Florida's electoral votes will be called into doubt—or purport to be withdrawn," at a time when appeals would go beyond December 12, and thus "jeopardize the 'conclusive' effect of any . . . determination for Congress' counting purposes." Uncorrectable harm would result, therefore, "unless this Court acts immediately."[19]

But as Gore's reply brief pointed out, the "action" Bush needed was not a stay, for such action was "*completely* irrelevant to [his] claimed injury."

> [The governor] can achieve his objective of a conclusive resolution to this dispute by December 12 in only one of two ways: (1) the count can go forward and the [Florida] courts can enter a final judgment [for him] by December 12, or (2) this Court can grant review and determine that Governor Bush is entitled to prevail in the contest by that date. A stay of the count obviously does nothing to advance either of those goals.[20]

In a supplemental memo of December 9, the Bush forces altered their irreparable-harm argument in a way showing that what really bothered them went beyond the timing of court decisions. If the "confusing, inconsistent and largely standardless process" begun in Florida was "not stayed" they argued, "the integrity of this presidential election could be seriously undermined," due to the fact that "whatever tabulations result from this process *will be incurable in the public consciousness* and, once announced, cannot be retracted."[21]

Such a claim of harm, while based on purely political perceptions, was not implausible in the context of 2000, though Laurence Tribe later raised a First Amendment objection to it that the Gore lawyers didn't get a chance to explore on December 8 and 9. "Freedom of speech and of the press," Tribe felt, "quite plainly prevent government from suppressing information that lies at the political core of free expression on the theory that the minds of adult citizens would be irreversibly polluted" if arguably valid recount results were later declared invalid.[22]

In any case, no argument Bush might make could obscure the fact that the harm inflicted on the vice president by a stay unquestionably outweighed the harm inflicted on him, since "what a stay would do," quite simply, was "prevent Vice President Gore from *ever* gaining the benefit of the Section 5 [safe harbor] presumption. A stay would essentially ensure that if this Court either denies review or affirms the decision below—even prior to the Section 5 deadline—the counting of the ballots would push a 'final determination' well beyond that date."[23] Bush might gain the safe harbor under a stayed recount; Gore never could. There was little question that the "balance of harms" traditionally considered in stay applications was on the side of the Democratic candidate. (It was also clear that the vice president's lawyers had abandoned the notion hinted at in their contest brief, that all adjudication *must* end by December 12. The Bush lawyers appeared to take the same position.)

End Game?

Gore's case seemed strong. Yet at 2:45 P.M. on Saturday, December 9, the United States Supreme Court issued an order approving the Bush application for a stay. The application was also treated as a writ of certiorari and was granted, for both the Article II and equal-protection issues. Oral argument was set for 11 A.M. on Monday, December 11, with briefs due on Sunday at 4 P.M.[24]

The stay was approved at the price of the tenuous unity achieved in *Bush v. Palm Beach County Canvassing Board*. The vote was 5-4. Justices Stevens, Souter, Ginsburg, and Breyer were the predictable dissenters. Justice Stevens wrote an angry dissent for the four. In a highly unusual move, Justice Scalia answered Stevens in a lone concurrence with the stay order.

There was only one reason the Court could have taken the action it did. The majority justices did not simply "believe," in Justice Scalia's words, "that the petitioner has a substantial probability of success [on the merits]."[25] They were absolutely certain they were going to rule against the vice president and declare the just-launched Florida recount illegal. The stoppage of the counting was the functional equivalent of overturning *Gore v. Harris.*

Some of the precedents governing stays do in fact adjust or downplay the balance of harms between litigants if the outcome of a case is virtually assured.[26] As Judge Posner notes, "It would be absurd to say that a party that had a 99 percent chance of prevailing when its appeal was heard should not be entitled to a stay just because the irreparable harm to him from the denial of the stay would be exceeded . . . by the irreparable harm to his opponent from the grant of the stay."[27]

Knowing their eventual judgment on the Florida recount, the majority could place considerations of "national interest" above any concerns of the vice president's. "One of the principal issues in the appeal we have accepted," wrote Justice Scalia, "is precisely whether the votes that have been ordered to be counted are, under a reasonable interpretation of Florida law, 'legally cast vote[s].' The counting of votes that are of questionable legality does in my view threaten irreparable harm to petitioner, and to the country, by casting a cloud upon what he claims to be the legitimacy of his election. Count first, and rule upon legality afterwards, is not a recipe for producing election results that have the public acceptance democratic stability requires."[28]

Scalia also claimed that "permitting the count to proceed on [an] erroneous basis will prevent an accurate recount from being conducted . . . later, since it is generally agreed that each manual [count] produces a degradation of the ballots, which renders a subsequent recount inaccurate."[29]

This was not "generally agreed," and was not heard from again in the litigation. Such reasoning, however, allowed Justice Scalia to overlook an important countervailing consideration regarding stays followed by subsequent recounting, especially in a presidential election. To stop such a counting process, even because the original recount would be declared unconstitutional, deprived election officials of important raw material they could use in implementing the standards dictated by a court decision, thus saving them invaluable time. As Louis Seidman of Georgetown Law School argues,

> Had the recount been allowed to proceed while the matter was under review, the difficulties that the Court ultimately discerned might never have materialized. The circuit judge, charged by the Florida Supreme Court with overseeing the recount, might have resolved disputes under a uniform standard. Even if he failed to do so, the canvassing boards con-

ducting the recount might have determined the number of ballots falling into various categories. Had the United States Supreme Court at that point decided that a uniform standard was constitutionally compelled, the state court could simply have imposed the standard on the already counted ballots.[30]

That all sixty-three counties across Florida would have exercised such diligence in preparing for a ruling from Washington can be doubted. In any event, it was already questionable on December 9 whether the ballots in Florida would ever undergo further "degradation," or whether Judge Lewis and the canvassing boards would ever be rearranging neatly stacked piles of them. While we cannot be certain, it is entirely possible that after reading *Gore v. Harris*, the same Supreme Court majority that decided by December 9 to invalidate the Florida recount also resolved on that date to close down the Florida contest for good a few days later, to set the drop-dead deadline for December 12. The strictly legal justification for taking this action was sorely lacking, as we shall see. And if, as appears likely, it was not a move born of purely judicial considerations, there is reason to believe that the move was agreed upon by the time of the stay.

Justice Stevens's dissent may have flowed from an awareness of what *Bush*'s ultimate outcome would be. The issuing of the stay, he noted, was "'tantamount to a decision . . . in favor of the applicants.'" Then he added, *"Preventing the recount from being completed* will inevitably cast a cloud on the legitimacy of the election."[31]

On that fateful Saturday, the Gore strategists saw defeat on the merits as certain, even if not fully aware of what was in store for them. When the vice president decided to replace Laurence Tribe with David Boies for the Supreme Court oral argument, Bill Daley told him, "It doesn't matter, because we're going to lose anyway."[32] Tribe, who still agreed to work on the Gore brief, felt "it's very uphill," and David Boies put the chances of success at "not much better than 5 percent."[33]

Notes

1. Hearing Before Judge Terry Lewis, Appendix to *Bush v. Gore*, "Brief on the Merits of Katherine Harris, Secretary of State," p. 11.
2. Ibid., p. 25.
3. Ibid., pp. 13-14.
4. Ibid., pp. 14, 12, 14.
5. Ibid., p. 25.
6. *Gore v. Harris*, 2nd Judicial Circuit, "Objection to and Supporting Memorandum Concerning Spoiled Miami-Dade Ballots," p. 1.
7. "Contest Trial Before Judge Sauls," p. 506, www.flcourts.org.
8. Ana Acle, "Miami Dade County 'Undervote' Ballots Separated," *Miami Herald*, November 20, 2000, p. A15.

9. "Hearing Before the Honorable Jorge LaBarga," November 22, 2000, p. 57. Courtesy of Gregory Barnhart.

10. *Gore v. Harris*, "Objection to and Supporting Memorandum," p. 9.

11. *Gore v. Harris*, "Order on Remand," p. 2, fn. 1.

12. Ibid., p. 3.

13. Ibid., p. 2.

14. Jeffrey Toobin, *Too Close to Call* (New York: Random House, 2001), p. 243.

15. *Gore v. Harris*, "Objections of Secretary of State and Elections Canvassing Commission," Appendix to Harris Brief.

16. Howard Gillman, *The Votes That Counted: How the Court Decided the 2000 Presidential Election* (Chicago: University of Chicago Press, 2001), p. 121; Toobin, *Too Close to Call*, p. 255.

17. *Gore v. Harris*, "Response of County Canvassing Board of Duval County to Court's Order," p. 3.

18. Robert Zelnick, *Winning Florida* (Stanford: Hoover Institution Press, 2001), pp. 143–144.

19. *Bush v. Gore*, "Emergency Application for a Stay of Enforcement of the Judgment Below," pp. 39–40.

20. *Bush v. Gore*, "Opposition of Respondent, Albert Gore Jr. to Emergency Motion for a Stay," p. 8.

21. *Bush v. Gore*, "Supplemental Memorandum in Support of Emergency Application," pp. 5–6 (italics added).

22. Laurence H. Tribe, "Comment," 110 *Harvard Law Review* (2001), pp. 170, 286.

23. *Bush v. Gore*, "Opposition of Respondent Albert Gore Jr.," p. 9.

24. *Bush v. Gore*, "Emergency Application for a Stay," 148 L Ed 2d 553.

25. Ibid., p. 554.

26. See *Michigan Coalition of Radioactive Material Users Inc. v. Griepentrag*, 945 F. 2d 150 (6th Cir. 1991); *Cuomo v. Nuclear Regulatory Commission*, 772 F. 2d 972 (D.C. Cir. 1985); see also Larry D. Kramer's brilliant essay, "The Supreme Court in Politics," in Jack N. Rakove (ed.), *The Unfinished Election of 2000* (New York: Basic Books, 2001), pp. 137–141.

27. Richard Posner, *Breaking the Deadlock: The 2000 Election, the Constitution, and the Courts* (Princeton, N.J.: Princeton University Press, 2001), p. 164, fn. 17.

28. *Bush v. Gore*, "Emergency Application for a Stay," p. 554.

29. Ibid.

30. Louis Michael Seidman, "What's So Bad About *Bush v. Gore*?" 47 *Wayne Law Review* (2001), pp. 953, 969–970.

31. *Bush v. Gore*, "Emergency Application for a Stay," p. 555 (italics added). Stevens is quoting from his own in-chambers opinion in *National Socialist Party of America v. Skokie*, 434 US 1327, 1328 (1977).

32. Toobin, *Too Close to Call*, p. 258.

33. David Kaplan, *The Accidental President* (New York: William Morrow, 2001), pp. 247, 250.

24

The Bush Brief in *Bush v. Gore*

Bush's attorneys argued vigorously that the Florida Supreme Court had distorted the contest statute in violation of Article II. They also expanded upon the equal-protection arguments that hadn't gotten past the certiorari brief in the previous trip to Washington. Possibly their most important claim was that the court-ordered recount proposed to examine undervotes, but none of the 110,000 overvotes.

The Bush team beclouded its case a bit, however, by relying upon a contention made originally only in the last stages of the litigation in Florida, that the state supreme court actually lacked jurisdiction to hear the contest appeal from Judge Sauls. The United States Supreme Court justices thought little of this notion, and Bush lawyers later acknowledged their mistake in bringing it up.

I-A. The Decision Below Overrides
Numerous Provisions of Florida Election Law....

[T]he decision below treats a contest as a *de novo* proceeding in which courts may treat the judgments of the canvassing boards and of the Secretary of State—including certification—as purely hortatory pronouncements. Those judgments thus become legally meaningless, since the circuit court *must* adjudicate the dispute without regard to any reasons, however compelling, that the canvassing boards or the executive may have had for certifying results as they did. Plaintiffs in the position of the Gore respondents thus need not "contest" the "*certification*," for the court will—indeed must—simply *ignore* it. In fact, under the ruling below, *certified* election returns are treated with *less* dignity than returns that have not been certified

From Brief for Petitioners, *Bush v. Gore,* www.supremecourtus.gov, pp. 21–25, 28–29, 40–44.

by either the county canvassing boards or the state election commission. While the *certified* election results from *all* other counties (except Broward and Volusia, where manual recounts produced over 700 additional Gore votes) are presumed *incorrect* and will be subject to *de novo* judicial review, the decision below requires that the *uncertified* results of manual recounts in Palm Beach County (adding 176 or 215 Gore votes) and Miami-Dade County (with 168 additional Gore votes based solely on partial results) be certified without *any* judicial review of their correctness (or any review of whether the certified results from these counties, in fact, "rejected legal votes").

The consequence of the court's ruling is nothing less than the evisceration of the internal coherence of the legislature's design. The legislature provided for canvassing boards, not courts, to count votes.... By revoking the canvassing board's legislatively conferred authority and ordering the *circuit court* to "commence the tabulation of the Miami-Dade ballots" and conduct its own *de novo* examination of which ballots are valid, the court below overrode the will of the legislature to repose responsibility for examining ballots in election officials with presumed expertise in this field (subject to the ultimate interpretive authority of the Secretary of State), and thereby violated Article II, § 1....

Moreover, the legislature clearly anticipated that some elections might be close, and clearly provided rules on how to deal with that situation. In particular, the legislature has never prescribed manual recounts as the exclusive, or even preferred, methodology for discerning the intent of voters or for distinguishing "legal" from "illegal" votes. Instead, when an initial count of the election results demonstrates that the margin of victory for a candidate is less than one-half of one percent, an *automatic* recount must take place, unless the losing candidate does not desire such a recount. *See* Fla. Stat. § 102.141(4). A manual recount *may* be ordered at the protest stage, subject to detailed requirements—including the requirement that "all ballots" must be counted when such a recount is ordered. *See* Fla. Stat. § 102.166. Under the scheme devised by the court below, however, there literally is no point in the safeguards provided for such recounts at the protest stage. Indeed, there is no point in any candidate or canvassing board *ever* going through the protest process or in conducting a manual recount. To achieve the result reached by the court below, the legislature might as well have dispensed with the bulk of the election code and simply provided for the shipment of all ballots to the circuit court immediately following the certification of the election results. Indeed, if Florida law could plausibly be read in the manner announced by the court below, the court's own earlier efforts—merely two weeks ago—to extend the certification deadline so as to permit additional manual recounts are completely inexplicable.

The Florida Supreme Court also approved the inclusion in the statewide election results of ballots (such as those from Broward County) that were counted as valid votes on the basis of mere "dimples" or indentations on the ballot. The Florida legislature has *never* provided that dimpled ballots should be counted as valid votes. To the contrary, counting "dimpled" ballots as valid votes violates the very statute relied on by the court below, Fla. Stat. § 101.5614(5), which requires "a *clear indication* of the intent of the voter as determined by the canvassing board" (emphasis added)....

I-B. Article II Precludes the Florida Supreme Court's Exercise of Jurisdiction

The Supreme Court of Florida lacked jurisdiction, as a matter of federal law, to enter the judgment below. Under Florida law, assuming *arguendo* that the legislature has authorized contest actions in presidential elections, only the circuit court possessed legislatively conferred jurisdiction to resolve the Gore respondents' claims. *See* Fla. Stat. § 102.168(1) (permitting election certifications to be "contested in the circuit court"); *id.* § 102.168(8) (authorizing "[t]he circuit judge to whom the contest is presented" to resolve contests).

By contrast, the Florida Legislature granted *no* such jurisdiction to the Florida Supreme Court—a point seemingly recognized by the court below, which rationalized its authority to overturn the circuit court's judgment on the sole basis of the Florida Constitution.... Article II, § 1 of the United States Constitution, however, does not permit state constitutions to circumscribe in any way a state legislature's selection of the manner of choosing presidential electors.... Thus, because the Florida *Legislature* has conferred no role in reviewing contests over the results of a presidential election on the Florida Supreme Court, the court below lacked authority to enter its judgment....

III. The Florida Supreme Court's Decision Violates Equal Protection and Due Process Guarantees

The Florida Supreme Court's decision is a recipe for electoral chaos. The court below has not only condoned a regime of arbitrary, selective and standardless manual recounts, but it has created a new series of unequal after-the-fact standards. This unfair, new process cannot be squared with the Constitution.

III-A. Equal Protection....

The Equal Protection Clause prohibits government officials from implementing an electoral system that gives the votes of similarly situated voters different effect based on the happenstance of the county or district in which those voters live....

As this Court has long recognized, the right to vote is "denied by a debasement or dilution of the weight of a citizen's vote just as effectively as by wholly prohibiting the free exercise of the franchise." *Reynolds*, 377 U.S. at 555.

[And] [a]s in...*Reynolds*, the necessarily disparate manual recounts ordered by the Florida Supreme Court arbitrarily treat voters differently based solely on where they happen to reside. For example, where there is a partial punch or stray mark on a ballot, that ballot may be counted as a "vote" in some counties but not others. The court's order also requires that ballots counted as part of the contest proceedings are evaluated under a different standard than ballots in other counties that have already completed manual recounts. Indeed, the "standards" used in those earlier manual recounts themselves constituted equal protection violations, since, to the extent "standards" existed at all, they varied widely from county to county, and even changed from day to day or hour to hour within a single Florida county....

In addition, the decision below manifestly violates equal protection by mandating the inclusion of 168 votes based on a manual recount of 20 percent of the ballots in Miami-Dade County (from predominantly Democratic precincts), while ordering that only approximately 9,000 of the remaining 80 percent of the ballots be recounted—even though many of those ballots were cast by voters in predominantly Hispanic (and Republican-leaning) precincts. This patent violation is compounded by the fact that the judgment below disenfranchises numerous voters in Miami-Dade County and elsewhere whose ballots were rejected by the machine count as so-called "over-votes" but might upon manual inspection reflect a clear intent to vote for a particular candidate....

The manual recount in Miami-Dade and the rest of the counties in Florida presents yet another intractable equal protection problem. The undisputed evidence at trial established that the very process of segregating undervotes from the rest of the ballots inevitably will identify as undervotes ballots that were *already counted* in the first (or second) machine counts, but not in the third pass through the machine. (34 precincts in Miami-Dade had more undervotes after segregating undervotes than were reported after the first recount.) Votes that have already been included in the count may be counted *again*, after examination, as undervotes. Such double-counting of votes is a plain dilution of the votes of the remaining voters in violation of the equal protection clause. That equal protection violation with respect to Miami-Dade has already occurred, and would be exacerbated if more ballots were counted. Moreover, the decision below orders the rest of the counties in Florida to engage in the same sort of selective manual recount. Some "undervotes" would be segregated in that process that have already been included in the certified count, with the result that some votes would be counted and included twice.

By requiring further inconsistent and standardless recounts, the court's order guarantees disparate treatment for similarly situated voters.

25

The Gore Brief

The brief submitted by Laurence Tribe and his associates decimated Bush's newfound jurisdictional argument, pointing out, among other things, that the new contest statute of 1999 was enacted against a "settled background" of Florida practice, mandating appellate review of circuit court trial decisions. This was an ironic reversal of roles, Gore's attorneys relying here on 102.168's codification of contest litigation, with no apparent concern about its effect on their view of "rejection of legal votes," and the Bush lawyers claiming codification of prior practice, so important to one phase of their Article II argument, was irrelevant to another.

Gore's brief did not attempt a detailed step-by-step rebuttal to *Bush* on the structure and purpose of the contest process. Its answer to the charge of equal-protection violations is vigorous and nuanced, but is based on a general defense of the intent of the voter standard, noting how, like the standard in negligence cases, it could permissibly vary in individual applications. There was no discussion of how widely variant local conditions could affect interpretations. Nor does the brief mention overvotes.

Tribe later contended that *Bush v. Gore* fell under the political-question doctrine, notwithstanding its equal-protection components. This can be legitimately debated, but in any event Tribe did not raise the matter in his brief, no doubt realizing it was useless.

From Brief of Respondent, *Bush v. Gore,* www.supremecourtus.gov, pp. 11, 13–16, 35–39, 41–46.

I. Article II Provides No Basis to
Override the Florida Supreme Court's Decision....

I-I. Recognizing that they have no good claim under the Article II theory presented to this Court just six days ago, petitioners now put forward a radical new proposition in the name of Article II: that the highest appellate court of the state may not exercise its ordinary appellate jurisdiction over decisions of lower state courts where its *jurisdiction* is granted by the state constitution rather than in legislation dealing specifically with presidential elections.

Even apart from the absurd theory that *McPherson* requires everything relevant to a state's process for choosing electors to be packed into a specialized presidential electoral code, the very premise of petitioner's argument is fatally flawed because the Florida Legislature re-enacted the contest statute in 1999 against the settled background rule that decisions of circuit courts in contest actions are subject to appellate review....

Even petitioners do not try to explain why the Legislature would have wanted to endow a single circuit judge with final authority to decide these cases. Instead, all indications are that the Legislature intended this statute to be governed by the settled principle of Florida law that the state supreme court has appellate jurisdiction over all matters determined in the lower courts unless the Legislature expressly precludes such review....

I-2. In any event, the Florida Legislature *itself* drafted, proposed, and approved through bicameral passage the very provisions of its constitution that provide for appellate jurisdiction....

Under Florida law, an amendment or revision to the state constitution may be undertaken "by joint resolution agreed to by three-fifths of the membership of each house of the legislature." Fla. Const. art II, § I. Pursuant to that method, the Legislature drafted, proposed, and approved the constitutional provision that confers jurisdiction on the state supreme court....

Nor is this [process invalidated] by the fact that state constitutional provisions in Florida, after proposal and passage by the Legislature, are ultimately ratified or adopted by the voters. Indeed, this Court has squarely held that the analogous constitutional provision in Article I, § 4, which vests state legislatures with the power to prescribe the manner for selecting representatives to Congress, is consistent with a legislative exercise of authority made subject to popular referenda. *See State ex rel. Davis v. Hildebrant*, 241 U.S. 565 (1916). [The decision upheld the application of a state law to a popular referendum on the state's congressional redistricting plan.]...

III. The Fourteenth Amendment
Affords No Basis for This Court to Set Aside
Florida's Established Statutory Proceedings for
Determining the Proper Outcome of the Election.

III-A. There Is No Violation of the Equal Protection Clause....

Petitioners' Fourteenth Amendment arguments rest principally on the assertion that, if the manual count proceeds, similar ballots will be treated dissimilarly in different parts of the State. We note that, insofar as this argument is directed at pre-contest tabulations, it is out of place here; petitioners should have raised such claims in an election contest of their own. But more fundamentally, petitioners' contention simply finds no support in the law, and has sweeping implications for the conduct of elections. The court below was quite insistent that the counting of ballots must be governed by a *single* uniform standard: the intent of the voter must control. Of course, so long as the count is conducted by humans, it undeniably will be possible to allege some degree of inconsistency in the treatment of individual ballots—as is the case whenever the application of any legal standard (*e.g.*, negligence, public forum) is at issue. That will be true in *every* one of the many jurisdictions that provide for manual recounts; it is true whenever States provide for variation in the methods of voting from county to county (*e.g.*, optical scanners as opposed to less reliable punch card ballots), which is now the case in *every* State; and it was true *everywhere* prior to the introduction of mechanical voting machines, when all ballots were counted by hand. Petitioners' theory would mean that all of these practices violate the Fourteenth Amendment. Moreover, if petitioners mean to say that all votes must be tabulated under a fixed and mechanical standard (*e.g.*, the "two-corner chad rule"), their approach would render unconstitutional the laws of States that hinge the meaning of the ballot on the intent of the voter—and also would mean that the Constitution requires the disenfranchisement of many voters whose intent is clearly discernible. This argument, in our view, is wholly insubstantial. Similar arguments regarding the conduct of elections uniformly have been rejected by the courts.

In any event, if the standard set out by the Florida court is not applied consistently, applicants will have recourse to the Leon County Circuit Court and, on appeal, to the Florida Supreme Court, either of which will be able to eliminate any inconsistency by determining itself which ballots meet the statutory standard.

1. The Florida Supreme Court's order to review the ballots from Miami-Dade County is consistent with established state law. The Florida Supreme Court's order to "remand this cause for the circuit court to immediately tabulate by hand the approximately 9,000 Miami-Dade ballots, which the counting machine registered as non-votes, but which have never been manually reviewed," was consistent with established state law for handling contest actions. As such, it raises no substantial federal questions....

Fashioning such a remedy in no way violates the U.S. Constitution in general, or its Equal Protection Clause specifically. Targeting the vote count to those ballots that had not registered on machines that were found not to be accurate by the trial court was a narrowly tailored remedy authorized under state law, that certainly does not discriminate against any group of voters on its face. Indeed, it is the exclusion of these ballots, not their inclusion, that would raise questions of unequal treatment. The Florida Supreme Court's order does nothing more than place the voters whose votes were not tabulated by the machine on the same footing as those whose votes were so tabulated....

2. The Florida Supreme Court's order of a manual tabulation of ballots that were recorded as "no votes" is consistent with state law. The gravamen of petitioners' complaint concerning the manual recount has been its selectivity. Yet, in this case, the Florida Supreme Court ordered not a "selective" recount but a *statewide* recount of undervotes in every Florida county that had not already completed a manual recount....

It is important to note that petitioners do not claim that the Florida Supreme Court's order is discriminatory in any invidious manner; they do not claim that any citizens of Florida were improperly denied their right to vote; and there is no claim of any fraudulent interference with the right of anyone to vote. Petitioners make none of these claims, which in certain circumstances have provided the basis for federal intervention in state election procedures and/or findings of invalidity of such procedures. Instead, petitioners' contention here seems to be that there is some constitutional defect in a state procedure that permits manual recounts to occur for some votes which may have been missed (undervotes), but not all votes (*i.e.*, votes that were effectively counted by automated processes). The Florida process, however, provides citizens of each county, and candidates for office within each county, with equal rights: No votes can be "diluted" in the constitutional sense by a process that seeks simply to count the legally cast votes of citizens participating in an election whose votes may not have been recognized by an initial machine count. All undervotes are treated the same way under the Florida Supreme Court's order. The Equal Protection Clause does not require that the Florida Supreme Court ignore the most accurately counted vote totals while seeking to ensure that all votes are counted.

The use of different vote tabulating systems undoubtedly will generate tabulation differences from county to county. But this will be true "[u]nless and until each electoral county in the United States uses the exact same

automatic tabulation (and even then there may be system malfunctions)."
Siegel v. LePore [120 F. Supp. 2d 1041, 1052]....

3. The "voter intent" standard set by Florida law does not violate the Equal Protection Clause.... [T]he contention that the "intent of the voter" standard violates equal protection (or due process) is nothing more than an argument that the contest and recount procedures of Florida's election code, which mirror those that have long existed in one form or another in numerous States, are on their face unconstitutional. Manual counting and recounting of ballots under the intent of the voter standard has been the *rule*, not the exception, in this country for generations—indeed, for most of the period since its founding....

Even in states that have adopted statutory guidelines to assist in ascertaining voter intent, the ultimate goal is to determine how a voter intended to vote. For example, the election code of Texas provides as follows:

(d) Subject to Subsection (e), in any manual count conducted under this code, a vote on a ballot on which a voter indicates a vote by punching a hole in the ballot may not be counted unless:
(1) at least two corners of the chad are detached:
(2) light is visible through the hole;
(3) an indentation on the chad from the stylus or other object is present and indicates a clearly *ascertainable intent of the voter* to vote; or
(4) the chad reflects by other means a clearly *ascertainable intent of the voter* to vote.
(e) Subsection (d) does not supersede any clearly *ascertainable intent of the voter.* Tex. Elec. Code § 127.130 (emphasis added).

The Oral Argument

The oral argument in *Bush v. Gore* on December 11 had a foredoomed air, with the participants aware they were probably just going through the motions. The most important development, potentially, was Justice Souter's, and Justice Breyer's, sympathy with the equal-protection claim of the petitioners, and their apparent attempt to get Anthony Kennedy to agree that the case could, and should, be sent back to Florida, even after December 12, for the purpose of setting uniform standards.

Both justices tried to get Theodore Olson and David Boies to identify what those standards might be. But Olson did not want to concede that an accurate count was doable, and David Boies had too much of a vested interest in the existing standard to abandon it now.

If Gore got any boost from the argument, it came from the distaste expressed by Justices Kennedy and O'Connor for Bush's jurisdictional claims. But the two also expressed distaste (along with Justice Scalia) for the entire performance of the Florida Supreme Court, Kennedy reiterating some of his concerns from the first oral argument.

David Boies was grilled on the overvotes by Chief Justice Rehnquist and several of his colleagues. Other jabs by the chief and Scalia pointed most directly to the ultimate resolution of *Bush v. Gore*.

On the afternoon of the oral argument, the Florida Supreme Court's decision on remand of *Bush v. Palm Beach* came down, too late to be a factor. The decision followed up on the indications in *Gore v. Harris* that December 12 was the date on which contests must end. In a footnote, the Florida justices repeated their reference to the "outside deadline set forth in 3 U.S.C. § 5 of December 12, 2000" (772 So. 2d 1273, 1290, fn. 22).

From The Oral Argument, *Bush v. Gore,* www.supremecourtus.gov, pp. 3, 5–7, 17–21, 23–24, 37–41, 43–44, 58, 61–70, 49–50, 52–54.

Oral Argument of Theodore B. Olson
on Behalf of the Petitioners

CHIEF JUSTICE REHNQUIST: We'll hear argument now on number 00-949, George W. Bush and Richard Cheney, versus Albert Gore, et al. Before we begin the arguments, the Court wishes to commend all of the parties to this case on their exemplary briefing under very trying circumstances. We greatly appreciate it. Mr. Olson....

JUSTICE O'CONNOR: [Y]ou think then there is no appellate review in the Supreme Court of what a circuit court does?

MR. OLSON: Certainly the legislature did not have to provide appellate review.

JUSTICE O'CONNOR: Well, but it seemed apparently to just include selection of electors in the general election law provisions. It assumed that they would all be lumped in together somehow....

MR. OLSON:...[But] [t]here is a specific grant of authority to the circuit courts. There is no reference to an appellate jurisdiction. It may not be the most powerful argument we bring to this Court.

JUSTICE KENNEDY: I think that's right.

MR. OLSON: Because notwithstanding, notwithstanding....

JUSTICE KENNEDY: Well, this is a serious business because it indicates how unmoored, untethered the legislature is from the constitution of its own state, and it makes every state law issue a federal question....

MR. OLSON:...[But] if you read the statutes...in the context of a presidential election, to stop this process at the circuit court, and not provide layers of appeal because given the time deadline, especially in the context of this election, the way it's played out, there is not time for an appellate court.

JUSTICE O'CONNOR: I have the same problem Justice Kennedy does, apparently, which is, I would have thought you could say that Article II certainly creates a presumption that the scheme the legislature has set out will be followed even by judicial review in election matters, and that 3 U.S. code section 5 likewise suggests that it may inform the reading of statutes crafted by the legislature so as to avoid having the law changed after the election. And I would have thought that that would be sufficient…to raise an appropriate federal question, rather than to say there's no judicial review here in Florida….

JUSTICE BREYER:…[I]f [the recount] were to start up again…, I understand that you think that the system that's set up now is very unfair because it's different standards in different places. What in your opinion would be a fair standard, on the assumption that it starts up missing the 12th deadline but before the 18th?

MR. OLSON: Well, one fair standard, and I don't know the complete answer to that, is that there would be a uniform way of evaluating the manner in which—there was Palm Beach, for example—

JUSTICE BREYER: All right, a uniform way of evaluating. What would the standard be, because this is one of your main arguments….

MR. OLSON: Well, the standard—

JUSTICE BREYER: You say the intent of the voter is not good enough. You want substandards….

MR. OLSON: Well, certainly at minimum, Justice Breyer, the penetration of the ballot card would be required. Now, that's why I mentioned the Palm Beach standard….

JUSTICE BREYER: [This is provided for] basically [in] Indiana. Is Indiana, in your opinion or pre—or 1990 Palm Beach, are either of those fair, or what else?

MR. OLSON: It's certainly a starting point….

JUSTICE SOUTER: If this were remanded to the Leon County Circuit Court and the judge of that court addressed the Secretary of State, who arguably either is or could be made a party, and said please tell us what the standard ought to be, we will be advised by your opinion, that would be feasible, wouldn't it?

MR. OLSON: I think it would be feasible....

JUSTICE BREYER: But I would still like to get your view as to what would be the fair standard.

MR. OLSON: Well, certainly one that would—I don't—I haven't crafted it entirely out. That is the job for a legislature.

JUSTICE BREYER: I would still like to get your opinion insofar as you could give it.

MR. OLSON: I think part of that standard is it would have to be applied uniformly. It...would have to be at minimum a penetration of the chad in the ballot, because indentations are no standards at all....

JUSTICE SOUTER:...Is it your position that if any official, judicial or executive, at this point were to purport to lay down a statewide standard which went to a lower level, a more specific level than intent of the voter, and said, for example, count dimpled chads or don't count dimpled chads. In your judgment, would that be a violation of Article II?...

MR. OLSON: If we went from the standard that existed before, the dimpled chads, that that had not been a standard anywhere in Florida, if that change was made, we would strongly urge that that would be a violation of Article II.... It would be a complete change.

JUSTICE SCALIA: It is also part of your case, is it not...that there is no wrong when a machine does not count those ballots that it's not supposed to count?

MR. OLSON: That's absolutely correct, Justice Scalia.

JUSTICE SCALIA: The voters are instructed to detach the chads entirely, and the machine, as predicted, does not count those chads where those instructions are not followed, there isn't any wrong.

MR. OLSON: That's correct, they've been euphemistically—this has been euphemistically referred to as legal votes that haven't been counted....

Oral Argument of David Boies
on Behalf of the Respondents

JUSTICE KENNEDY: The Supreme Court of Florida said that it took, that it was cognizant, *and the legislature was cognizant of* 3 U.S.C. Section 5....When the Supreme Court used that word, I assume it used it in a legal sense. Cognizance means to take jurisdiction of, to take authoritative notice. Why doesn't that constitute an acceptance by the Supreme Court of the proposition that 3 USC section 5 must be interpreted in this case?...

CHIEF JUSTICE REHNQUIST: There really—Mr. Boies, there are really two parts to that sentence of section 5 we're talking about. One is the law in effect at the time and the other is finally determined six days before the date for choosing the electors. Do you think the Florida court meant to acknowledge—it seems to me since it's cited generally, *they must have acknowledged both of those provisions.*

MR. BOIES: I don't know exactly what was in the Florida Supreme Court's mind, but I think that in general what the Florida Supreme Court made quite clear is that the thing that was constraining it was the desire to fit its remedy within the safe harbor provision....

JUSTICE KENNEDY: Let me ask, could the legislature of the State of Florida, after this election, have enacted a statute to change the contest period by truncating it by 19 days?...

MR. BOIES: I think that it would be unusual. I haven't really thought about that question. I think they probably could not—

JUSTICE KENNEDY: [B]ecause that would be a new law under section 5, wouldn't it?

MR. BOIES: Yes, because it would be a legislative enactment as opposed to a judicial interpretation of an existing law....

JUSTICE KENNEDY: But if we assume the legislature would run contrary to the new law prohibition in the statute, wouldn't the Supreme Court do it if it does exactly the same thing?

MR. BOIES: Except what I'm saying, Your Honor, is that it wasn't doing exactly the same thing because it wasn't passing a new law. It was interpreting the existing law. . . .

JUSTICE KENNEDY: I'm not sure why—if the legislature does it it's a new law and when the supreme court does it, it isn't....

JUSTICE O'CONNOR:...Does...not [Article II] mean that a court has to, in interpreting a legislative act, give special deference to the legislature's choices insofar as a presidential election is concerned? I would think that is a tenable view anyway....

MR. BOIES: I think, Your Honor, that if the Florida Supreme Court in interpreting the Florida law, I think the Court needs to take into account the fact that the legislature does have this plenary power. I think when the Florida Supreme Court does that, if it does so within the normal ambit of judicial interpretation, that is a subject for Florida's Supreme Court to take.

JUSTICE O'CONNOR: You are responding as though there were no special burden to show some deference to legislative choices. In this one context, not when courts review laws generally for general elections, but in the context of selection of presidential electors, isn't there a big red flag up there, watch out?

MR. BOIES: I think there is in a sense, Your Honor, and I think the Florida Supreme Court was grappling with that.

JUSTICE O'CONNOR: And you think it did it properly?

MR. BOIES: I think it did do it properly.

JUSTICE O'CONNOR: That's, I think, a concern that we have, and I did not find really a response by the Florida Supreme Court to this Court's remand in the case a week ago. It just seemed to kind of bypass it and assume that all those changes and deadlines were just fine and they would go ahead and adhere to them, and I found that troublesome....

MR. BOIES: [According to Judge Burton] another thing that they counted [in Palm Beach] was [this:] they discerned what voters sometimes did was instead of properly putting the ballot in where it was supposed to be, they laid it on top, and then what you would do is you would find the punches went not through the so-called chad, but through the number.

JUSTICE O'CONNOR: Well, why isn't the standard the one that voters are instructed to follow, for goodness sakes? I mean, it couldn't be clearer. I mean, why don't we go to that standard?...

MR. BOIES:...Now, I would point out that we asked to have the Miami-Dade ballots reviewed. We also asked to have the 3,300 Palm Beach ballots reviewed, but the supreme court said no to us on that. They said yes, you can have the 9,000 Miami-Dade ballots reviewed. They also said, which we didn't ask for, they said as a matter of remedy, we want to review the undervotes all around the state.

CHIEF JUSTICE REHNQUIST: Mr. Boies, one of the dissenting justices in the Supreme Court of Florida said that meant 177,000 ballots. Was he correct in your view?

MR. BOIES: No. That is a result of adding the so-called undervotes that were mentioned and the so-called overvotes that were mentioned....

CHIEF JUSTICE REHNQUIST: So if you disagree that 177,000 ballots will be involved in this recount, how many do you think there are?

MR. BOIES: It's approximately 60,000, I think, Your Honor. It turns out to be less than that because of the recounts that have already been completed, but I think the total sort of blank ballots for the presidency start at around 60,000.

JUSTICE STEVENS: Mr. Boies, can I ask, ask you this question. Does that mean there are 110,000 overvotes?

MR. BOIES: That's right.

JUSTICE STEVENS: And if that's the case, what is your response to the Chief Justice of Florida's concern that the recount relates only to undervotes and not overvotes?

MR. BOIES: Well first, nobody asked for a contest of the overvotes....

JUSTICE KENNEDY: But as a matter of remedy it's ordered a statewide recount in counties where the ballots were not contested, and that's where I'm having some difficulty, and it goes back to...the answer you are giving to Justice Stevens....Why is it that you say... these weren't part of the contest, but now all of a sudden we are talking about statewide, not all of which were contested, but we are not talking about the overvotes?...

MR. BOIES: There is nothing in the record that suggests that there are such votes. If anybody had contested the overvotes, it would have been a relatively simple process to test that because you could simply test it as to whether the double vote was a write-in vote or was another candidate.

CHIEF JUSTICE REHNQUIST: I gathered from the opinion of the Supreme Court of Florida that the Vice President did not ask for as broad a recount as the Supreme Court granted, but that it thought that to do just what he wanted would be unfair and therefore out of fairness, they granted the wider recount, am I correct in that?

MR. BOIES: I think that's right. I think that's the way I would interpret it, Mr. Chief Justice....

JUSTICE KENNEDY: My concern is that the contest period as we have been talking about requires the setting of standards, judicial review, and...this period has been truncated by 19 days, causing the time frame of which we are all so conscious, making it difficult for appellate review....

MR. BOIES:... It's absolutely clear under Florida law...what the contest is about, so at the contest stage, the only question is can you complete the contest of the contested ballots in the time available?
Everything that's in the record is, that we could have and indeed we still may be able to, if that count can go forward.

CHIEF JUSTICE REHNQUIST: Including appeals to the Supreme Court of Florida, and another petition to this Court?

MR. BOIES: Excuse me, Your Honor?

CHIEF JUSTICE REHNQUIST: I said after the circuit judge says that the contest comes out this way, surely there is going to be an appeal to the Supreme Court of Florida and likely another petition to this Court. *Surely that couldn't have been done by December 12th, could it?*

MR. BOIES: Your Honor, I think, I think the appeal to the Florida Supreme

Court could have and indeed the schedule that was set up would have made that quite possible. There is about another day or so, except for, except for four or five counties, all of the counties would be completed in about another day. And maybe even those counties could be now because as I understand it some of them have taken advantage of the time to get the procedures ready to count.

CHIEF JUSTICE REHNQUIST: Just a minute, Mr. Boies. Wouldn't the Supreme Court of Florida want briefs and wouldn't the parties have needed time to prepare briefs?

MR. BOIES: Yes, Your Honor, but as we did in this Court, we have done in the Florida Supreme Court a number of times and that is to do the briefs and have the argument the next day and a decision within 24 hours.

JUSTICE SCALIA: After the counts are conducted in the individual counties, wouldn't the Leon County circuit judge have to review those counts? After all, it's—I mean, the purpose of the scheme is to have a uniform determination.

MR. BOIES: To the extent that there are contested or disputed ballots—

JUSTICE SCALIA: Right.

MR. BOIES: —I think that may be so, Your Honor.

JUSTICE SCALIA: Well, wouldn't that take a fair amount of time and is that delegable? I assume he would have to do that personally.

MR. BOIES: We believe that it could be done in the time available....

JUSTICE SCALIA: Mr. Boies, would you explain to me again how the protest and the contest fits in. You said that the—let's assume that my complaint that I want to protest is the failure to do undercounts to those ballots that were undercounted, okay? That's my protest.

MR. BOIES: Right.

JUSTICE SCALIA: Why would I ever bring that in a protest proceeding? Why wouldn't I just go right to the contest because it doesn't matter whether I win or lose the protest proceeding. It's de novo at the contest stage. What possible advantage is there to go through the protest proceeding?

MR. BOIES: If you've identified the ballots, you could presumably wait and do it at the contest phase. There's no particular advantage to doing that. The fact—

JUSTICE O'CONNOR: I thought the advantage [of having a protest] might be as described in the Florida case, *Boardman v. Esteva*, saying that the certified election returns which occur after the protest period are presumptively correct, and they must be upheld unless clearly outside legal requirements. I thought that was Florida law.

MR. BOIES: Your Honor....

JUSTICE O'CONNOR: I think the Florida court has sort of ignored that old Boardman case....

(Earlier in Mr. Boies' argument, the following exchanges took place.)

JUSTICE KENNEDY: Do you think that in the contest phase, there must be a uniform standard for counting the ballots?

MR. BOIES: I do, Your Honor. I think there must be a uniform standard. I think there is a uniform standard.... The standard is whether or not the intent of the voter is reflected by the ballot. That is the uniform standard throughout the State of Florida.

JUSTICE KENNEDY: That's very general. It runs throughout the law. Even a dog knows the difference in being stumbled over and being kicked....
      In this case...what we are concerned with is an intent that focuses on this little piece of paper called a ballot, and...from the standpoint of [the] equal protection clause, could each county give their own interpretation to what intent means, so long as they are in good faith and with some reasonable basis finding intent?... Could that vary from county to county?

MR. BOIES: I think it can vary from individual to individual. I think that just as these findings—

JUSTICE KENNEDY: So that, so that even in one county can vary from table to table on counting these ballots?

MR. BOIES: I think on the margin, on the margin, Your Honor, whenever you are interpreting intent, whether it is in the criminal law, an administrative practice, whether it is in local government, whenever somebody is coming to government—

JUSTICE KENNEDY: But here you have something objective. You are not just reading a person's mind. You are looking at a piece of paper....

JUSTICE SOUTER: ...I think...what's bothering Justice Kennedy, Justice Breyer, me and others, is, we're assuming there's a category in which there just is no other—there is no subjective appeal. All we have are [ballots with] certain physical characteristics. Those physical characteristics we are told are being treated differently from county to county. In that case, where there is no subjective counter indication, isn't it a denial of equal protection to allow that variation?

MR. BOIES: I don't think, I don't think so, Your Honor.... Maybe if you had specific objective criteria in one county that says we're going to count indented ballots and another county that said we're only going to count the ballot if it is punched through. If you knew you had those two objective standards and they were different, then you might have an equal protection problem.

JUSTICE SOUTER: All right, [but] we're going to assume that we do have that. We can't send this thing back for more fact finding. If, if we respond to this issue and we believe that the issue is at least sufficiently raised to require a response, we've got to make the assumption, I think at this stage, that there may be such variation, and I think we would have a responsibility to tell the Florida courts what to do about it.
    On that assumption, what would you tell them to do about it?

MR. BOIES: Well, I think that's a very hard question.

JUSTICE SCALIA: You would tell them to count every vote.

MR. BOIES: I would tell them to count every vote....

JUSTICE STEVENS: Let me ask you this question, Mr. Boies. Is it really, does not the procedure that is in place there contemplate ... that the uniformity will be achieved by having the final results all reviewed by the same judge?

MR. BOIES: Yes, that's what I was going to say.

Final Judicial Opinions: *Bush v. Gore*

Soon after the oral argument, Chief Justice Rehnquist circulated a draft
of what he wanted to be the opinion of the Court in *Bush v. Gore*. It
was based on Article II grounds, and would have automatically ended
the Florida contest by decreeing that the state supreme court's election
law interpretations had usurped the legislature's prerogative of determining the "Manner" for appointment of presidential electors. Scalia
and Thomas quickly joined the opinion. Breyer, following up on the
concerns he and Souter raised during oral argument, crafted a compromise designed to snare either O'Connor's or, more likely, Kennedy's
vote. Justice Breyer agreed there were equal-protection concerns (not
violations necessarily), but proposed sending the case back to the
Florida courts for rectification of the problem. Justice Souter joined
him in this conclusion, though his eventual opinion did cite equal-protection violations.

But O'Connor and Kennedy went their own decisive way. In an
opinion eventually headed per curiam, but expressing in full only those
two justices' views, they decided that Florida's recount system did
indeed violate the equal-protection clause. They seized above all upon
the lack of uniform standards for the counting of the ballots, and the
fact that undervotes could be retrieved by the manual recount, but not
overvotes. The opinion (apparently written by Kennedy) also seized on
the egregious action by the Florida Supreme Court in adding Miami-
Dade votes to the certification with no certainty the county totals
would ever be complete.

It criticized in addition the logistical arrangements for the recount

From Final Judicial Opinions: *Bush v. Gore,* 148 LEd 2d 388, 398–402, 403–409,
409–413, 413–417, 417–418, 420–423, 423–425, 428–431.

decreed by Judge Lewis, but this seemed to raise questions under the due process clause of the Fourteenth Amendment rather than under the equal-protection clause.

The language on overvotes was a bit equivocal; still, the opinion made it extremely unlikely they could be ignored if there were further recount proceedings.

But there was in fact no way to fix the Florida system according to Kennedy, because of the Florida legislature's definite intention to take advantage of the safe-harbor option offered by Section 5. Hence, the uncompleted contest proceedings must end.

Rehnquist, Scalia, and Thomas joined the opinion, agreeing with its views on the December 12 deadline, and turning Rehnquist's original effort into a concurrence. Predictably, neither the per curiam opinion nor the concurrence mentioned the political-question doctrine.

While not claiming that Congress possessed exclusive authority to decide presidential election disputes, Justice Breyer's dissent argued strongly that as a matter of prudence the justices should have exercised restraint and not accepted the Bush-Gore controversy (a point with which all the dissenters agreed). Justice Souter offered the most succinct critique of Rehnquist's foray into the Florida statutes, though Breyer also dealt with this issue.

Justices Stevens and Ginsburg dissented from all aspects of the per curiam opinion and the concurrence. Ginsburg focused on the deference normally paid by the Supreme Court to state court interpretations of state law. Justice Stevens penned a particularly vehement and controversial denunciation of his colleagues' actions (joined by Breyer as well as by Ginsburg).

Except for Breyer, none of the dissenters addressed the majority's logic on the December 12 issue.

The opinions in *Bush* were distributed at 10 P.M. on Tuesday, December 12.

Bush v. Gore, Per Curiam

II-B

The individual citizen has no federal constitutional right to vote for electors for the President of the United States unless and until the state legislature chooses a statewide election as the means to implement its power to appoint members of the Electoral College. U.S. Const., Art. II, § 1. This is the source for the statement in *McPherson v. Blacker*, 146 U.S. 1, 35 (1892), that the State legislature's power to select the manner for appointing electors is plenary; it may, if it so chooses, select the electors itself.... History has now favored the voter, and in each of the several States the citizens themselves vote for Presidential electors. When the state legislature vests the right to vote for President in its people, the right to vote as the legislature has prescribed is fundamental; and one source of its fundamental nature lies in the equal weight accorded to each vote and the equal dignity owed to each voter. The State, of course, after granting the franchise in the special context of Article II, can take back the power to appoint electors....

[But] [t]he right to vote is protected in more than the initial allocation of the franchise. Equal protection applies as well to the manner of its exercise. Having once granted the right to vote on equal terms, the State may not, by later arbitrary and disparate treatment, value one person's vote over that of another. See, *e.g., Harper v. Virginia Board of Elections*, 383 U.S. 663, 665 (1966) ("[O]nce the franchise is granted to the electorate, lines may not be drawn which are inconsistent with the Equal Protection Clause of the Fourteenth Amendment"). It must be remembered that "the right of suffrage can be denied by a debasement or dilution of the weight of a citizen's vote just as effectively as by wholly prohibiting the free exercise of the franchise." *Reynolds v. Sims*, 377 U.S. 533, 555 (1964).

There is no difference between the two sides of the present controversy on these basic propositions. Respondents say that the very purpose of vindicating the right to vote justifies the recount procedures now at issue. The question before us, however, is whether the recount procedures the Florida Supreme Court has adopted are consistent with its obligation to avoid arbitrary and disparate treatment of the members of its electorate.

Much of the controversy seems to revolve around ballot cards designed to be perforated by a stylus but which, either through error or deliberate omission, have not been perforated with sufficient precision for a machine to count them. In some cases a piece of the card—a chad—is hanging, say by two corners. In other cases there is no separation at all, just an indentation.

The Florida Supreme Court has ordered that the intent of the voter be discerned from such ballots. For purposes of resolving the equal protection challenge, it is not necessary to decide whether the Florida Supreme Court had the authority under the legislative scheme for resolving election disputes to define what a legal vote is and to mandate a manual recount implementing that definition. The recount mechanisms implemented in response to the decisions of the Florida Supreme Court do not satisfy the minimum requirement for non-arbitrary treatment of voters necessary to secure the fundamental right. Florida's basic command for the count of legally cast votes is to consider the "intent of the voter."... This is unobjectionable as an abstract proposition and a starting principle. The problem inheres in the absence of specific standards to ensure its equal application. The formulation of uniform rules to determine intent based on these recurring circumstances is practicable and, we conclude, necessary.

The law does not refrain from searching for the intent of the actor in a multitude of circumstances; and in some cases the general command to ascertain intent is not susceptible to much further refinement. In this instance, however, the question is not whether to believe a witness but how to interpret the marks or holes or scratches on an inanimate object, a piece of cardboard or paper which, it is said, might not have registered as a vote during the machine count. The factfinder confronts a thing, not a person. The search for intent can be confined by specific rules designed to ensure uniform treatment.

The want of those rules here has led to unequal evaluation of ballots in various respects.... As seems to have been acknowledged at oral argument, the standards for accepting or rejecting contested ballots might vary not only from county to county but indeed within a single county from one recount team to another.

The record provides some examples. A monitor in Miami-Dade County testified at trial that he observed that three members of the county canvassing board applied different standards in defining a legal vote.... And testimony at trial also revealed that at least one county changed its evaluative standards during the counting process. Palm Beach County, for example, began the process with a 1990 guideline which precluded counting completely attached chads, switched to a rule that considered a vote to be legal if any light could be seen through a chad, changed back to the 1990 rule, and then abandoned any pretense of a *per se* rule, only to have a court order that the county consider dimpled chads legal. This is not a process with sufficient guarantees of equal treatment....

The State Supreme Court ratified this uneven treatment. It mandated that the recount totals from two counties, Miami-Dade and Palm Beach, be included in the certified total. The court also appeared to hold *sub silentio* that the recount totals from Broward County, which were not completed until after the original November 14 certification by the Secretary of State, were to be considered part of the new certified vote totals even though the county certification was not contested by Vice President Gore. Yet each of the counties used varying standards to determine what was a legal vote. Broward County used a more forgiving standard than Palm Beach County, and uncovered almost three times as many new votes, a result markedly disproportionate to the difference in population between the counties.

In addition, the recounts in these three counties were not limited to so-called undervotes but extended to all of the ballots. The distinction has real consequences. A manual recount of all ballots identifies not only those ballots which show no vote but also those which contain more than one, the so-called overvotes. Neither category will be counted by the machine. This is not a trivial concern. At oral argument, respondents estimated there are as many as 110,000 overvotes statewide. As a result, the citizen whose ballot was not read by a machine because he failed to vote for a candidate in a way readable by a machine may still have his vote counted in a manual recount; on the other hand, the citizen who marks two candidates in a way discernable by the machine will not have the same opportunity to have his vote count, even if a manual examination of the ballot would reveal the requisite indicia of intent. Furthermore, the citizen who marks two candidates, only one of which is discernable by the machine, will have his vote counted even though it should have been read as an invalid ballot. The State Supreme Court's inclusion of vote counts based on these variant standards exemplifies concerns with the remedial processes that were under way.

That brings the analysis to yet a further equal protection problem. The votes certified by the court included a partial total from one county, Miami-Dade. The Florida Supreme Court's decision thus gives no assurance that the recounts included in a final certification must be complete. Indeed, it is respondent's submission that it would be consistent with the rules of the recount procedures to include whatever partial counts are done by the time of final certification, and we interpret the Florida Supreme Court's decision to permit this (noting "practical difficulties" may control outcome of election, but certifying partial Miami-Dade total nonetheless). This accommodation no doubt results from the truncated contest period established by the Florida Supreme Court in *Bush I*, at respondent's own urging. The press of time does not diminish the constitutional concern. A desire for speed is not a general excuse for ignoring equal protection guarantees.

In addition to these difficulties the actual process by which the votes were to be counted under the Florida Supreme Court's decision raises further concerns. That order did not specify who would recount the ballots. The county canvassing boards were forced to pull together ad hoc teams comprised of judges from various Circuits who had no previous training in handling and interpreting ballots. Furthermore, while others were permitted to observe, they were prohibited from objecting during the recount.

The recount process, in its features here described, is inconsistent with the minimum procedures necessary to protect the fundamental right of each voter in the special instance of a statewide recount under the authority of a single state judicial officer. Our consideration is limited to the present circumstances, for the problem of equal protection in election processes generally presents many complexities.

The question before the Court is not whether local entities, in the exercise of their expertise, may develop different systems for implementing elections. Instead, we are presented with a situation where a state court with the power to assure uniformity has ordered a statewide recount with minimal procedural safeguards. When a court orders a statewide remedy, there must be at least some assurance that the rudimentary requirements of equal treatment and fundamental fairness are satisfied.

Given the Court's assessment that the recount process underway was probably being conducted in an unconstitutional manner, the Court stayed the order directing the recount so it could hear this case and render an expedited decision. The contest provision, as it was mandated by the State Supreme Court, is not well calculated to sustain the confidence that all citizens must have in the outcome of elections. The State has not shown that its procedures include the necessary safeguards. The problem, for instance, of the estimated 110,000 overvotes has not been addressed, although Chief Justice Wells called attention to the concern in his dissenting opinion....

Upon due consideration of the difficulties identified to this point, it is obvious that the recount cannot be conducted in compliance with the requirements of equal protection and due process without substantial additional work. It would require not only the adoption (after opportunity for argument) of adequate statewide standards for determining what is a legal vote, and practicable procedures to implement them, but also orderly judicial review of any disputed matters that might arise. In addition, the Secretary of State has advised that the recount of only a portion of the ballots requires that the vote tabulation equipment be used to screen out undervotes, a function for which the machines were not designed. *If a recount of overvotes were also required,* perhaps even a second screening would be necessary. [Italics added.] Use of the equipment for this purpose, and any new software developed for it, would have to be evaluated for accuracy by the Secretary of State....

The Supreme Court of Florida has said that the legislature intended the State's electors to "participat[e] fully in the federal electoral process," as provided in 3 U.S.C. § 5.... That statute, in turn, requires that any controversy or contest that is designed to lead to a conclusive selection of electors be completed by December 12. That date is upon us, and there is no recount procedure in place under the State Supreme Court's order that comports with minimal constitutional standards. Because it is evident that any recount seeking to meet the December 12 date will be unconstitutional for the reasons we have discussed, we reverse the judgment of the Supreme Court of Florida ordering a recount to proceed.

Seven Justices of the Court agree that there are constitutional problems with the recount ordered by the Florida Supreme Court that demand a remedy.... The only disagreement is as to the remedy. Because the Florida Supreme Court has said that the Florida Legislature intended to obtain the safe-harbor benefits of 3 U.S. C. § 5, JUSTICE BREYER's proposed remedy—remanding to the Florida Supreme Court for its ordering of a constitutionally proper contest until December 18—contemplates action in violation of the Florida election code, and hence could not be part of an "appropriate" order authorized by Fla. Stat. § 102.168 (8) (2000).

None are more conscious of the vital limits on judicial authority than are the members of this Court, and none stand more in admiration of the Constitution's design to leave the selection of the President to the people, through their legislatures, and to the political sphere. When contending parties invoke the process of the courts, however, it becomes our unsought responsibility to resolve the federal and constitutional issues the judicial system has been forced to confront.

The judgment of the Supreme Court of Florida is reversed, and the case is remanded for further proceedings not inconsistent with this opinion....

It is so ordered.

Chief Justice Rehnquist, Concurring
(Joined by Justices Scalia and Thomas)

We join the *per curiam* opinion. We write separately because we believe there are additional grounds that require us to reverse the Florida Supreme Court's decision.

I

We deal here not with an ordinary election, but with an election for the President of the United States....

In most cases, comity and respect for federalism compel us to defer to the decisions of state courts on issues of state law. That practice reflects our understanding that the decisions of state courts are definitive pronouncements of the will of the States as sovereigns. Cf. *Erie R. Co. v. Tompkins*, 304 U.S. 64 (1938). Of course, in ordinary cases, the distribution of powers among the branches of a State's government raises no questions of federal constitutional law, subject to the requirement that the government be republican in character. See U.S. Const., Art. IV, § 4. But there are a few exceptional cases in which the Constitution imposes a duty or confers a power on a particular branch of a State's government. This is one of them. Article II, § 1, cl. 2, provides that "[e]ach State shall appoint, in such Manner as the *Legislature* thereof may direct," electors for President and Vice President. [Italics added.] Thus, the text of the election law itself, and not just its interpretation by the courts of the States, takes on independent significance....

In order to determine whether a state court has infringed upon the legislature's authority, we necessarily must examine the law of the State as it existed prior to the action of the court. Though we generally defer to state courts on the interpretation of state law...there are of course areas in which the Constitution requires this Court to undertake an independent, if still deferential, analysis of state law.

For example, in *NAACP v. Alabama ex. rel. Patterson*, 357 U.S. 449

(1958), it was argued that we were without jurisdiction because the petitioner had not pursued the correct appellate remedy in Alabama's state
courts. Petitioners had sought a state-law writ of certiorari in the Alabama
Supreme Court when a writ of mandamus, according to that court, was
proper. We found this state-law ground inadequate to defeat our jurisdiction
because we were "unable to reconcile the procedural holding of the
Alabama Supreme Court" with prior Alabama precedent. *Id.*, at 456. The
purported state-law ground was so novel, in our independent estimation,
that "petitioner could not fairly be deemed to have been apprised of its
existence." *Id.*, at 457.

Six years later we decided *Bouie v. City of Columbia*, 378 U.S. 347
(1964), in which the state court had held, contrary to precedent, that the
state trespass law applied to black sit-in demonstrators who had consent to
enter private property but were then asked to leave. Relying upon *NAACP*,
we concluded that the South Carolina Supreme Court's interpretation of a
state penal statute had impermissibly broadened the scope of that statute
beyond what a fair reading provided, in violation of due process. See 378
U.S., at 361-362. What we would do in the present case is precisely parallel: Hold that the Florida Supreme Court's interpretation of the Florida
election laws impermissibly distorted them beyond what a fair reading
required, in violation of Article II. [An accompanying footnote says in part:
In one of our oldest cases, we similarly made an independent evaluation of
state law in order to protect federal treaty guarantees. In *Fairfax's Devisee
v. Hunter's Lessee*, 7 Cranch 603 (1813), we disagreed with the Supreme
Court of Appeals of Virginia that a 1782 state law had extinguished the
property interests of one Denny Fairfax, so that a 1789 ejectment order
against Fairfax supported by a 1785 state law did not constitute a future
confiscation under the 1783 peace treaty with Great Britain.]

This inquiry does not imply a disrespect for state *courts* but rather a
respect for the constitutionally prescribed role of state *legislatures*. To
attach definitive weight to the pronouncement of a state court, when the
very question at issue is whether the court has actually departed from the
statutory meaning, would be to abdicate our responsibility to enforce the
explicit requirements of Article II.

II....

In its first decision, *Palm Beach Canvassing Bd. v. Harris*,...the Florida
Supreme Court extended the 7-day statutory certification deadline established by the legislature. This modification of the code, by lengthening the
protest period, necessarily shortened the contest period for Presidential
elections. Underlying the extension of the certification deadline and the
shortchanging of the contest period was, presumably, the clear implication

that certification was a matter of significance: The certified winner would enjoy presumptive validity, making a contest proceeding by the losing candidate an uphill battle. In its latest opinion, however, the court empties certification of virtually all legal consequence during the contest, and in doing so departs from the provisions enacted by the Florida Legislature.

The court determined that canvassing boards' decisions regarding whether to recount ballots past the certification deadline (even the certification deadline established by *Harris I*) are to be reviewed *de novo*.... Moreover, the Florida court held that all late vote tallies arriving during the contest period should be automatically included in the certification regardless of the certification deadline..., thus virtually eliminating both the deadline and the Secretary's discretion to disregard recounts that violate it.

Moreover, the court's interpretation of "legal vote," and hence its decision to order a contest-period recount, plainly departed from the legislative scheme. Florida statutory law cannot reasonably be thought to *require* the counting of improperly marked ballots. Each Florida precinct before election day provides instructions on how properly to cast a vote.... In precincts using punch-card ballots, voters are instructed to punch out the ballot cleanly:

> AFTER VOTING, CHECK YOUR BALLOT CARD TO BE SURE YOUR VOTING SELECTIONS ARE CLEARLY AND CLEANLY PUNCHED AND THERE ARE NO CHIPS LEFT HANGING ON THE BACK OF THE CARD....

No reasonable person would call it "an error in the vote tabulation," FLA. STAT. § 102.166 (5), or a "rejection of legal votes," FLA. STAT. § 102.168 (3) (c), when electronic or electromechanical equipment performs precisely in the manner designed, and fails to count those ballots that are not marked in the manner that these voting instructions explicitly and prominently specify. [An accompanying footnote states: It is inconceivable that what constitutes a vote that must be counted under the "error in the vote tabulation" language of the protest phase is different from what constitutes a vote that must be counted under the "legal votes" language of the contest phase.] The scheme that the Florida Supreme Court's opinion attributes to the legislature is one in which machines are *required* to be "capable of correctly counting votes," § 101.5606 (4), but which nonetheless regularly produces elections in which legal votes are predictably *not* tabulated, so that in close elections manual recounts are regularly required. This is of course absurd. The Secretary of State, who is authorized by law to issue binding interpretations of the election code...rejected this peculiar reading of the statutes.... The Florida Supreme Court, although it must defer to the Secretary's interpretations...rejected her reasonable interpretation and embraced the peculiar one....

But as we indicated in our remand of the earlier case, in a Presidential election the clearly expressed intent of the legislature must prevail. And there is no basis for reading the Florida statutes as requiring the counting of improperly marked ballots, as an examination of the Florida Supreme Court's textual analysis shows. We will not parse that analysis here, except to note that the principal provision of the election code on which it relied, § 101.5614 (5), was, as the Chief Justice pointed out in his dissent from *Harris II*, entirely irrelevant.... The State's Attorney General (who was supporting the Gore challenge) confirmed in oral argument here that never before the present election had a manual recount been conducted on the basis of the contention that "undervotes" should have been examined to determine voter intent [as documented in *Broward County Canvassing Board v. Hogan*, 607 So. 2d 508-509]....

III

The scope and nature of the remedy ordered by the Florida Supreme Court jeopardizes the "legislative wish" to take advantage of the safe harbor provided by 3 U.S.C. § 5.... December 12, 2000, is the last date for a final determination of the Florida electors that will satisfy § 5....

Surely when the Florida Legislature empowered the courts of the State to grant "appropriate" relief, it must have meant relief that would have become final by the cut-off date of 3 U.S.C. § 5. In light of the inevitable legal challenges and ensuing appeals to the Supreme Court of Florida and petitions for certiorari to this Court, the entire recounting process could not possibly be completed by that date.

Dissent of Justice Stevens
(Joined by Justices Ginsburg and Breyer)

[P]etitioners...are [not] correct in asserting that the failure of the Florida Supreme Court to specify in detail the precise manner in which the "intent of the voter"...is to be determined rises to the level of a constitutional violation. We found such a violation when individual votes within the same State were weighted unequally, see, *e.g., Reynolds v. Sims*, 377 U.S. 533, 568 (1964), but we have never before called into question the substantive standard by which a State determines that a vote has been legally cast. And there is no reason to think that the guidance provided to the fact-finders, specifically the various canvassing boards, by the "intent of the voter" standard is any less sufficient—or will lead to results any less uniform—than, for example, the "beyond a reasonable doubt" standard employed everyday by ordinary citizens in courtrooms across this country.

Admittedly, the use of differing substandards for determining voter intent in different counties employing similar voting systems may raise serious concerns. Those concerns are alleviated—if not eliminated—by the fact that a single impartial magistrate will ultimately adjudicate all objections arising from the recount process. Of course, as a general matter, "[t]he interpretation of constitutional principles must not be too literal. We must remember that the machinery of government would not work if it were not allowed a little play in its joints." *Bain Peanut Co. of Tex. v. Pinson*, 282 U.S. 499, 501 (1931) (Holmes, J.). If it were otherwise, Florida's decision to leave to each county the determination of what balloting system to employ—despite enormous differences in accuracy—might run afoul of equal protection. So, too, might the similar decisions of the vast majority of state legislatures to delegate to local authorities certain decisions with respect to voting systems and ballot design.

Even assuming that aspects of the remedial scheme might ultimately be found to violate the Equal Protection Clause, I could not subscribe to the majority's disposition of the case.... [T]he appropriate course of action would be to remand to allow a more specific general standard to be established.

In the interest of finality, however, the majority effectively orders the disenfranchisement of an unknown number of voters whose ballots reveal their intent—and are therefore legal votes under state law—but were for some reason rejected by ballot-counting machines. It does so on the basis of the deadlines set forth in Title 3 of the United States Code. *Ante*, at 11. But…those provisions merely provide rules of decision for Congress to follow when selecting among conflicting slates of electors…. They do not prohibit a State from counting what the majority concedes to be legal votes until a bona fide winner is determined….Thus, nothing prevents the majority, even if it properly found an equal protection violation, from ordering relief appropriate to remedy that violation without depriving Florida voters of their right to have their votes counted….

Finally, neither in this case, nor in its earlier opinion in *Palm Beach County Canvassing Bd. v. Harris*…did the Florida Supreme Court make any substantive change in Florida electoral law. Its decisions were rooted in long-established precedent and were consistent with the relevant statutory provisions, taken as a whole. It did what courts do—it decided the case before it in light of the legislature's intent to leave no legally cast vote uncounted. In so doing, it relied on the sufficiency of the general "intent of the voter" standard articulated by the state legislature, coupled with a procedure for ultimate review by an impartial judge, to resolve the concern about disparate evaluations of contested ballots. If we assume—as I do—that the members of that court and the judges who would have carried out its mandate are impartial, its decision does not even raise a colorable federal question.

What must underlie petitioners' entire federal assault on the Florida election procedures is an unstated lack of confidence in the impartiality and capacity of the state judges who would make the critical decisions if the vote count were to proceed. Otherwise, their position is wholly without merit. The endorsement of that position by the majority of this Court can only lend credence to the most cynical appraisal of the work of judges throughout the land. It is confidence in the men and women who administer the judicial system that is the true backbone of the rule of law. Time will one day heal the wound to that confidence that will be inflicted by today's decision. One thing, however, is certain. Although we may never know with complete certainty the identity of the winner of this year's Presidential election, the identity of the loser is perfectly clear. It is the Nation's confidence in the judge as an impartial guardian of the rule of law.

I respectfully dissent.

Dissent of Justice Souter
(Joined by Justice Breyer, and Joined by Justices Stevens and Ginsburg with Regard to All Except Part C [the Equal Protection Section])

The Court should not have reviewed either *Bush v. Palm Beach County Canvassing Bd., ante* . . . (*per curiam*), or this case, and should not have stopped Florida's attempt to recount all undervote ballots...by issuing a stay of the Florida Supreme Court's orders during the period of this review.... If this Court had allowed the State to follow the course indicated by the opinions of its own Supreme Court, it is entirely possible that there would ultimately have been no issue requiring our review, and political tension could have worked itself out in the Congress following the procedure provided in 3 U.S.C § 15. The case being before us, however, its resolution by the majority is another erroneous decision....

There are three issues: whether the State Supreme Court's interpretation of the statute providing for a contest of the state election results somehow violates 3 U.S.C. § 5; whether that court's construction of the state statutory provisions governing contests impermissibly changes a state law from what the State's legislature has provided, in violation of Article II, § 1, cl. 2, of the national Constitution; and whether the manner of interpreting markings on disputed ballots failing to cause machines to register votes for President (the undervote ballots) violates the equal protection or due process guaranteed by the Fourteenth Amendment. None of these issues is difficult to describe or to resolve.

A

The 3 U.S.C. § 5 issue is not serious. That provision sets certain conditions for treating a State's certification of Presidential electors as conclusive in the event that a dispute over recognizing those electors must be resolved in the Congress under 3 U.S.C. § 15. Conclusiveness requires selection under a legal scheme in place before the election, with results determined at least six days before the date set for casting electoral votes. But no State is required to conform to § 5 if it cannot do that (for whatever reason); the sanction for failing to satisfy the conditions of § 5 is simply loss of what has been called its "safe harbor." And even that determination is to be made, if made anywhere, in the Congress.

B

The second matter here goes to the State Supreme Court's interpretation of certain terms in the state statute governing election "contests," Fla. Stat. § 102.168 (2000); there is no question here about the state court's interpretation of the related provisions dealing with the antecedent process of "protesting" particular vote counts, § 102.166, which was involved in the previous case, *Bush v. Palm Beach County Canvassing Board.* The issue is whether the judgment of the state supreme court has displaced the state legislature's provisions for election contests....

The starting point for evaluating the claim that the Florida Supreme Court's interpretation effectively rewrote § 102.168 must be the language of the provision on which Gore relies to show his right to raise this contest: that the previously certified result in Bush's favor was produced by "rejection of a number of legal votes sufficient to change or place in doubt the results of the election." Fla. Stat. § 102.168 (3) (c) (2000)....

B-1. The statute does not define a "legal vote," the rejection of which may affect the election. The State Supreme Court was therefore required to define it, and in doing that the court looked to another election statute, § 101.5614 (5), dealing with damaged or defective ballots, which contains a provision that no vote shall be disregarded "if there is a clear indication of the intent of the voter as determined by a canvassing board." The court read that objective of looking to the voter's intent as indicating that the legislature probably meant "legal vote" to mean a vote recorded on a ballot indicating what the voter intended.... It is perfectly true that the majority might have chosen a different reading. See, *e.g.*, Brief for Respondent Harris et al. 10 (defining "legal votes" as "votes properly executed in accordance with the instructions provided to all registered voters in advance of the election and in the polling places"). But even so, there is no constitutional violation in following the majority view; Article II is unconcerned with mere disagreements about interpretative merits.

B-2. The Florida court next interpreted "rejection" to determine what act in the counting process may be attacked in a contest. Again, the statute does not define the term. The court majority read the word to mean simply a failure to count.... That reading is certainly within the bounds of common sense, given the objective to give effect to a voter's intent if that can be determined. A different reading, of course, is possible. The majority might have concluded that "rejection" should refer to machine malfunction, or that a ballot should not be treated as "reject[ed]" in the absence of wrong-doing by election officials, lest contests be so easy to claim that every election will end up in one…. There is, however, nothing nonjudicial in the Florida majority's more hospitable reading.

B-3.   The same is true about the court majority's understanding of the phrase "votes sufficient to change or place in doubt" the result of the election in Florida. The court held that if the uncounted ballots were so numerous that it was reasonably possible that they contained enough "legal" votes to swing the election, this contest would be authorized by the statute. While the majority might have thought (as the trial judge did) that a probability, not a possibility, should be necessary to justify a contest, that reading is not required by the statute's text, which says nothing about probability. Whatever people of good will and good sense may argue about the merits of the Florida court's reading, there is no warrant for saying that it transcends the limits of reasonable statutory interpretation to the point of supplanting the statute enacted by the "legislature" within the meaning of Article II.

In sum, the interpretations by the Florida court raise no substantial question under Article II….

C

It is only on the third issue before us that there is a meritorious argument for relief, as the Court's *Per Curiam* opinion recognizes. It is an issue that might well have been dealt with adequately by the Florida courts if the state proceedings had not been interrupted, and if not disposed of at the state level it could have been considered by the Congress in any electoral vote dispute. But because the course of state proceedings has been interrupted, time is short, and the issue is before us, I think it sensible for the Court to address it.

Petitioners have raised an equal protection claim…in the charge that unjustifiably disparate standards are applied in different electoral jurisdictions to otherwise identical facts. It is true that the Equal Protection Clause does not forbid the use of a variety of voting mechanisms within a jurisdiction, even though different mechanisms will have different levels of effectiveness in recording voters' intentions; local variety can be justified by concerns about cost, the potential value of innovation, and so on. But evidence in the record here suggests that a different order of disparity obtains under rules for determining a voter's intent that have been applied (and could continue to be applied) to identical types of ballots used in identical brands of machines and exhibiting identical physical characteristics (such as "hanging" or "dimpled" chads).... I can conceive of no legitimate state interest served by these differing treatments of the expressions of voters' fundamental rights. The differences appear wholly arbitrary.

In deciding what to do about this, we should take account of the fact that electoral votes are due to be cast in six days. I would therefore remand the case to the courts of Florida with instructions to establish uniform standards for evaluating the several types of ballots that have prompted differing treatments, to be applied within and among counties when passing on such identical ballots in any further recounting (or successive recounting) that the courts might order.

Unlike the majority, I see no warrant for this Court to assume that Florida could not possibly comply with this requirement before the date set for the meeting of electors, December 18. Although one of the dissenting justices of the State Supreme Court estimated that disparate standards potentially affected 170,000 votes,...the number at issue is significantly smaller. The 170,000 figure apparently represents all uncounted votes, both undervotes...and overvotes.... But as JUSTICE BREYER has pointed out, no showing has been made of legal overvotes uncounted, and counsel for Gore made an uncontradicted representation to the Court that the statewide total of undervotes is about 60,000.... To recount these manually would be a tall order, but before this Court stayed the effort to do that the courts of Florida were ready to do their best to get that job done. There is no justification for denying the State the opportunity to try to count all disputed ballots now. I respectfully dissent.

Dissent of Justice Ginsburg
(Joined by Justice Stevens, and Joined by Justices Souter and Breyer with Regard to Part I [the Article II Section])

I

The CHIEF JUSTICE acknowledges that provisions of Florida's Election Code "may well admit of more than one interpretation."... But instead of respecting the state high court's province to say what the State's Election Code means, the CHIEF JUSTICE maintains that Florida's Supreme Court has veered so far from the ordinary practice of judicial review that what it did cannot properly be called judging. My colleagues have offered a reasonable construction of Florida's law. Their construction coincides with the view of one of Florida's seven Supreme Court justices.... I might join the CHIEF JUSTICE were it my commission to interpret Florida law. But disagreement with the Florida court's interpretation of its own State's law does not warrant the conclusion that the justices of that court have legislated. There is no cause here to believe that the members of Florida's high court have done less than "their mortal best to discharge their oath of office," *Sumner v. Mata*, 449 U.S. 539, 549 (1981), and no cause to upset their reasoned interpretation of Florida law.

This Court more than occasionally affirms statutory, and even constitutional, interpretations with which it disagrees. For example, when reviewing challenges to administrative agencies' interpretations of laws they implement, we defer to the agencies unless their interpretation violates "the unambiguously expressed intent of Congress." *Chevron U.S.A. Inc. v. Natural Resources Defense Council, Inc.* 467 U.S. 837, 843 (1984). We do so in the face of the declaration in Article I of the United States Constitution that "All legislative Powers herein granted shall be vested in a Congress of the United States." Surely the Constitution does not call upon us to pay more respect to a federal administrative agency's interpretation of its own State's law. And not uncommonly, we let stand state-court interpretations of *federal* law with which we might disagree. Notably, in the habeas context, the Court adheres to the view that "there is no intrinsic reason why the fact that a man is a federal judge should make him more competent, or conscientious, or learned with respect to [federal law] than his neighbor in the state courthouse." *Stone v. Powell*, 428 U.S. 465, 494, n. 35 (1976) (quoting Bator, Finality in Criminal Law and Federal Habeas Corpus For State Prisoners, 76 Harv. L. Rev. 441, 509 (1963)....

Rarely has this Court rejected outright an interpretation of state law by a state high court. *Fairfax's Devisee v. Hunter's Lessee*, 7 Cranch 603 (1813), *NAACP v. Alabama ex rel. Patterson*, 357 U.S. 449 (1958), and *Bouie v. City of Columbia*, 378 U.S. 347 (1964), cited by the CHIEF JUS-TICE, are three such rare instances.... But those cases are embedded in historical contexts hardly comparable to the situation here. *Fairfax's Devisee*, which held that the Virginia Court of Appeals had misconstrued its own forfeiture laws to deprive a British subject of lands secured to him by federal treaties, occurred amidst vociferous States' rights attacks on the Marshall Court.... The Virginia court refused to obey this Court's *Fairfax's Devisee* mandate to enter judgment for the British subject's successor in interest. That refusal led to the Court's pathmarking decision in *Martin v. Hunter's Lessee*, 1 Wheat. 304 (1816). *Patterson*, a case decided three months after *Cooper v. Aaron*, 358 U.S. 1 (1958), in the face of Southern resistance to the civil rights movement, held that the Alabama Supreme Court had irregularly applied its own procedural rules to deny review of a contempt order against the NAACP arising from its refusal to disclose membership lists. We said that "our jurisdiction is not defeated if the nonfederal ground relied on by the state court is without any fair or substantial support." 357 U.S., at 455. *Bouie*, stemming from a lunch counter "sit-in" at the height of the civil rights movement, held that the South Carolina Supreme Court's construction of its trespass laws—criminalizing conduct not covered by the text of an otherwise clear statute—was "unforeseeable" and thus violated due process when applied retroactively to the petitioners. 378 U.S., at 350, 354.

The CHIEF JUSTICE's casual citation of these cases might lead one to believe they are part of a larger collection of cases in which we said that the Constitution impelled us to train a skeptical eye on a state court's portrayal of state law. But one would be hard pressed, I think, to find additional cases that fit the mold.... [And] this case involves nothing close to the kind of recalcitrance by a state high court that warrants extraordinary action by this Court. The Florida Supreme Court concluded that counting every legal vote was the overriding concern of the Florida Legislature when it enacted the State's Election Code. The court surely should not be bracketed with state high courts of the Jim Crow South.

The CHIEF JUSTICE says that Article II, by providing that state legislatures shall direct the manner of appointing electors, authorizes federal superintendence over the relationship between state courts and state legislatures, and licenses a departure from the usual deference we give to state court interpretations of state law.... The Framers of our Constitution, however, understood that in a republican government, the judiciary would construe the legislature's enactments. See U.S. Const., Art. III; The Federalist No. 78 (A. Hamilton). In light of the constitutional guarantee to States of a "Republican Form of Government," U.S. Const., Art. IV, § 4, Article II can hardly be read to invite this Court to disrupt a State's republican regime. Yet the CHIEF JUSTICE today would reach out to do just that. By holding that Article II requires our revision of a state court's construction of state laws in order to protect one organ of the State from another, the CHIEF JUSTICE contradicts the basic principle that a State may organize itself as it sees fit.... Article II does not call for the scrutiny undertaken by this Court.

The extraordinary setting of this case has obscured the ordinary principle that dictates its proper resolution: Federal courts defer to state high courts' interpretations of their State's own law. This principle reflects the core of federalism, on which all agree. "The Framers split the atom of sovereignty. It was the genius of their idea that our citizens would have two political capacities, one state and one federal, each protected from incursion by the other." *Saenz v. Roe*, 526 U.S. 489, 504, n. 17 (1999) (citing *U.S. Term Limits, Inc. v. Thornton*, 514 U.S. 779, 838 (1995) (KENNEDY, J., concurring). The CHIEF JUSTICE's solicitude for the Florida Legislature comes at the expense of the more fundamental solicitude we owe to the legislature's sovereign. U.S. Const., Art II, § 1, cl. 2 ("Each *State* shall appoint, in such Manner as the Legislature *thereof* may direct," the electors for President and Vice President) (emphasis added).... Were the other members of this Court as mindful as they generally are of our system of dual sovereignty, they would affirm the judgment of the Florida Supreme Court.

II

I agree with JUSTICE STEVENS that petitioners have not presented a substantial equal protection claim. Ideally, perfection would be the appropriate standard for judging the recount. But we live in an imperfect world, one in which thousands of votes have not been counted. I cannot agree that the recount adopted by the Florida court, flawed as it may be, would yield a result any less fair or precise than the certification that preceded that recount....

Even if there were an equal protection violation, I would agree with JUSTICE STEVENS, JUSTICE SOUTER, and JUSTICE BREYER that the Court's concern about the December 12 date...is misplaced. Time is short in part because of the Court's entry of a stay on December 9, several hours after an able circuit judge in Leon County had begun to superintend the recount process. More fundamentally, the Court's reluctance to let the recount go forward—despite its suggestion that "[t]he search for intent can be confined by specific rules designed to ensure uniform treatment,"…ultimately turns on its own judgment, about the practical realities of implementing a recount, not the judgment of those much closer to the process.

Equally important,…the December 12 date for bringing Florida's electoral votes into 3 U.S.C. § 5's safe harbor lacks the significance the Court assigns it. Were that date to pass, Florida would still be entitled to deliver electoral votes Congress *must* count unless both Houses find that the votes "ha[d] not been…regularly given." 3 U.S.C. § 15. The statute identifies other significant dates. See, *e.g.*, § 7 (specifying December 18 as the date electors "shall meet and give their votes"); § 12 (specifying "the fourth Wednesday in December"—this year, December 27—as the date on which Congress, if it has not received a State's electoral votes, shall request the state secretary of state to send a certified return immediately). But none of these dates has ultimate significance in light of Congress' detailed provisions for determining, on "the sixth day of January," the validity of electoral votes. § 15.… In sum, the Court's conclusion that a constitutionally adequate recount is impractical is a prophecy the Court's own judgment will not allow to be tested. Such an untested prophecy should not decide the Presidency of the United States. I dissent.

Dissent of Justice Breyer
(Joined by Justices Steven and Ginsburg with Regard to All Except Part I-A-I [the Equal Protection Section], and Joined by Justice Souter with Regard to Part I [the Equal Protection and Article II Sections])

The Court was wrong to take this case. It was wrong to grant a stay. It should now vacate that stay and permit the Florida Supreme Court to decide whether the recount should resume.

I

The political implications of this case for the country are momentous. But the federal legal questions presented, with one exception, are insubstantial.

I-A-I. The majority raises three Equal Protection problems with the Florida Supreme Court's recount order: first, the failure to include overvotes in the manual recount; second, the fact that *all* ballots, rather than simply the undervotes, were recounted in some, but not all, counties; and third, the absence of a uniform, specific standard to guide the recounts. As far as the first issue is concerned, petitioners presented no evidence, to this Court or to any Florida court, that a manual recount of overvotes would identify additional legal votes. The same is true of the second....

The majority's third concern does implicate principles of fundamental fairness. The majority concludes that the Equal Protection Clause requires that a manual recount be governed not only by the uniform general standard of the "clear intent of the voter," but also by uniform subsidiary standards (for example, a uniform determination whether indented, but not perforated, "undervotes" should count). The opinion points out that the Florida Supreme Court ordered the inclusion of Broward County's under-counted "legal votes" even though those votes included ballots that were not perforated but simply "dimpled," while newly recounted ballots from other counties will likely include only votes determined to be "legal" on the basis of a stricter standard. In light of our previous remand, the Florida Supreme Court may have been reluctant to adopt a more specific standard than that provided for by the legislature for fear of exceeding its authority under Article II. However, since the use of different standards could favor one or the other of the candidates, since time was, and is, too short to permit the lower courts to iron out significant differences through ordinary judicial review, and since the relevant distinction was embodied in the order of the State's highest court, I agree that, in these very special circumstances, basic principles of fairness should have counseled the adoption of a uniform standard to address the problem....

I-A-2. Nonetheless, there is no justification for the majority's remedy, which is simply to reverse the lower court and halt the recount entirely. An appropriate remedy would be, instead, to remand this case with instructions that, even at this late date, would permit the Florida Supreme Court to require recounting *all* undercounted votes in Florida, including those from Broward, Volusia, Palm Beach, and Miami-Dade Counties, whether or not previously recounted prior to the end of the protest period, and to do so in accordance with a single-uniform substandard.... Of course, it is too late for any such recount to take place by December 12, the date by which election disputes must be decided if a State is to take advantage of the safe harbor provisions of 3 U.S.C. § 5. Whether there is time to conduct a recount prior to December 18, when the electors are scheduled to meet, is a matter for the state courts to determine. And whether, under Florida law, Florida could or could not take further action is obviously a matter for Florida courts, not this Court, to decide....

By halting the manual recount, and thus ensuring that the uncounted legal votes will not be counted under any standard, this Court crafts a remedy out of proportion to the asserted harm. And that remedy harms the very fairness interests the Court is attempting to protect....

I-B

The remainder of petitioners' claims, which are the focus of the CHIEF JUSTICE's concurrence, raise no significant federal questions. I cannot agree that the CHIEF JUSTICE's unusual review of state law in this case, see...(GINSBURG, J., dissenting opinion), is justified by reference either to Art. II, § 1, or to 3 U.S.C. § 5. Moreover, even were such review proper, the conclusion that the Florida Supreme Court's decision contravenes federal law is untenable....

II

Despite the reminder that this case involves "an election for the President of the United States," *ante*, at 1 (REHNQUIST, C.J., concurring), no preeminent legal concern, or practical concern related to legal questions, required this Court to hear this case, let alone to issue a stay that stopped Florida's recount process in its tracks. With one exception, petitioners' claims do not ask us to vindicate a constitutional provision designed to protect a basic human right. See, e.g., *Brown v. Board of Education*, 347 U.S. 483 (1954).... And [this] fundamental equal protection claim might have been left to the state court to resolve if and when it was discovered to have mattered. It could still be resolved through a remand conditioned upon issuance of a uniform standard; it does not require reversing the Florida Supreme Court.

Of course, the selection of the President is of fundamental national importance. But that importance is political, not legal. And this Court should resist the temptation unnecessarily to resolve tangential legal disputes, where doing so threatens to determine the outcome of the election.

The Constitution and federal statutes themselves make clear that restraint is appropriate. They set forth a road map of how to resolve disputes about electors, even after an election as close as this one. That road map foresees resolution of electoral disputes by *state* courts. See 3 U.S.C. § 5 (providing that, where a "State shall have provided, by laws enacted prior to [election day], for its final determination of any controversy or contest concerning the appointment of...electors...by *judicial* or other methods," the subsequently chosen electors enter a safe harbor free from congressional challenge). But it nowhere provides for involvement by the United States Supreme Court.

To the contrary, the Twelfth Amendment commits to Congress the authority and responsibility to count electoral votes. A federal statute, the Electoral Count Act, enacted after the close 1876 Hayes-Tilden Presidential election, specifies that, after States have tried to resolve disputes (through "judicial" or other means), Congress is the body primarily authorized to resolve remaining disputes....

The Act goes on to set out rules for the congressional determination of disputes about those votes....

Given this detailed, comprehensive scheme for counting electoral votes, there is no reason to believe that federal law either foresees or requires resolution of such a political issue by this Court. Nor, for that matter, is there any reason to think that the Constitution's Framers would have reached a different conclusion. Madison, at least, believed that allowing the judiciary to choose the presidential electors "was out of the question."

Madison, July 25, 1787 (reprinted in 5 Elliot's Debates on the Federal Constitution 363 (2d ed. 1876)).

The decision by both the Constitution's Framers and the 1886 Congress to minimize this Court's role in resolving close federal presidential elections is as wise as it is clear. However awkward or difficult it may be for Congress to resolve difficult electoral disputes, Congress, being a political body, expresses the people's will far more accurately than does an unelected Court. And the people's will is what elections are about.

Moreover, Congress was fully aware of the danger that would arise should it ask judges, unarmed with appropriate legal standards, to resolve a hotly contested Presidential election contest. Just after the 1876 Presidential election, Florida, South Carolina, and Louisiana each sent two slates of electors to Washington.... In order to choose between the two slates of electors, Congress decided to appoint an electoral commission composed of five Senators, five Representatives, and five Supreme Court Justices....

The Commission divided along partisan lines, and the responsibility to cast the deciding vote fell to Justice [Joseph] Bradley. He decided to accept the votes of the Republican electors, and thereby awarded the Presidency to Hayes.

Justice Bradley immediately became the subject of vociferous attacks. Bradley was accused of accepting bribes, of being captured by railroad interests, and of an eleventh-hour change in position after a night in which his house "was surrounded by the carriages" of Republican partisans and railroad officials. C. Woodward, Reunion and Reaction 159-160 (1966). Many years later, Professor [Alexander] Bickel concluded that Bradley was honest and impartial. He thought that "the great question for Bradley was, in fact, whether Congress was entitled to go behind election returns or had to accept them as certified by state authorities," an "issue of principle." The Least Dangerous Branch 185 (1962). Nonetheless, Bickel points out, the legal question upon which Justice Bradley's decision turned was not very important in the contemporaneous political context. He says that "in the circumstances the issue of principle was trivial, it was overwhelmed by all that hung in the balance, and it should not have been decisive." *Ibid.*

For present purposes, the relevance of this history lies in the fact that the participation in the work of the electoral commission by five Justices, including Justice Bradley, did not lend that process legitimacy. Nor did it assure the public that the process had worked fairly, guided by the law. Rather, it simply embroiled Members of the Court in partisan conflict, thereby undermining respect for the judicial process. And the Congress that later enacted the Electoral Count Act knew it.

This history may help to explain why I think it not only legally wrong, but also most unfortunate, for the Court simply to have terminated the Florida recount. Those who caution judicial restraint in resolving political disputes have described the quintessential case for that restraint as a case marked, among other things, by the "strangeness of the issue," its "intractability to principled resolution," its "sheer momentousness,…which tends to unbalance judicial judgment," and "the inner vulnerability, the self-doubt of an institution which is electorally irresponsible and has no earth to draw strength from." Bickel, *supra*, at 184. Those characteristics mark this case.…

And, above all, in this highly politicized matter, the appearance of a split decision runs the risk of undermining the public's confidence in the Court itself. That confidence is a public treasure. It has been built slowly over many years, some of which were marked by a Civil War and the tragedy of segregation. It is a vitally necessary ingredient of any successful effort to protect basic liberty, and indeed, the rule of law itself. We run no risk of returning to the days when a President (responding to this Court's efforts to protect the Cherokee Indians) might have said, "John Marshall has made his decision; now let him enforce it!" Loth, Chief Justice John Marshall and The Growth of the American Republic 365 (1948). But we do risk a self-inflicted wound—a wound that may harm not just the Court, but the Nation.

I fear that in order to bring this agonizingly long election process to a definitive conclusion, we have not adequately attended to that necessary "check upon our own exercise of power," "our own sense of self-restraint." *United States v. Butler*, 297 U.S. 1, 79 (1936) (Stone, J., dissenting). Justice Brandeis once said of the Court, "The most important thing we do is not doing." Bickel, *supra*, at 71. What it does today, the Court should have left undone. I would repair the damage as best we now can, by permitting the Florida recount to continue under uniform standards. I respectfully dissent.

On Remand from the United States Supreme Court: The Brief That Never Was

To the public, as well as most of the media, *Bush v. Gore* ended the 2000 election struggle. But the U.S. Supreme Court actually remanded the case to the Florida Supreme Court "for further proceedings not inconsistent with this opinion," and while it was hard to see how any continuation of the recount could be "consistent," the justices had not sent the dispute back with explicit instructions to dismiss.

Thus Ron Klain and other Gore attorneys wanted to fight on, to get the Florida justices to respond to Washington's peremptory view of *their* view of the safe harbor, and even to order the contest resumed under altered, uniform standards. Late into the night of December 12, Klain, David Boies, and others worked on a brief, much of which was drafted by Richard Cordray, who had once clerked for Justice Kennedy.

The document argued powerfully against the Supreme Court's reasoning on the December 12 deadline, and claimed there was still time to complete a corrected count before the Electoral College met, even if it had to include overvotes. While calling attention to the iffy language in the per curiam, the Gore lawyers seemed reconciled to the Florida Supreme Court's being compelled to order such votes assessed. Gore's brief also pleaded one last time that the standard in *Delahunt v. Johnston* be used in the final count.

Having spoken to Dexter Douglass, however, and after sleeping on the matter, Vice President Gore decided that a further appeal was futile, that the justices in Washington had indeed spoken the last word. At 9 P.M. on the evening of December 13, Albert Gore conceded the presidential election.

Reprinted by permission of Ron Klain and Richard Cordray.

Introduction

This case is before this Court on remand from the U.S. Supreme Court, which has returned the case for further proceedings "not inconsistent with this opinion." *Bush v. Gore* [148 L Ed 2d, 388, 402.] An appropriate response to the U.S. Supreme Court's decision is a clarification of key points of statutory construction under Florida state law. The U.S. Supreme Court suggested that *this Court* has held that in a Presidential election, Florida law places primacy on trying to meet the so-called "safe harbor" provision in 3 U.S.C. s5 (which is *never even mentioned* in the Florida statutes) rather than on ensuring the fundamental democratic principle that the will of the people not be frustrated in accurately ascertaining the outcome of a popular election.... Yet this Court has never so held, and Florida's elections laws cannot remotely bear such a construction. This Court should respond to the U.S. Supreme Court's remand with a statement of Florida law that clarifies this point.

The U.S. Supreme Court has identified limited equal protection problems with the recount of undervotes this Court had ordered to complete a full and fair tally of the votes cast in this election.... The Court's opinion also suggests some need to address the question of so-called "overvote" ballots. As discussed below, these conditions could be met by an immediate order of this Court, and a full and accurate tally of the votes could be achieved, just as this Court directed as a matter of state law five days ago.

At bottom, the issue here is whether this Court—on a fundamental issue of state law which it holds the definitive authority to construe— believes that a mere "legislative wish to take advantage of the 'safe harbor'" afforded by federal law, *Bush v. Palm Beach County Canvassing Bd.* [148 L Ed 2d, 366, 372] (Dec. 4, 2000), trumps the intent of the Legislature, which runs deeply and constantly through Florida's elections law: *i.e.*, that "the right of Florida's citizens to vote and to have elections determined by the will of Florida's voters [are] important policy concerns of the Florida Legislature in enacting Florida's elections code." *Palm Beach County Canvassing Bd. v. Harris*, Slip op. 31 (Fla. Dec. 11, 2000). The proposition is particularly unpersuasive now that the Legislature has provided powerful new evidence in its current special session that it is more concerned about making a selection of electors than in meeting the supposed December 12th "safe harbor" deadline.

If instead, as we believe, this Court's recent provision for a "manual recount" of undervotes to determine accurately the rightful winner of the election should not be "eviscerated and rendered meaningless" by a time limit that is not mandatory, but should "accommodate the manual recount," *id.* at 22, then the Florida Supreme Court has the lawful authority, on remand, to correct this misunderstanding about Florida law, and to order a resumption of the manual recounts, to be completed within 48 hours. [T]his Court could exercise such authority properly under the U.S. Supreme Court's remand, and in so doing, would vindicate democracy and the rule of law in Florida before the Electoral College convenes on December 18, 2000.

I. The Clear and Consistent Intent of Florida Law Is That Elections Must Faithfully Reflect the Popular Will.

Three days ago, this Court stressed the importance "to remind ourselves that the Florida Legislature has expressly vested in the voters of Florida the authority to elect the presidential electors who will ultimately participate in choosing a president." *Palm Beach County, supra,* Slip op. 31 (citing 103.011, Fla. Stat. [2000]). In that case, the Court held that an arguably mandatory deadline "must be construed in a flexible manner to accommodate the manual recount" needed to ensure an accurate count of the votes cast in this very election. *Id.* at 22. In large part, the Court reached this conclusion because of the "important policy concerns of the Florida Legislature in enacting Florida's election code" to preserve and protect "the right of Florida's citizens to vote and to have elections determined by the will of Florida's voters." *Id.* at 31.

Nor, as this Court noted, was this the first time that an apparent deadline in the Florida election laws was extended to accommodate competing policy concerns. In particular, the overseas ballots must be counted if they are received any time up to ten days after the election pursuant to an administrative rule that balanced competing concerns of related federal and state laws. *Id.* at 25.

Moreover, this Court has repeatedly stressed that the fundamental purpose of Florida's election laws is to determine and effectuate the will of the people. *See, e.g., Harris,* Slip op. 31 (Fla. Dec. 11, 2000) ("Courts must not lose sight of the fundamental purpose of election laws: The laws are intended to facilitate and safeguard the right of each voter to express his or her will in the context of our representative democracy"); *Chappell v. Martinez,* 536 So. 2d 1007, 1008 (Fla. 1988) (the people effecting their will through "balloting, not the hypertechnical compliance with statutes, is the object of holding elections"); *Boardman v. Esteva,* 323 So. 2d 259, 267 (Fla. 1975) ("It is the policy of the law to prevent as far as possible the disenfranchisement of electors who have cast their ballots in good faith")....

Thus, where putative deadlines or matters of administrative convenience would cause legal votes cast not to be counted or otherwise frustrate the will of the people, they must give way to this paramount concern.... The same overriding concern with enfranchising as many citizens as possible is reflected in Florida's universal standard for determining the legal validity of ballots that are cast in elections. *See, e.g., Darby v. State*, 75 So. 411, 412 (Fla. 1917) (ballot marked to plainly indicate voter's intent should be counted "unless some positive provision of law would be thereby violated"); *State ex rel. Carpenter v. Barber*, 198 So. 49 (Fla. 1940) (vote should be counted "if the will and intention of the voter can be determined"); *Nuccio v. Williams*, 120 So. 310 (Fla. 1929). Hence, in a case of allegedly mismarked ballots, this Court held that the Florida courts "should not frustrate the will of the voters." *Beckstrom v. Volusia County Canvassing Bd.*, 707 So. 2d 720, 726 (Fla. 1998).

Weighing against this bedrock policy of Florida law is not the need to comply with any firm, mandatory deadline, but consideration of a voluntary choice of whether to strive to meet a provision of federal law that *both parties have agreed* offers only encouragement and some penumbral protection for the electoral votes that Florida submits to Congress. As the U.S. Supreme Court noted: "The parties before us agree that whatever else may be the effect of [3 U.S.C. § 5], it creates a 'safe harbor' for a State insofar as congressional consideration of its electoral votes is concerned." *Bush I* [at 372.] The parties were unable to find any more meaning or substance in this provision, which has been characterized as "all carrot and no stick." *Indeed, this year 21 states did not even bother to submit their paperwork to the National Archives by the prescribed date....* One reason for this unconcern may be that a successful challenge to a state's electors requires the concurrence of both chambers in Congress, which is virtually impossible if different parties control the two chambers when Congress meets to count the electoral votes, as is true this year.

What is important, however, is that a mere "safe harbor" provision designed to offer encouragement to the states cannot sensibly be transformed into a deadly vortex that sucks into its maw the rights of voters, the rights of candidates, and all of the legal and democratic procedures established under Florida state law. Noting that all provisions of the Florida election statutes must be read *in pari material*, this Court held that a "comprehensive reading" of the laws "required that there be time for an elections contest pursuant to section 102.168." *Harris II*, Slip op. 30, n. 22. As a matter of statutory construction, therefore, this Court fashioned a remedial system carefully designed to safeguard the mandatory judicial contest provided by the Florida Legislature.... Once again, there is nothing to commend a reading of Florida law that would cast overboard the contest proceeding, and with it any hope of an accurate rendition of the people's will, merely for an ephemeral date that need not even be followed, has no practical effect in this instance, and in fact is widely ignored....

The U.S. Supreme Court's opinion rests on a confused reading of Florida law that this Court should clarify... [Title 3's]...'safe harbor'" [is a] "safe harbor" [that] cannot be transformed from a shield for this State into a sword dangling above *this* Court. Moreover, the assertion that "the Florida Supreme Court has said that the Florida Legislature intended to obtain the safe-harbor benefits of 3 U.S.C. § 5" [*Bush v. Gore*, at 402] comes from a passage in *Harris I* that does not even support the statement. Under Florida law, judicial contests, along with the rights of voters and candidates they are designed to safeguard, cannot be terminated to achieve compliance with an administrative deadline that approximately half the states honor only in the breach.

On remand, this Court may want to consider the U.S. Supreme Court's opinion as effectively certifying the following question to the Florida Supreme Court: "Does Florida law hold that the state *may* select electors by December 12, 2000, or does Florida law hold that the state *shall* select electors by that date?"

The answer here…must be informed by the importance in Florida law of preserving and protecting the will of the voters. And that answer must be that Florida law makes compliance with the safe harbor date preferable, but not compulsory. As Justice Breyer noted, though the proceedings to date rendered it impossible to qualify for the "safe harbor," it would be possible to complete all manual recounts necessary to conclude the contest proceedings by December 18, 2000, the date the Electoral College convenes. The Court did not disagree, but expressed the view that it was bound by the Florida Supreme Court's supposed construction of Florida law to end all such proceedings on December 12….

III. This Court Need Not Order Counting of Over-Votes; If Such a Count Is Ordered, an Appropriate Procedure for Counting These Votes Can Be Easily Established….

A. Overvotes Do Not Need to Be Included in a Recount

While the U.S. Supreme Court did raise issues concerning the exclusion of overvotes from a recount, it did *not* mandate that such ballots be included on remand. *See, e.g., Bush II* [at 402] ("*If* a recount of the overvotes were also required…"). Thus, this Court is under no obligation to order such a count on remand.

There are ample reasons not to include such ballots in a recount. First, as Justice Breyer pointed out, "[the defendants] presented no evidence, to this Court or any Florida court, that a manual recount of overvotes would identify additional legal votes." *Bush II* [at 423] (Breyer, J., dissenting). Neither at trial, nor on appeal, did the defendants present any evidence concerning the nature of the ballots found to be overvotes….

The U.S. Supreme Court noted two distinct types of overvotes:

- First, voters whose ballots reflect two marks, but whose intent can nonetheless be discerned (such as a voter who punched and wrote-in for the same candidate or mistakenly marked in the area designated for another candidate but then also for the candidate of choice);
- Second, ballots counted by machines as legitimate votes, that were indeed illegal overvotes.

Neither category merits inclusion in a statewide recount.

First, while there may be some ballots that fall into the first category, defendants did not produce at trial, nor does the record contain, any evidence that they are particularly numerous in nature—or that they tend to favor one candidate over the other. To the extent that evidence exists in other judicial proceedings concerning this same election, it suggests that a large number of overvote ballots may have reflected an intent to vote for Vice President Gore, not Governor Bush....

With regard to the second problem—a voter who marks two votes on his ballot, only to have a single vote read by the machine (and thereby, has his illegal ballot counted as a legal vote)—what the U.S. Supreme Court fails to recognize is that if inclusion of these votes presents constitutional issues, the same issues are presented by the earlier certified vote tallies. That is, such ballots are included—not just in any certification to emerge from this proceeding—but from the two certifications that the Court suggests were somehow more legitimate. Yet those earlier certifications included all ballots that the machine read, *whether or not they were true overvotes.*

In the end, there is no reason to include so-called overvotes in any statewide recount....

B. If This Court Orders Counting of All Ballots That Have Not Been Counted by Vote-Counting Machinery, There Is a Practicable Manner for Completing It Fairly Quickly.

If this Court concludes that a count of the so-called overvotes is required or desirable, it can be completed practicably and efficiently.

This...can be accomplished in the time remaining before December 18. It does not require that every ballot in the State of Florida be manually recounted....

The process for segregating machine-countable from non-machine countable ballots is well-developed. The Supreme Court's opinion, in an attempt to make remedial action here appear impossible, expressed concern that:

> The Secretary of State has advised that the recount of only a portion of the ballots requires that the vote tabulation equipment be used to screen out undervotes, a function for which the machines were not designed. If a recount of overvotes were also required, perhaps even a second screening would be necessary.... [*Bush v. Gore*, at 402.]

However, this vastly overstates the logistical difficulty. In fact, most if not all vote-counting machines in Florida, whether they use a punchcard or opti-scan type ballot, are already equipped to segregate uncounted ballots.... Indeed, plaintiffs believe that segregation of undervote ballots was already completed or in progress in every county where such segregation was necessary in response to the order of this Court and the Circuit Court when the Supreme Court issued its Stay Order on December 9. The same technology can segregate overvotes as well as undervotes by simply changing the designation on the vote segregation and tabulation system. It does not require new software as implied in the Supreme Court's opinion. For those counties whose machines do not have that capacity now, the necessary software is readily available, free of charge....

Although the number of ballots is large—approximately six million were cast in the State of Florida—the recount we propose can be timely completed. The machine segregation and count will take only a short time. The manual inspection of an estimated 177,000 undervote and overvote ballots will be spread across the State. Most counties will have little trouble finishing their count in under a day. Plaintiffs estimate that 43 of Florida's 67 counties will have to inspect less than a thousand ballots. An additional fourteen counties will have to inspect less than 4,000 ballots. And, as this election season has amply demonstrated, Florida's counties have the resources and dedication to complete their ballot count quickly and efficiently when called upon.

Reactions to *Bush v. Gore*

The immediate reaction of the legal academy to *Bush v. Gore* was predominantly negative. Scholars such as Professor Ackerman and his distinguished Yale colleague Akhil Reed Amir weighed in with strong denunciations of the Supreme Court's logic and honesty, Ackerman arguing that in response to the Court's decision the United States Senate should refuse to confirm any future nominations to it offered by President Bush. One of the nation's leading opponents of the death penalty, Anthony Amsterdam of New York University Law School penned an especially passionate comment.

Among the relatively few defenders of *Bush v. Gore* was Nelson Lund of the George Mason Law School.

Should We Trust Judges?

Akhil Reed Amir

What will I tell my law students in the aftermath of *Bush vs. Gore,* in which five Republican judges handed the presidency to Republican George W. Bush? It will be my painful duty to say, "Put not your trust in judges." Don't misunderstand me. I am a true believer in the rule of law. I have devoted my professional life to the study of the U.S. Constitution. I consider myself a friend of the U.S. Supreme Court and of many of its current justices.

The court, in its long history, has made many mistakes. I do not hide these from my students. We read large chunks of the Dred Scott and *Plessy vs. Ferguson* decisions, which promoted slavery and racism. We discuss the court's Gilded Age transformation of amendments drafted to promote freedom and equality into doctrines protecting the rich and powerful, while ignoring the rights of others. We debate the various failures of legal analysis in *Roe vs. Wade* and its progeny. We critique the court's perverse criminal-procedure doctrines, which often help guilty defendants at the expense of innocent defendants and innocent victims.

And now, to the list of dubious precedents that I must teach, I will add *Bush vs. Gore.* I will teach it as I teach most other cases—by parsing its language and logic. Since students will be graded on their work, I will need to show them what counts as good legal analysis and what cannot count. In effect, I grade court opinions as a way of illustrating how I will grade exams and papers.

Judged by ordinary standards of legal analysis, *Bush vs. Gore* gets low marks. The core idea is that because the Florida recount was proceeding under somewhat uneven standards, it violated constitutional principles of equal protection. In some counties, dimpled chads might be counted; in other counties, not. And so on.

The Los Angeles Times, December 17, 2000, p. M1. Reprinted by permission.

At first, this argument sounds plausible. But let's test it by traditional legal tools. As a matter of logic: If the Florida recount was constitutionally flawed, why wasn't the initial Florida count equally, if not more, flawed? It, too, featured uneven standards from county to county. Different counties used different ballots (including the infamous butterfly ballot); and even counties using the same ballot used different interpretive standards in counting them. This happened not just in Florida, but across the country. Are all these elections unconstitutional?

Now think about history and tradition. The idea that the Constitution requires absolute perfection and uniformity of standards in counting ballots is novel, to put it gently. Americans have always been asked to put their "X" marks in boxes, and human umpires have had to judge if the "X" is close enough to the box to count. On election day, different umpires in different precincts have always called slightly different strike zones. If these judgments are made in good faith and within a small zone of "close calls," why are they unconstitutional? If they are unconstitutional, then every election America has ever had is unconstitutional. And the *Bush* court nowhere claimed or showed any special bad faith that might render the recount more suspicious than, say, the initial count (which occurred without judicial oversight).

Now think about precedent. The *Bush* court failed to cite a single case that, on its facts, comes close to supporting the majority's analysis and result. There is forceful voting-equality language in Supreme Court case law—but, on their facts, these are cases about citizens simply being denied the right to vote (typically on race or class lines); or being assigned formally unequal voting power, with some (typically white) districts being over-represented at the expense of other (typically black) districts. As a precedent for future cases, the *Bush* court majority tries to limit its ruling to its unique facts—recounts presided over by judges—but fails to support this ad hoc limitation with any neutral principle: The justices might as well have said, "We promise to follow this case in all future cases captioned *Bush vs. Gore,* but not elsewhere." Indeed, the fact that the *Bush* case involved recounts monitored by judges cuts precisely against the court majority: Less cheating in tabulation is likely when judges and special masters—and the eyes of the world—are watching.

As a matter of constitutional text and history, the equal protection clause was, first and foremost, designed to remedy the inequalities heaped upon blacks in America. The 15th Amendment extended this idea by prohibiting race discrimination with respect to the vote. Yet, governments in the South mocked these rules for most of the 20th century—and with the court's blessing. For decades, most American blacks were simply not allowed to vote. When Congress finally acted to even things up in the 1960s, inequality persisted as a practical matter.

In Florida, for example, black precincts typically have much glitchier voting machines, which generate undercounts many times the rate of wealthier (white) precincts with sleek voting technology. Undermaintenance of voting machines, chad build-up and long voting lines in poor precincts—these are the real ballot inequalities today. If we are serious about real equality, as envisioned by the architects of Reconstruction, we should not ignore the voting-machine skew. Rather, we should do our best to correct for it, albeit imperfectly, via manual recounts. Even if such recounts are not required by equality, surely they are not prohibited by equality. In fixating on the small glitches of the recount rather than on the large and systemic glitches of the machines, the justices turned a blind eye to the real inequality staring them in the face, piously attributing the problem to "voter error" and inviting "legislative bodies" to fix the mess for future elections....

Finally, consider issues of constitutional statecraft. The Florida courts, the Florida Legislature and Congress are all electorally accountable. The U.S. Supreme Court is not, yet it snatched the case away from these alternative decision-makers. The biggest electoral check on the court is the ability of presidents to appoint new justices, yet the five justices who Al Gore directly criticized during his campaign handed the presidency over to his opponent by preventing a recount that might have proved that he was indeed the choice of Florida's voters, as well as the nation's. The court majority reached this result by a single vote. By refusing to consider equality issues in its first review of the Florida fiasco several weeks ago, the court denied itself the benefits of amicus briefs from scholars and experts who might have helped clarify the real issues at stake.

Ironies abound. Justices who claim to respect states savage state judges. Jurists who purport to condemn new rules make up rules of breathtaking novelty in application. A court that frowns on ad hoc decision-making gives us a case limited to its facts. A court that claims it is defending the prerogatives of the Florida Legislature unravels its statutory scheme vesting power in state judges and permitting geographic variations. The real problems in Florida identified by the justices were problems in the election laws themselves, not the Florida courts. The case that bears the name of a professed strict constructionist is as activist a decision as I know.

When my students ask about the case, I will tell them that we should and must accept it. But we need not, and should not, respect it.

The Law Is Left Slowly Twisting in the Wind

Anthony Amsterdam

In 1987, the U.S. Supreme Court held, 5 to 4, that evidence of race discrimination in Georgia's use of the death penalty was not enough to invalidate a
death sentence under the equal protection clause of the federal Constitution
[*McCleskey v. Kemp*, 481 US 279]. During the court's private deliberations
(as Justice Thurgood Marshall's papers have disclosed), Justice Antonin
Scalia admitted that the evidence did show Georgia death sentences were
being handed out on grounds of race, but Scalia urged the court to disregard
this violation of equal protection in order to allow the states to get on
promptly with the business of killing. The published opinion of the
Supreme Court engineered Scalia's proposed result in a less forthright way,
using a parade of rhetorical tricks to conceal the majority justices' aim of
expediting the execution of death sentences.

Now, in its ruling for George W. Bush, a majority of the Supreme
Court intones solemnly that: "A desire for speed is not a general excuse for
ignoring equal protection guarantees."

In 1983, a majority of the Supreme Court rejected a claim by a condemned Florida inmate that the Florida courts had violated his federal constitutional rights by flagrantly disregarding clear, long-settled rules of
Florida law in sentencing him to death. The U.S. Supreme Court opinion,
written by Justice William Rehnquist, declared that the federal courts and
the federal Constitution could have nothing to do with the matter, because
Florida law is whatever the Florida courts say it is, and their interpretations
of Florida law are unreviewable by federal Supreme Court justices [*Barclay
v. Florida*, 463 US 939].

Now, in its ruling for Bush, a majority of the federal Supreme Court

The Los Angeles Times, December 17, 2000, p. M5. Reprinted by permission of
Anthony Amsterdam.

289

suddenly discovers that it has the power to second-guess Florida court decisions of Florida law.

The important point to notice in the presidential election case is not simply the Supreme Court's abandonment of any pretense at behaving like a court of law. It is not even the sickening hypocrisy and insincere constitutional posturing with which the court's foray into president-making is dressed up. It is that the court finally has revealed unmistakably what it does all the time and usually gets away with: making result-driven, political, unprincipled decisions in the guise of obedience to rules of law which the justices feel completely free to twist and retwist to suit their purposes.

To steal an election in this way is bad but is not the worst of it. To take human life by decisions made in this way—as the court has done again and again in the past two decades—is among the greater crimes for which the court can now be held accountable on the record it has made for history and eternity.

An Act of Courage

Nelson Lund

Generations of law students have learned that the U.S. Supreme Court should avoid entanglement in "political" cases in order to preserve its reputation for impartiality. Unless, of course, such cases involve certain selectively chosen constitutional principles, which invariably call for the uninhibited expenditure of this carefully husbanded political capital.

Some of the more conservative justices have bought into this excessive and asymmetrical concern with protecting the Court's reputation. The decision in *Bush v. Gore*, however, suggests that a majority are now willing to enforce the law more evenhandedly, even when that very evenhandedness will subject the Court to strident political attacks.

The High Court's decision at first glance looks important primarily for its effect on this one presidential contest. The holding is deliberately narrow, and seems unlikely to have significant effects on future elections. The broader significance lies in a passage near the end of the majority opinion, where the justices stress their sensitivity to the limits of judicial authority and the wisdom of leaving the selection of the president to the political sphere. Despite these considerations, they say, it sometimes "becomes our unsought responsibility to resolve the federal and constitutional issues the judicial system has been forced to confront."

The Court could easily have avoided this responsibility, and that is what many observers expected. These expectations had a real foundation. In 1992, for example, the Court reaffirmed the judicially created right to abortion, even while strongly hinting that some of those who voted to do so had serious misgivings. One important reason they gave for their decision was a fear that overruling *Roe v. Wade* would be *perceived* as a capitulation to political pressure [*Planned Parenthood of Southeastern Pennsylvania v. Casey*, 505 US 833].

Weekly Standard, December 25, 2000, pp. 19–20. Reprinted by permission.

Bush v. Gore rejects this beguiling logic. The majority, including two justices who had joined the 1992 abortion opinion, recognized that their decision would subject them to merciless, politically motivated attacks. But rather than take the easy way out, they courageously accepted their "unsought responsibility" to require that the Florida court comply with the Constitution.

The significance of this act of courage comes into focus when we consider the strongest argument offered by the dissenters. Justice Breyer, who admitted that the Florida court's decision was arbitrary and unconstitutional, suggested that the Twelfth Amendment assigns Congress (rather than the federal courts) the responsibility for correcting such problems. This is a plausible interpretation of the Constitution, especially if one also concludes (as Justice Breyer did not) that the Constitution authorized the Florida legislature to override the Florida court's attempted retroactive rewrite of the state election statute.

But Justice Breyer's position does not rest on a disinterested interpretation of the Constitution. Rather, it is based on the tired theory that "the appearance of a split decision runs the risk of undermining the public's confidence in the Court itself.". . .

[And] [i]f the Twelfth Amendment argument is the best that the *Bush v. Gore* dissenters had to offer, the worst was Justice Stevens's claim that Governor Bush irresponsibly impugned the impartiality of the Florida judges by appealing their ruling. Justice Stevens also noted that the real loser in this year's election will be the nation's "confidence in the judge as an impartial guardian of the rule of law." It is certainly true that almost no one will believe that *all* the judges who ruled in the election cases were impartial, or devoted to the rule of law. Justice Stevens, however, was entirely wrong to place the blame for that fact on his colleagues and on Governor Bush.

The blame rests squarely on Florida's supreme court, which violated the Constitution, and on the High Court dissenters, who would have let the Florida judges get away with it. "Impartial guardians of the rule of law" are willing to enforce the law even when they know they will be excoriated for doing so. Which is why the majority decision in *Bush v. Gore* deserves a spirited defense.

30

Comment: Was the Court's Decision Sound and Principled?

Mark Whitman

Bush v. Gore stirred more controversy, quite understandably, than any Supreme Court decision since *Roe v. Wade*. Detailed analysis by legal scholars, most, though not all of it negative, focused on all aspects of the decision: the strength of the constitutional contentions set out in the per curiam opinion, in Chief Justice Rehnquist's concurrence, and in the dissents; evidence that the majority justices thought they were serving the national welfare by acting as they did, whatever the doctrinal coherence of their arguments; indications, even, that rank partisanship may have played a role in the controversy.

What should not be forgotten, however, is the desperate haste with which the parties prepared their cases and the justices composed their decisions, particularly the lack of time available to both to command and evaluate information. This paucity of breathing space played a significant and sometimes decisive role in shaping the final product. As Michael Herz of the Cardozo School of Law puts it,

> The risks of [a] mad dash . . . were painfully on display in *Bush v. Gore*. First, rather than giving their considered judgment, the Justices were shooting from the hip on extremely difficult legal issues. They were completely without time for reflection, study, or debate, all the things one wants when faced with a difficult problem. In addition, the Court was without the usual assistance from the parties or other judges. The parties themselves had had very little time to develop, refine, and brief the issues. The equal protection issue, on which the case turned, had received no consideration from any other court or individual judge before it was laid before the Supreme Court. As the Court in other circumstances has emphasized, it benefits from the "percolation" of legal issues in the lower courts before it decides them. Thus, many basic structures designed to give the Court the best chance of getting it right were absent.[1]

The Article II Slant

In what he saw initially as the majority opinion in *Bush*, the chief justice followed up on the comments made in the earlier remand. While "comity and respect for federalism" usually compelled deference to state court interpretations of state law, this was the "exceptional case" where the Constitution, in the form of Article II, conferred power on a "particular branch" of a state's government.[2] Hence, "the text of the election law itself, and not just its interpretation by the courts of the States, takes on independent significance."[3]

This suggested Article II set a far more suspicious criterion for acceptance of state glosses on such election laws than was normally true—if not "de novo" review of state decisions, at least "reduced deference."[4] The chief justice failed to answer, however, Justice Ginsburg's query as to why, if this was so, the Supreme Court habitually deferred to administrative agency interpretations of federal law without the text of the law taking on an "independent" status, "in the face" of Article I's declaration that "'All legislative powers . . . granted shall be vested in a Congress of the United States.'"[5]

Nor does the concurrence cite any historical support for its conclusions about Article II, an odd omission for an opinion endorsed by jurists such as Scalia and Thomas, who always professed devotion to the original intent of any constitutional provision. Scalia had written in 1997 that "what I look for in the Constitution is precisely what I look for in a statute, the original meaning of the text."[6] Thomas, joined by Scalia, had earlier argued that the Eighth Amendment proscription against cruel and unusual punishments could not extend to violent abuse by correctional authorities of people already in prison, since the amendment applied "only to tortuous punishments meted out by statutes or sentencing judges, and not . . . to any hardship that might befall a prisoner during incarceration."[7]

While disagreeing on the outcome, both also applied strict original-intent analysis to a 1995 case rejecting a state's right to outlaw anonymous campaign literature. "I agree with the majority's conclusion," Thomas wrote. "[But] instead of asking whether 'an honorable tradition' of anonymous speech has existed throughout American history, or what the 'value' of anonymous speech might be, we should determine whether the phrase 'freedom of speech and of the press,' as originally understood, protected anonymous political leafleting."[8] Scalia dissented, though conceding, "The question posed by the . . . case is not the easiest sort to answer for those who adhere to the Court's (and the society's) traditional view that the *Constitution bears its original meaning and is unchanging*."[9]

Yet the concurring opinion in *Bush* paid no attention to Article II's pri-

mal meaning, even ignoring one of the best-known guides to the subject—
and one which scarcely approved the notion that the framers wished to lav-
ish inviolable powers on the state legislatures. The vices of these bodies,
wrote James Madison in 1787, "so frequent and so flagrant as to alarm the
most steadfast friends of Republicanism . . . contributed more to that
uneasiness which produced the [Constitutional] Convention . . . than those
which accrued to our national character and interest from the inadequacy of
the Confederation to its immediate objects."[10]

None of this made much practical difference, though, because the chief
justice's assault on the Florida Supreme Court indicated he felt their decisions could not survive even the most forgiving deference. The concurrence
was a blunderbuss aimed at every aspect of the lower court's performance.
Its "interpretation of the Florida election laws impermissibly distorted them
beyond what a fair reading required," was "absurd," could be accepted by
"no reasonable person."[11]

Rehnquist's condemnation, indeed, is not limited to the contest issue
under direct consideration in *Bush v. Gore*, but repeats Secretary Harris's
original contention that manual recounts in the protest phase are only justified by machine failure. He reproduces the instructions he mistakenly
claims were posted in all "precincts using punch-card ballots," directing the
voter to "be sure . . . there are no chips left hanging on the back of the
card."[12] Then, yoking the protest and contest provisions of Florida law, he
maintains "no reasonable person would call it 'an error in the vote tabulation,' . . . or a 'rejection of legal votes,' . . . when electronic or electromechanical equipment performs precisely in the manner designed, and fails
to count those ballots that are not marked in the manner that these voting
instructions explicitly and prominently specify."[13]

But this "error in the vote tabulation" from the protest phase, as we
have seen, is determined only after a sample manual count in which canvassers must search, under Section 166(7), for the "intent of the voter," and
where critical numbers of votes, both then and in a full recount, can be
adjudged legal despite the fact that the machines failed to count them. The
concurrence (like *Palm Beach County v. Harris*) never mentions the "intent
of the voter" section, however, simply citing Chief Justice Wells's dissent
in *Gore v. Harris* to prove "that the principal provision of the election code
on which" the Florida Supreme Court did rely in emphasizing voter
intent—101.5614(5)—was "entirely irrelevant," because the provision
referred only to defective ballots.[14] Again, like the Florida justices,
Rehnquist overlooks the passage in *Beckstrom* defining 5614(5). "We construe 'defective ballot' to include a ballot which is marked in a manner such
that it cannot be read by a scanner,"[15] a definition that certainly seems to
"encompass incompletely punched-through ballots."[16]

The chief justice professed himself scandalized by the "scheme that the Florida Supreme Court's opinion attributes to the legislature," a scheme in which, by statute, machines are supposed to count votes correctly, "but which nonetheless regularly produces elections [where] legal votes are predictably *not* tabulated, so that in close elections manual recounts are regularly required."[17] Yet this was the system Florida (and many other jurisdictions) had, and, unlike the chief, no knowledgeable observer in the state would have been surprised to learn that machine runs of ballots regularly produced results such as the ones found in the *Miami Herald* survey, where 1,500 fully punched ballots registered as undervotes, as did 1,400 two- and three-corner hangers, whose exact replicas in many cases were undoubtedly counted by the machines as valid votes.[18]

The chief justice's tying of "error in the vote tabulation" to "rejection of legal votes" in order to discredit manual searches for voter intent is the obverse, it seems, of Professor Friedman's attempt to legitimize them by his contention that "an error" in the vote tabulation is really "the counting of illegal votes or the failure to count legal votes . . . the standard explicitly adopted by the contest statute."[19] If these two terms are not in fact fully congruent, if ballots harvested during manual recounts that reflect the "intent of the voter" are later adjudged not to be "legal votes" during the contest phase, it is, as Professor Greene says, because "officials had perfectly legal, valid reasons for not counting [such ballots]—even . . . where the voter's intent was clear."[20]

This "critique of the Florida Supreme Court was Bush's strongest."[21] Consequently, Chief Justice Rehnquist did "draw blood"[22] in his concurrence when he asserted that "Florida statutory law cannot reasonably be thought to *require* the counting of [all] improperly marked ballots," and when he noted that having lengthened the protest phase of the 2000 election—"the clear implication [being] certification was a matter of significance"—the Florida justices then "emptie[d] certification of virtually all legal consequence during the contest."[23] (This was the only mention of the extended protest deadline, but the chief justice did not treat it as a constitutional violation per se.)

Rehnquist also returned to the protest phase to condemn the state court's peremptory dismissal of the original November 13 opinions of the secretary of state, "who is authorized by law to issue binding interpretations of the election code."[24] It was a little late, however, to scuttle the whole Florida process on this basis.

An Article II argument focused on the contest phase might well have been a stronger one. But that it would have won over both Justices Kennedy and O'Connor is doubtful; the latter's intense dislike of the Florida Supreme Court made it most unlikely she was put off by the chief's furious attack. This was just not the way she wished to go.

The Perplexing Levels of Scrutiny

The basic equal-protection argument in *Bush v. Gore*—that "the standards for accepting or rejecting contested ballots [in the court-ordered recount] might vary not only from county to county but indeed within a single county"[25]—fared far better than the Article II representations, gaining the votes of six justices and the de facto concurrence of Justice Breyer.[26] The per curiam followed the pattern of Bush's brief in holding that the recount structure intruded on a right that was "fundamental,"[27] and did so in a manner analogous to the actions condemned in *Reynolds v. Sims.* ("'[T]he right of suffrage can be denied by a debasement or dilution . . . of a citizen's vote just as effectively as by wholly prohibiting the free exercise of the franchise.'")[28]

The invocation of *Reynolds* seemed to indicate that a fundamental right being involved, Florida's actions were subject to judgment under the highest, most rigorous standard of scrutiny applied in equal-protection cases. This was so-called strict scrutiny, as opposed to the intermediate scrutiny used in gender and illegitimacy cases, and to the most forgiving level, rational-basis review, employed, among other things, in looking at business regulations. Under strict-scrutiny analysis, a law or regulation could treat similarly situated people, like Florida voters, unequally only if it served an overriding,"compelling" state interest, and was narrowly tailored to that end.[29]

Reynolds itself preceded the Court's formal use of this vocabulary of fundamental rights and strict scrutiny, but seems to anticipate it in stating that because the franchise "is . . . preservative of other basic civil and political rights, any alleged infringement of the right of citizens to vote must be carefully and meticulously scrutinized."[30]

The per curiam does not mention levels of scrutiny at all. But the majority justices stated at one point that the "question before us" was whether the recount procedures avoided "arbitrary and disparate treatment of the members of [the] electorate," and concluded that these mechanisms "do not satisfy the minimum requirement for non-arbitrary treatment of voters necessary to secure the fundamental right."[31] This strongly hints at the failure of the Florida setup to pass even the rational-basis test, particularly in the use of the word "arbitrary."[32] Justice Souter's opinion uses the same language. "I can conceive of no legitimate state interest served by these differing treatments of the expressions of voters' fundamental rights. The differences appear wholly arbitrary."[33]

A decision based on this lower-tier criterion would be condemning practices used for decades by most states as "'so unrelated to the achievement of any combination of legitimate purposes that we can only conclude that the [government's] actions were irrational'" (in language defining the rational-basis test used by Justice O'Connor earlier in 2000).[34] But there is no follow-through in *Bush v. Gore* on this potentially explosive point.

The failure to discuss levels of scrutiny, combined with a bow in the direction of the rational-basis test, could have flowed from the desire of Kennedy and O'Connor to be moderate but also to get a majority for their central equal-protection claim. Thus Chief Justice Rehnquist had long held that unless equal-protection classifications involved "means of sorting people which the draftsmen of the [Fourteenth] Amendment sought to prohibit"[35]—by race most obviously, or perhaps by nationality—they fell under the rational-basis standard of judgment. For him, then, Florida's counting system could be unconstitutional *only* because it failed a test under which, as he phrased it a few months later, "'*any reasonably conceivable state of facts*'" provided justification.[36]

Justice Scalia carried even greater baggage. He was on record as believing that in equal-protection (and First Amendment) controversies, "'when a practice not explicitly prohibited by the text of the Bill of Rights bears the endorsement of a long tradition of open, widespread, and unchallenged use [dating] back to the beginning of the Republic, we have no proper basis for striking it down.' . . . The same applies . . . to a practice asserted to be in violation of the post–Civil War Fourteenth Amendment."[37] The practice of hand counting votes without any uniform, overriding standards bore exactly this endorsement. (Justice Thomas, though, whatever his exact views on *Bush,* had written in 1993 that the rational-basis test did not apply to "statutory classification[s] that . . . proceed along suspect lines [or] *infringe fundamental constitutional rights.*"[38])

Actually, none of the three had to approve of the per curiam's dominant equal-protection holding in order to join it. They were necessarily drawn to the opinion through O'Connor's and Kennedy's willingness to bring the Florida crisis to a definitive end by decreeing that the state legislature had made December 12 the drop-dead date. This was the functional equivalent of their belief that violations of Article II automatically voided the recount.

And had these three not endorsed the per curiam, the historic judgment in *Bush v. Gore,* awaited breathlessly by America and the world, would have come down as an utterly bewildering collage. The public would have learned that a six-person majority had overruled the Florida Supreme Court decision, but without a majority rationale, three justices acting on Article II grounds, three on equal-protection grounds. Reports would also have indicated that a bare majority of the justices effectively ended the election contest, but again with no one opinion articulating the reason for this action.

The Root Holding

The idea that criteria for counting votes raised matters of constitutional dimension was certainly a novel one in U.S. law. *Bush v. Gore* was very much a case of first impression; the most recent precedent cited in the per curiam opinion, *Moore v. Ogilvie*, dates from 1969, before any of the justices who decided *Bush* joined the Court. Neither *Moore* nor any of the other cases cited, including *Reynolds v. Sims*, are, or could be, directly on point.

Yet the central contention of the per curiam (of Kennedy and O'Connor, basically) is not aberrant, radiating, to the contrary, a certain commonsense appeal. In the form, at least, in which the election dispute came before the justices, it did not seem "entirely crazy" to "extend the principle of 'one person, one vote' from the question of how districts are apportioned before the election to the question of how the votes are tabulated after the election."[39]

The most obvious objection to such an approach is that it seems a bit hypocritical, that tolerating a non-uniform system of recounts in Florida in 2000 was ultimately no different from tolerating the system that held sway during the original counts (and in hundreds of previous elections), where jurisdictions with different voting technologies produced widely varying numbers of spoiled ballots. But as Michael McConnell notes, these contentions, for one thing, are irrelevant to the 2000 election. "If the use of different voting machines by different [Florida] counties" raised "a constitutional issue" in 2000, it had to be "challenged before the election," the only time "it could be remedied."[40] And as for future elections, "Why *not* require every state to adopt a uniform vote-counting system?"[41]

Still, the Court's rationale for condemning different standards of recounting points to myriad possible intrusions on state election processes that go beyond the matter of voting machines. The design of ballots, the way absentee ballots are handled, alleged differences between the way elderly voters are treated in different counties, even different poll closing times, could all be subjects of litigation, something totally at odds with the federalist passion of the Rehnquist court.[42] "To subject all of these diverse practices and rules to equal protection review," argues Richard Briffault of Columbia Law School, "could ultimately result in a federal court-ordered, nationwide standardization of the mechanics of elections. . . . The real tension between *Bush v. Gore* and federalism is that the gravamen of the particular equal protection violation at the heart of *Bush v. Gore* is the value at the heart of federalism itself—decentralized decision-making and the resulting variations in governmental action."[43]

Awareness of such difficulties almost surely explains why the majority justices tried a widely criticized tactic in *Bush*. They sought to reconcile the hasty manner in which they had to render their decision with the broader constitutional philosophies they espoused by sharply restricting the decision's reach. "Our consideration is limited to the present circumstances, for the problem of equal protection in election processes generally presents many complexities."[44]

A number of scholars found this statement disingenuous at best, pointing out that constitutional disputes in most areas present "many complexities," yet the whole point of Supreme Court decisions is to lay down precedents that apply, in varying degrees, to future cases.[45] The majority was trying to limit the damage in *Bush*, felt Michael Herz, by saying in essence, "[H]ere's our gut reaction, but don't hold us to it."[46] We need "not take *Bush v. Gore's* [equal-protection] holding seriously," concludes Richard Hasen of Loyola Law School, "because the Court itself did not take its holding seriously."[47]

The Weight of Time

Perhaps the most important effect of the frantic circumstances under which *Bush v. Gore* developed was the way those circumstances shaped the basic form of the case—defined, as it were, the constitutional universe both the litigants and the justices inhabited. This universe was largely a mirage.

The justices operated in an equal-protection order where they saw, above all, differing standards in Palm Beach and Broward Counties for assessing "identical types of ballots used in identical brands of machines."[48] Gore's brief did not really attack such factual premises; up through the contest phase, his lawyers had downplayed technical differences among the punch-card counties themselves, since they sought to get dimpled ballots credited everywhere. Their submission to the Supreme Court focused on the *systemic* "inconsistency in the treatment of individual ballots" that would always exist, "so long as the count is conducted by humans."[49]

But there were examples of a far messier situation on the ground. Thus, Palm Beach voters did not all use the much-discussed Votomatic machines in 2000. Many were stuck with a cheap "knockoff" of the device named Data-Punch, much less reliable than the Votomatic, and very poorly maintained at the time of the election. Officials testing the machines on November 7 found many of them defective, not capable of facilitating a clean punch, yet due to the exigencies of the day the devices stayed in service. Investigation by the *Miami Herald* showed "Data-Punch machines . . . plagued by worn out parts, including plastic springs that had been discontinued years earlier by their manufacturer because they were associated with spoiled votes."[50]

These defects helped contribute to an undervote rate of 4.4 percent among those who used Data-Punch, as opposed to 1.6 percent among those using the Votomatic.[51] (Only one punch-card county had a total undervote rate that got above 2.5 percent, at 2.58.) The Data-Punch machines also contributed to around two-thirds of the 6,789 dimpled ballots found in Palm Beach County; Broward County, with 20 percent more voters, had 2,060 dimpled cards.[52]

Under less constraint of time, Gore's legal team might have developed this matter with precinct and county authorities, and pressed their demand for counting of the Palm Beach dimples by means of an alternate legal rationale, which focused on the peculiar difficulties experienced in the county. Whatever the merits of this more specific argument, and whatever its fate had been before the Palm Beach canvassing board or the state courts, it would have presented the U.S. Supreme Court with a very different picture than it saw of equal-protection problems in disparate jurisdictions.

The Critical Overvotes

Time clearly would have been on the side of the majority justices, however, with regard to the claim that equal protection required the search for overvotes as well as for undervotes in the court-ordered recount.

The matter was one for legitimate debate in the December 12 opinions. The per curiam made a sound case simply by noting that 110,000 overvotes existed in the state, particularly a state in which the vast majority of them remained untouched. If the Florida Supreme Court was "actually . . . seeking to ascertain the 'will of the voters,'" as Nelson Lund argues, "that would have required . . . at an absolute minimum . . . reexamining all the 'overvotes' . . . as well as the undervotes. . . . Once one assumes that the 'intent of the voter' should be honored even when the voter failed to comply with the instructions on how to vote, these two categories of ballots become logically indistinguishable." Although the "machine counts were undoubtedly imperfect, there could be no legitimate, let alone compelling, interest in substituting hand recounts unless those recounts could reasonably have been expected to be *more accurate as a whole* than the machine recounts."[53] Overvotes also promised, in theory, a higher rate of recovery than undervotes. Many people could deliberately have skipped the presidential race, but no one, presumably, set out to vote for two candidates.

Still, on the facts before the Court, Justice Breyer could justifiably point to the lack of evidence that overvoted ballots really yielded valid votes. The petitioners, he noted, had presented no documentation on this matter "to any Florida court,"[54] in contrast to Gore's repeated demonstrations that undervotes required scrutiny because there were five times as many of them in punch-card counties as in the rest of Florida. (Judge Burton's contest trial testimony did discuss whether certain punch cards were properly treated as valid votes or overvotes. But he was discussing cards displaying a clean punch in the presidential race combined with a dimple, ballots a machine would count as undervotes.)[55] Gore's final brief endorsed Justice Breyer's dissent with the reminder that "neither at trial, nor on appeal, did [Bush] present any evidence concerning the nature of the ballots found to be overvotes."[56]

Yet lying within the justices' reach was proof of a very significant pattern in the unscouted territory, a pattern Bush surely would have called attention to had there been further litigation. The appendix to Judge Ed Carnes's Eleventh Circuit opinion of December 6, dissenting from denial of Governor Bush's last injunction request, contained a list of the total percentage of spoiled ballots, undervotes and overvotes, in all of Florida's counties.[57] Arranged separately for punch-card and optical-scanning counties, this document revealed that, despite their known paucity of undervotes, it was the optical-scanning jurisdictions that contained eight of the top twelve percentages of rejected ballots. Gadsden County, at 12.4 percent, led the state. These eight counties, it turned out, were all ones where ballots were not counted at the precinct level, and mistakes corrected, but at a central location. The fifteen counties of this sort in Florida came up with an average spoilage rate of 7.32 percent, more than 90 percent of them overvotes,[58] compared to 3.92 percent in the punch-card counties (and only 1.16 percent in counties with optical scanners and counting in each precinct). This certainly warranted a look at the overvotes, even granted just 16,000 or so of them were in the central-location counties.[59]

Indeed, the *USA Today–Miami Herald* survey of the Florida overvotes showed that even optical-scanning counties that counted in each precinct, despite their low overall percentage of spoiled ballots, validated 1,220 overvotes, 461 for Bush, 759 for Gore. The central-location counties, however, came up with 1,649 such overvotes, 649 for Bush, 1,000 for Gore. The punch-card counties as a whole had only 110 retrievable overvotes, 78 for Bush, 110 for Gore; Palm Beach, as noted, had just 12 such ballots, Miami-Dade 20, and Broward only 4.[60] The overvotes in the optical scanning counties occurred most often because voters would color in the oval for a candidate but also put a mark next to his party. Or they would fill in the Bush or Gore oval, then write the candidate's name on the ballot as well.

The *USA Today–Miami Herald* study concluded that even with the margin of 682 he gained in overvotes, the vice president still would have needed dimpled ballots to win, though under the Palm Beach standard for crediting such ballots he would have come out on top by 242 votes.[61] A survey by the National Opinion Research Center indicates the addition of overvotes would have produced a Gore victory, using recount standards county officials said they would have used.[62] Prevailing in the Supreme Court, however, would have meant certain defeat for Gore.

The False Bottom

The culminating section of *Bush v. Gore*, laying down the December 12 deadline, is generally agreed to be its weakest. Whatever the Florida Supreme Court's intimations on this matter, it never said flatly that the Florida legislature had opted for the safe harbor, and the legislature itself had never decreed by law or by resolution that it intended at all costs to take advantage of Section 5's protections, as other states have done.[63] In the absence of such a declaration, it is impossible to be certain this is what the house and senate wanted. The amicus brief in *Bush v. Gore* (again by Charles Fried, Einer Elhauge, and Roger Magnuson) assumes that it was the "Florida Legislature's wish" to embrace Section 5, because manual recounts completed after December 11 "are not binding on Congress when it counts the electoral results."[64] But as Michael Klarman of the University of Virginia argues,

> It is one thing to say that the Florida legislature would have wished, all things being equal, to take advantage of the federal safe harbor provision. It is another thing entirely to say that the legislature would have wanted the availability of the safe harbor provision to trump any and all competing considerations, such as ensuring that every vote be counted. The outcome of the 2000 presidential election quite possibly turned on this aspect of the *Bush* decision, a rationale that is, to put it bluntly, a complete fabrication.[65]

By December 12, actually, the legislature was at work naming its own slate of electors, with none of its leaders proclaiming the contest must automatically end.

In any event, it is ironic that the per curiam should rely so heavily on the supposed wisdom of the Florida Supreme Court in reaching its conclusion about the safe harbor. Justice Kennedy does not even quote the passages from prior opinions that most help his case, such as the references in *Gore v. Harris* to "an outside deadline established by federal law," or to the Florida election statutes being "derived from 3 U.S.C. § 5."[66] Instead, in his haste, Kennedy quotes from the original protest opinion, the very opinion that was remanded in part because it didn't deal with the state legislature's take on Section 5. *"The Supreme Court of Florida* has said that the legislature intended the State's electors to 'participat[e] fully in the federal electoral process' as provided in 3 U.S.C. § 5."[67] This passage, as we have seen, refers to a secretary of state's authority to rely on Section 5 in setting protest deadlines; as Justice Leander Shaw noted in Florida's final decision on remand (issued December 22, 2000), the passage does not definitively establish "a *court's* obligation to stop a recount in a post-certification *contest* action."[68]

In *Bush I*, Chief Justice Rehnquist and his colleagues were emphatic in declaring that *Palm Beach County Canvassing Board v. Harris* had not addressed a possible "legislative wish to take advantage of the 'safe harbor.'"[69] Now they were claiming the decision of November 21 had settled the matter. Not surprisingly, the remedy arrived at "in *Bush* . . . had few defenders even among conservatives who defended the . . . decision on the merits"; a number of them felt that the appropriate action for the justices to have taken was to remand the case to the Florida Supreme Court with specific instructions to address the question of why, in the absence of an explicit legislative statement, that court *seemed* to be saying December 12 was the end of the line.[70]

Notes

1. Michael Herz, "The Supreme Court in Real Time: Haste, Waste, and *Bush v. Gore*," 35 *Akron Law Review* (2002), pp. 185, 190–191.
2. *Bush v. Gore*, 148 LEd 2d 388, 403 (2000).
3. Ibid.
4. Michael J. Klarman, "*Bush v. Gore* Through the Lens of Constitutional History," 89 *California Law Review* (2001), pp. 1721, 1734, 1735.
5. *Bush v. Gore*, p. 418.
6. Antonin Scalia, *A Matter of Interpretation* (Princeton, N.J.: Princeton University Press, 1997), p. 38.
7. *Hudson v. McMillan*, 503 US 1, 18 (1992).
8. *McIntyre v. Ohio Elections Commission*, 514 US 334, 358–359 (1995).
9. Ibid., at 371–372 (italics added).
10. Quoted in Gordon Wood, *The Creation of the American Republic, 1776–1787* (Chapel Hill: University of North Carolina Press, 1969), p. 467.
11. *Bush v. Gore*, pp. 405, 407, 407.
12. Ibid., p. 407.
13. Ibid.
14. Ibid., p. 408.
15. *Beckstrom v. Volusia County Canvassing Board*, 707 So. 2d 720, 722, fn. 4 (1998).
16. Lawrence Tribe, "Comment," 115 *Harvard Law Review* (2001), pp. 170, 200.
17. *Bush v. Gore*, p. 407.
18. Martin Merzer and the Staff of *The Miami Herald*, *The Miami Herald Report: Democracy Held Hostage* (New York: St. Martin's Press, 2001), p. 231.

19. Richard Friedman, "Trying To Make Peace with *Bush v. Gore*," 29 *Florida State University Law Review* (2001), pp. 811, 843.

20. Abner Greene, *Understanding the 2000 Election* (New York: New York University Press, 2001), p. 66.

21. Ibid., pp. 66–67.

22. Richard A. Epstein, "'In Such Manner as the Legislature Thereof May Direct': The Outcome in *Bush v. Gore* Defended," in Cass Sunstein and Richard A. Epstein (eds.), *The Vote: Bush, Gore, and the Supreme Court* (Chicago: University of Chicago Press, 2001), p. 33.

23. *Bush v. Gore*, pp. 407, 406, 407.

24. Ibid., 407.

25. Ibid., p. 399.

26. The issue has arisen as to whether in this equal-protection area, Governor Bush possessed legal standing to press the suit in *Bush v. Gore*. If anyone figured to be directly harmed by the court-ordered recounts, some commentators point out, it was various Florida voters, and since George Bush was assuredly not a Florida voter, he didn't suffer the direct harm requisite to bring a "case or controversy" under Article III of the Constitution. Assuming this is true, that Bush's injury of possibly losing the presidency was legally distinct from the injury to Florida voters, and was not direct enough to qualify him in itself, he might still have retained what is known as third-party standing in the case, standing to speak for the injured voters. Erwin Chemerinsky denies this is so, however, arguing that Governor Bush does not fall into the exceptions to the direct-standing rule that allow intervention. There was not "a close relationship between the advocate and the third party," like that between doctor and patient. Furthermore, there seemed to be no "substantial obstacles" to the Florida voters presenting their own case. "In response" to this second argument, he admits "it could be argued that no Florida voter could know if it [was] his or her ballot" that was going "uncounted; [and] thus no Florida voter [could] meet the requirements of standing." But if this was true, "the absence of a plaintiff for standing indicates that the matter is [properly] left to the political process and not to the courts" ("*Bush v. Gore* Was Not Justiciable," 76 *Notre Dame Law Review* [2001], pp. 1093, 1099–1100). Laurence Tribe maintains, though, that Governor Bush did have third-party standing, analogizing the situation in *Bush v. Gore* to the one in the 1991 case of *Powers v. Ohio*, where the U.S. Supreme Court allowed such standing to a white criminal defendant challenging the deliberate exclusion of African Americans from a jury pool. The defendant, said the Supreme Court, would clearly suffer "a cognizable injury" from the "discriminatory use of peremptory challenges by the prosecution"; he had through "voir dire . . . established a relation, if not a bond of trust, with the jurors," and both an "excluded juror and the criminal defendant have a common interest in eliminating racial discrimination from the courtroom"; finally, while it was not impossible for an excluded juror to bring a discrimination suit, "the barriers" to such a suit were "daunting" (499 US 400, 411, 413, 414). Tribe argued that the same situation existed in the *Bush* case. "[Bush's] injury was obvious: the Florida Supreme Court was in essence forcing the Governor of Texas to exchange twenty-five electoral votes the Florida Secretary of State had certified as his on November 26—a number sufficient to make him the next president—for a recount to be conducted by a process he regarded as an unconstitutional roulette game rigged in favor of his opponent"; he also "shared with all the voters a sufficiently common interest in protecting the integrity of the vote count to ensure his standing as third-party plaintiff." Hence, "Bush not only had [third-party] standing, but was particularly well placed to assert" the rights of voters who would face

"significant obstacles" in bringing a suit, because they typically could "not know whether [it was their vote that] had been miscounted." Those voters did not have to be abandoned to the political process ("Comment," 115 *Harvard Law Review* [2001], pp. 170, 230–231). Ultimately, however, it is clear that unless Bush's lack of standing was beyond dispute, the Supreme Court wasn't going to decide the case on this abstruse basis. The justices do not even mention standing.

27. *Bush v. Gore*, p. 398.
28. Ibid.
29. See *Shapiro v. Thompson*, 394 US 618, 631, 638 (1969); *Kramer. v. Union Free School District*, 395 US 621, 626 (1969); *Dunn v. Blumstein*, 405 US 330, 336, 342 (1972); *Memorial Hospital v. Maricopa County*, 415 US 250, 269 (1974).
30. *Reynolds v. Sims*, 377 US 533, 562 (1964).
31. *Bush v. Gore*, pp. 398, 399, 399.
32. See *Royster Guano Co. v. Virginia*, 253 US 412, 415 (1920); *Stanton v. Stanton*, 421 US 7, 14 (1975); *New Orleans v. Dukes*, 427 US 297, 303 (1976); *Cleburne v. Cleburne Living Center Inc.*, 473 US 432, 446 (1985).
33. *Bush v. Gore*, p. 417.
34. *Kimel v. Florida Board of Regents*, 528 US 62, 84 (2000), quoting *Vance v. Bradley*, 440 US 93, 97 (1979).
35. *Trimble v. Gordon,* 430 US 762, 785 (1977). Justice Rehnquist dissented in this case.
36. *Board of Trustees of University of Alabama v. Garrett*, 148 LEd 2d 866, 869 (2001), quoting *FCC v. Beach Communications Inc.,* 508 US 307, 313 (1993) (italics added).
37. *United States v. Virginia,* 518 US 515, 568 (1996), quoting from *Rutan v. Republican Party of Illinois*, 497 US 62, 95 (1990). Scalia dissented in both cases.
38. *FCC v. Beach Communications Inc.*, 508 US 307, 313 (1993) (italics added).
39. Jack Balkin, "*Bush v. Gore* and the Boundary Between Law and Politics," 110 *Yale Law Journal* (2001), pp. 1407, 1426.
40. Michael McConnell, "Two-and-a-Half Cheers for *Bush v. Gore*," in Sunstein and Epstein (eds.), *The Vote*, p. 117.
41. Ibid.
42. See Richard Briffault, "*Bush v. Gore* as an Equal Protection Case," 29 *Florida State University Law Review* (2001), pp. 325, 349–350; Peter M. Shane, "Disappearing Democracy," 29 *Florida State University Law Review* (2001), pp. 535, 572–573.
43. Briffault, "*Bush v. Gore* as an Equal Protection Case," pp. 350, 373.
44. *Bush v. Gore*, p. 401.
45. On this point, see Justice Scalia's dissenting opinion in *United States v. Virginia*, at 596.
46. Herz, "The Supreme Court in Real Time," p. 194.
47. Richard L. Hasen, "*Bush v. Gore* and the Future of Equal Protection Law in Elections," 29 *Florida State University Law Review* (2001), pp. 377, 387.
48. *Bush v. Gore*, p. 416.
49. *Bush v. Gore*, "Brief of Respondent Albert Gore Jr.," p. 36.
50. Merzer and the Staff of *The Miami Herald, The Miami Herald Report,* pp. 79–80.
51. Ibid., p. 79.
52. Ibid., pp. 283, 239; interview with David Kidwell, *Miami Herald.*
53. Nelson Lund, "The Unbearable Rightness of *Bush v. Gore*," 23 *Cardozo Law Review* (2002), pp. 1219, 1241, 1249.

54. *Bush v. Gore*, p. 423.

55. "Contest Hearing Before Judge Sauls," p. 263, www.flcourts.org.

56. "The Unfiled Gore Brief of December 13, 2000," reprinted in Jake Tapper, *Down and Dirty* (Boston: Little Brown, 2001), p. 496.

57. *Siegel v. LePore*, 234 F. 3d 1163, 1215–1216 (Chart C), 1217–1218 (Chart F).

58. See Correspondents of the *New York Times, 36 Days* (New York: Times Books, 2001), p. 285.

59. Ibid.

60. *USA Today–Miami Herald* Survey of Overvotes—County Summary. Courtesy of Dennis Cauchon.

61. Martin Merzer, "Overvotes Leaned to Gore but to Win, He Needed Help of Dimpled Ballots," *Miami Herald*, May 11, 2001, p. 1A.

62. Dan Keating and Dan Balz, "Florida Recounts Would Have Favored Bush, but Study Finds Gore Might Have Won Statewide Tally of All Uncounted Ballots," *Washington Post*, November 12, 2001, p. A1.

63. 28 *Cal Jur*, Elections, § 285; *Connecticut General Statutes Annotated*, § 9-323; *Iowa Code Annotation*, § 60.5.

64. *Bush v. Gore*, "Brief of the Florida House of Representatives and Florida Senate as *Amici Curiae* in Support of Neither Party and Seeking Reversal," pp. 18, 17.

65. Klarman, "*Bush v. Gore* Through the Laws of Constitutional History," p. 1733.

66. *Gore v. Harris*, 772 So. 2d 1243, 1261, 1248 (2000).

67. *Bush v. Gore*, p. 402 (italics added).

68. *Gore v. Harris*, 773 So. 2d 524, 529, fn. 12 (2000).

69. *Bush v. Palm Beach County Canvassing Board*, 148 LEd 2d 366, 372 (2000).

70. Ward Farnsworth, "'To Do a Great Right, Do a Little Wrong': A User's Guide to Judicial Lawlessness," 86 *Minnesota Law Review* (2001), pp. 227, 232. See McConnell, "Two-and-a-Half Cheers for *Bush v. Gore*," in Sunstein and Epstein (eds.), *The Vote*, pp. 117–120; Charles Fried, "'A Badly Flawed Election': An Exchange," *New York Review of Books*, February 22, 2002, p. 8; Ronald Cass, *The Rule of Law in America* (Baltimore: Johns Hopkins Press, 2001), pp. 93–95; John Yoo, "In Defense of the Court's Legitimacy," in Sunstein and Epstein (eds.), *The Vote*, p. 240. But see also Daniel Lowenstein in "A Principled Ruling to Some, A Disaster to Others," *Salon*, December 13, 2000, pp. 3–4; John O. McGinnis, "A Just and Wise Decision," *New York Post*, December 14, 2000.

PART 7

CONCLUSION

The Whys and the Wherefores

Mark Whitman

The failure of the majority justices to order a meaningful remand in *Bush v. Gore* is the prime source of suspicions that some of them carried a hidden agenda into the case—that institutional or prudential or rawly partisan aims lay behind the outcome.

The view most flattering to any extrajudicial motives the Court might have harbored is articulated by Judge Posner, in his characteristically thoughtful and elegant manner. He maintains the majority in *Bush v. Gore* very possibly acted, and was justified in acting, to save the country from the raucous and divisive national crisis that would have followed upon a continuing recount, especially if, by some chance, the recount had been completed and shown Gore on top. "Blacks and white liberals," Posner writes, "will not soon forgive the Supreme Court for dashing Gore's hopes. But the bitterness that lingers may be slight compared with what it would have been had the election outcome not been resolved until January."[1]

It is certainly easy to imagine dangerous, disruptive scenarios emerging in December 2000 and January 2001. If Gore had won a reconstituted and completed recount, the country could first have been treated to the spectacle of Secretary Harris wrangling with the Florida and federal courts over whether she had to sign a new certification, Governor Jeb Bush almost certainly refusing to sign a new certificate of ascertainment, and a Gore slate of electors casting votes in a Tallahassee hotel ballroom. Meanwhile, the Florida legislature would have designated its Bush slate of electors by now, perhaps, in a form Governor Bush was able to sign off on. Then the grand climax in an agonizingly divided Congress!

> Had the responsibility for determining who would be President fallen to Congress in January, there would have been a competition in indignation between the parties' supporters, with each side accusing the other of having stolen the election. Whatever Congress did would have been regarded

as the product of raw politics, with no tincture of justice. The new President would have been deprived of a transition period in which to organize his administration and would have taken office against a background of unprecedented bitterness. (Even the relatively brief delay in resolving the election deadlock delayed the formation of Bush's administration.) His "victory" would have been an empty one; he could not have governed effectively. The scenario that produces this dismal result is conjectural. But that there was a real and disturbing *potential* for disorder and temporary paralysis (I do not want to exaggerate) seems undeniable. That is why the Supreme Court's decision was greeted with relief by many people, not all of them Republicans. . . .

I do not see what the point would have been of risking precipitating a political and constitutional crisis merely in order to fuss with a statistical tie that—given the inherent subjectivity involved in hand counting spoiled ballots—can never be untied.[2]

In this context, Judge Posner feels the Supreme Court wisely traded in some of the respect in which it is held to serve the cause of national reconciliation.

Bush v. Gore may have done less harm to the nation by reducing the Supreme Court's prestige than it did good by heading off a significant probability of a Presidential selection process that would have undermined the Presidency and embittered American politics more than the decision itself did or is likely to do. Judges unwilling to sacrifice some of their prestige for the greater good of the nation might be thought selfish.[3]

(In hindsight, the tragic events of 2001 cut both ways for these arguments. Genuine crisis, it seems, will bring the nation together behind nearly any chief executive, no matter the circumstances surrounding his or her election. Still, September 11 suggests the vital importance of truncating as little as possible an already brief presidential transition period.)

Judge Posner's scenario is anything but beyond the realm of possibility. Yet it is also possible that a Supreme Court effort to "save the nation" could have ended by flaunting the will of Congress and changing the outcome of the presidential election. Suppose the count had been allowed to proceed, Gore had overcome the obstacles (some of them proper) placed in his path by the Supreme Court's recount order, and finished ahead in a recount regarded as legally sound by most observers. An upsurge in public opinion might well have demanded his election, a sentiment putting irresistible pressure on Republicans from moderate congressional districts, for the vice president "could then claim," as Professor Balkin notes, "that he had won a majority in Florida and a majority in the Electoral College as well as a majority in the popular vote. . . . The Republicans [could] have judged it politically very difficult to displace him with Bush, and their opposition on January 6 might have been much less fierce."[4]

In any case, United States Supreme Court justices do not "hold their positions by virtue of demonstrated skill at predicting the political consequences of decisions," writes Ward Farnsworth, in an incisive rebuttal to Judge Posner.[5] Besides,

> Most of the costs and benefits of prolonged litigation over the [2000] election were impossible to define without making initial decisions that had ideological content and that were the subject of the election itself. . . .
> Whether [in normal, non-crisis times, at least] a weak President Bush is better than a strong one, or better or worse than a weak or strong President Gore, is not possible to say from an apolitical standpoint. Ensuring that the winner of the election entered office in a position of strength thus was not an appropriate "good" for the Court to maximize. From a pragmatic standpoint, the outcome the Court ordered did not work especially well for those who opposed George Bush, and there is no reason to weight their interests less than those of his supporters.[6]

Frankly political decisions should only issue, Farnsworth argues, under controlled circumstances, and *Bush v. Gore* did not fit those circumstances, the "harm" avoided being by nature unquantifiable.

A Simpler Motive—Again, Time

There is a more modest version of the realpolitik logic for shutting down the recount.[7] The majority justices may well have believed, as early as December 9, and certainly by December 11, that the constitutional defects they saw in the recounts meant the election was over, since (state contest appeals aside) it was virtually impossible Florida officials could remedy those defects and complete the statewide recount by December 18, the day the Electoral College met. Even granting Rehnquist and his colleagues couldn't be positive December 12 represented the "drop-dead" date for completing recounts, it is safe to assume them certain December 18 *was* the date, a view shared by two of the dissenting justices (though not by Stevens and Ginsburg). The majority also believed the vice president was precluded from succeeding in court after December 18 on the basis of an incomplete count (as they affirmed in *Bush*). That he could not succeed in Congress, or with public opinion, appeared a reasonable proposition as well.

Hence, the purpose of insisting on December 12 was a prudential one in this view, designed to spare the country, and the candidates, further anguish, though one can surmise it blended in with the majority's lack of trust in the whole Florida recount enterprise, supervised by the authors of *Gore v. Harris*.

Of course, a decision terminating the election controversy for lack of time was a self-fulfilling prophecy in part, considering that the stay granted on December 9 kept many counties from getting information they could have used to readjust their undervote totals once standards were set. The justices may not have thought of such a possibility, believing, as Charles Fried later maintained, that "assuming . . . the equal protection violation, the recounting . . .would have had to be repeated."[8] Or they were firmly convinced any advantages gained from a doomed recount must be subordinated to the harm done to Bush and to the United States, if Gore crept ahead.

Still, it was highly unlikely that all sixty-four counties in Florida doing recounting could have avoided the necessity of another complete count of undervotes once standards came down from the Florida Supreme Count. Above all, there was the new matter of the overvotes. The issue was raised immediately in Bush's stay request of December 8. By the next day, the justices (and/or their clerks) had read Justice Harding's dissent in *Gore v. Harris*, speaking of 177,000 "no-votes" in the state,[9] and anyone conversant with the Florida situation knew most of them were overvotes. (The December 9 *Washington Post* contained a chart putting the number of undervotes to be counted at 45,170.)[10] If this was not enough to influence the majority's course of action, they pried the 110,000 figure out of David Boies on December 11.

Hence, they could well have concluded that even if they allowed the Florida justices to clarify (and likely moot) the December 12 deadline, the time needed to do this, then to set standards for and complete the counting of 177,000 ballots, then finally to get all the disputed ballots, perhaps thousands, packed up and shipped to Tallahassee for Judge Lewis's review—that all these tasks were just not doable in five days.

To clear up the deadline issue and set uniform counting standards would surely have claimed at least two days, and even three full days for the recount itself represented a tight fit at best. But it is very possible things would have been held up again before the recount started by an emergency appeal on Bush's part to the U.S. Supreme Court over some aspect of standards or protocol. Overvotes, after all, were coming before everyone for the first time. Furthermore, the necessarily hurried setting up of procedures for the new recount could have activated another due process grievance, to which the majority justices had already shown themselves generally receptive.

The vice president's lawyers were aware of these scheduling pressures. Understandably anxious to save time, their aborted brief of December 13 suggested that judicial review of disputed ballots in the recount be spread out among the circuit areas in which the various canvassing boards were located.[11] But remembering the reassurance that the Florida Supreme Court's best friends in *Bush v. Gore*, Justices Stevens and Ginsburg, had derived from believing some "*single impartial magistrate*" would "ultimately adjudicate all objections arising from the recount process,"[12] the

Bush lawyers undoubtedly would have appealed to Washington on due process grounds against any notion of fifteen judges of last resort.

If the majority justices in *Bush v. Gore* based their decision on matters of timing, they were very likely right as to what would have happened. Yet this still meant staking the presidency on a guess—however educated the guess might be.

Ultimate Motives

The Court's entire performance has led inevitably to accusations of the basest and most blatant partisanship, masquerading as judicial reasoning. "I am convinced," writes Alan Dershowitz, "—along with many academics, editorial writers, litigators, and ordinary citizens—that if it had been Bush rather than Gore who needed the Florida recount in order to have any chance of winning, at least some of the five justices who voted to stop the recount would instead have voted to allow it to go forward—that is, they would have failed the shoe-on-the-other-foot test."[13] Michael Klarman asks, "Had all the other facts in the Florida election imbroglio remained the same, but the situation of the two presidential candidates been reversed, does anyone seriously believe that the conservative Justices would have reached the same result?"[14]

There are defenses, as we have seen, for the justices' actions. But it is clear once the Supreme Court decided to get mixed up in the Bush-Gore controversy, its members, or at least some of them, could never avoid the suspicion that they were making nothing but a personal choice—even if not for crassly political resaons. Rehnquist and Scalia had labored openly and with deep conviction all their professional lives for something like the kind of Court over which the chief now presides. Why mightn't they have allowed the wish to be father to the thought in *Bush v. Gore*, when it could mean eight years of conservative appointments? Similarly, most important in assessing Justice O'Connor's possible motives is not the gaffe, however deplorable, that she made by bemoaning Gore's seeming victory at an election-night party,[15] but her commitment, and that of Justice Kennedy, to a jurisprudence causing them to markedly prefer George Bush.

We can never know for certain what role motivations of this sort played in the majority's decision, or would have played in *"Gore v. Bush."* We are on more open ground if we look at the broader philosophy behind the case the Court did decide, as revealed so strikingly in its handling of the December 12 deadline. Here was a Court that seemed to believe that, one way or another, judicial fiat should settle the Bush-Gore struggle, not the expedient maneuverings of senators and congresspeople. If there was an opening for the justices to act, they would do so, and do so emphatically.

This dominant characteristic of the Rehnquist era provides the key, most likely, to *Bush v. Gore*. The chief justice and his colleagues are scarcely the first to be accused of overreaching themselves. Cries of judicial usurpation ring throughout our history, not least at the time of Earl Warren. But John Yoo of Berkeley Law School, a former clerk to Justice Scalia and a supporter of the *Bush* decision, invokes brilliantly what some see as the special hubris of the contemporary Court, in words that parallel Rachel Barkow and other commentators.[16]

> What is important about the Court's recent track record is not just the frequency of the uses of judicial review, but their quality. Initially, the Marshall Court in *Marbury v. Madison* grounded judicial review in the Court's unique function in deciding cases or controversies that arise under federal law. As Thomas Jefferson argued, this basis for judicial review leaves ample room for the coordinate branches of government to interpret the Constitution in the course of performing their own constitutional functions. Under the Rehnquist court, this limited vision of judicial review has steadily been supplanted by assertions of judicial supremacy—that the Supreme Court is not just *an* interpreter of the Constitution, but *the* interpreter of the Constitution. . . .
>
> Such assertions of judicial supremacy belie any notions that the Rehnquist court generally has followed a course of restraint. If the Court is willing to go so far as to declare that its power to interpret the Constitution is supreme over the other branches, certainly it is no greater a step to intervene in a dispute about non-substantive, rarely-used election procedures. . . . Claims to judicial supremacy bespeak an arrogance that the Court has a special role in the American political system, one borne not just out of its unique function in deciding cases or controversies, but out of some vague vision of itself as a final resolver of national issues. The justices, in other words, have truly come to believe in Justice Jackson's famous aphorism that "[w]e are not final because we are infallible, but we are infallible only because we are final."[17]

A Final Word: The Future and the Past

Florida undertook extensive patching of its electoral system soon after experiencing the vicissitudes of 2000; it passed a state Election Reform Act the next year.[18] This legislation inevitably reflected the way the Republican senators and representatives wished the system had been constructed in the first place.

There was no longer any distinction between "shall" and "may" in determining deadlines. Returns "must" now come in by 5 P.M. on the eleventh day after a general election (extended from seven), and if they were "not received" by the Department of State at that time, "such returns *shall* be ignored."[19] Only an emergency could gain an extension for a canvassing board, and "emergency" was specifically, and rather melodramatically, defined as "any occurrence, or threat thereof, whether accidental, natural, or caused by human beings, in war or in peace, that results or may result in substantial injury or harm to the population or substantial damage to or loss of property to the extent it will prohibit an election officer's ability to conduct a safe and orderly election."[20]

The discretion of canvassing boards to grant manual recounts was also ended. If the election returns showed a margin of victory for one candidate of 0.25 percent or less of the total vote, a manual recount of all "the overvotes and undervotes cast in the entire geographic jurisdiction" was obligatory—obviously a statewide recount in a statewide election.[21] If the returns showed a margin of victory between 0.25 and 0.5 percent, the candidate who trailed was automatically entitled upon request to a recount of overvotes and undervotes.[22]

The "intent of the voter" standard no longer governed. Now, "If a counting team is unable to determine whether [a] ballot contains *a clear indication that the voter has made a definite choice*, the ballot shall be presented to the county canvassing board for a determination."[23] (The same language still controlled the evaluation of damaged ballots.)[24] The secretary of state was required to "adopt specific rules for . . . what constitutes a 'clear indication . . . that the voter has made a definite choice,'"[25] and the secretary issued guidelines in late 2001 for evaluation of optical-scan ballots. They provided, among other things, that such ballots counted as valid votes in a manual recount if the name of the candidate "is circled or underlined" (rather than the oval next to it colored in), if the "party abbreviation associated with a candidate's name is circled or underlined," or if the ballot contains "written words naming a specific candidate . . . such as 'Vote for Doe.'"[26] Optical-scan ballots are invalid if there is any "abbreviation, misspelling, or other minor variation" in a write-in choice, or when the voter writes in two names, even if one "is not a qualified . . . candidate."[27]

These initial instructions could be limited to optical-scan ballots, for in 2001 Florida discontinued the use of all punch-card machines and helped counties purchase more up-to-date equipment, either optical scanners or the newer touch-screen technology. The debut of the latter, at least in Miami-Dade and Broward Counties, was not auspicious. Voters flocking to the polls for the 2002 gubernatorial primary found that about 10 percent of Miami-Dade's 754 precincts had failed to open on time, because poll officials could not properly activate the touch-screen systems. At about 11 A.M., 32 precincts were still closed and 77 others were operating at less than half of capacity, due to machine malfunctions. There were similar, if less severe, problems in Broward County.[28]

Both counties then encountered serious difficulties with vote counting. The "master activators" in many of the touch-screen devices, which are supposed to transmit accurate vote totals electronically to county headquarters, turned out to be wildly inaccurate.[29] Thus, seven precincts in Miami-Dade originally reported Democratic turnouts of more than 100 percent of the registered Democrats in those precincts, but thirty-two polling places showed no Democratic ballots cast at all. Broward County had five such precincts. In eighty-one other precincts in Miami, the overall Democratic turnout was reported as less than 6 percent; eleven precincts in Broward reported turnout rates below 5 percent, including Democrats, Republicans, and independents.[30]

Broward and Miami-Dade election authorities, including the much-beset David Leahy, ordered a recheck of the election machines, each of which possesses backup technology capable of providing an accurate vote total. Repairing the glitches did not change the outcome of the marquee primary contest of 2002, the battle for the Democratic gubernatorial nomination won by William McBride over Janet Reno. The touch-screen system functioned smoothly in the general election.

Florida was not the only state undertaking electoral reform in the wake of 2000, though some of them deny the Bush-Gore farrago is the reason for their actions.[31] By the time of the 2002 elections, eleven states had passed legislation providing for the purchase of new voting machines and for the creation of much improved voter databases, depending upon federal funding to help with these improvements.

This funding became a reality at the end of 2001, on the authorization level at least, when Congress passed, and President Bush signed, the Federal Election Reform Act. The act earmarks $3.86 billion over four years to states undertaking improvements in their electoral processes. The legislation does not impose anything like uniform federal standards for elections. But as a condition of federal funding, states must submit a plan for reform to a new national agency, the Election Assistance Commission.

Some states did not wait for federal dollars. Georgia installed a uniform statewide touch-screen system in time for the 2002 elections, the most ambitious reform anywhere in the 2000–2002 period. Texas banned further acquisition of punch-card devices, and by the 2002 primaries Harris County (Houston) had become the largest county jurisdiction in the nation to switch entirely from punch-card voting to electronic machines. (It has 3.4 million people.)

Other states have approved new vote-counting or ballot standards. North Carolina banned the butterfly ballot. Mississippi and Missouri, which still have punch-card voting, explicitly adopted the two-corner rule for recounts; Nevada, by contrast, adopted a uniform system stipulating that if "one corner of [a] . . . chad . . . is detached from the ballot, the vote counts."[32] In Virginia and Wyoming, however, only ballots that are properly marked will now count. There will be no more attempts in the two states to divine "intent of the voter."

Is this, finally, the correct way to approach elections, the "hard-assed" view, in Andrew Sullivan's words, that holds "that a strict, clear, technical standard for a vote should be maintained at all costs"? Most states still think not, including Florida; its officials still assert, for instance, that an X instead of a marked-in oval next to a candidate's name, cannot be ignored as officials seek to reconstruct election tallies that reflect the "will of the people." Yet everyone knows that the will of those who went to the polls in Florida on November 7, 2000, includes about thirty thousand people who cast irretrievable overvotes on butterfly or two-page ballots, but most of whom meant to vote for Gore.

The 2000 election in Florida was a lesson in the imperfections of democracy, both operationally and philosophically. But that it took a flat statistical tie to demonstrate these things, in a state on which, incredibly, the presidency rested, is a reassuring thought.

Notes

1. Richard Posner, *Breaking the Deadlock* (Princeton, N.J.: Princeton University Press, 2001), p. 144.
2. Ibid., pp. 143–144, 147.
3. Ibid., p. 162.
4. Jack Balkin, "*Bush v. Gore* and the Boundary Between Law and Politics," 110 *Yale Law Journal* (2001), p. 1438.
5. Ward Farnsworth, "'To Do a Great Right, Do a Little Wrong': A User's Guide to Judicial Lawlessness," 86 *Minnesota Law Review* (2001), p. 242.
6. Ibid., pp. 243, 245.
7. See Posner, *Breaking the Deadlock*, pp. 136–137. Judge Posner does not develop this point as fully as his major thesis, but certainly opens the point for development. See also Michael McConnell, "Two-and-a-Half Cheers for *Bush v. Gore*," in Cass M. Sunstein and Richard A. Epstein (eds.), *The Vote: Bush, Gore and the Supreme Court* (Chicago: Chicago University Press, 2001), pp. 119–120.
8. Charles Fried and Ronald Dworkin, "'A Badly Flawed Election': An Exchange," *New York Review of Books*, February 22, 2001, p. 8, fn. 5.
9. *Gore v. Harris*, 772 So. 2d 1243, 1271, fn. 33.
10. "The Undervote," *Washington Post*, December 9, 2000, p. A20.
11. "The Unfiled Gore Brief of December 13, 2000," reprinted in Jake Tapper, *Down and Dirty* (Boston: Little Brown, 2001), p. 495.
12. *Bush v. Gore*, p. 411, italics added. Justice Breyer also joined this opinion, although his own opinion takes a different view on counting standards.
13. Alan Dershowitz, *Supreme Injustice* (New York: Oxford University Press, 2001), pp. 95–96.
14. Michael Klarman, "*Bush v. Gore* Through the Lens of Constitutional History," 89 *California Law Review* (2001), p. 1725.
15. See Jeffrey Toobin, *Too Close to Call* (New York: Random House, 2001), pp. 248–249.
16. See particularly the essay by Richard Pildes, "Democracy and Disorder," in Sunstein and Epstein (eds.), *The Vote*, p. 140.

17. John Yoo, "In Defense of the Court's Legitimacy," in Sunstein and Epstein (eds.), *The Vote*, pp. 237–238. Justice Jackson's comment is found in *Brown v. Allen,* 344 US 443, 540 (1953).

18. See Judge Robert W. Lee, "The Florida Election Canvassing System," 26 *Nova Law Review* (2002), pp. 851, 883–890.

19. *The 2002 Florida Statutes,* 102.112 (2) (3) (italics added), www.flcourts.org.

20. Ibid., 101.732 (3).

21. Ibid., 102.166 (1).

22. Ibid., 102.166 (2) (a).

23. Ibid., 102.166 (6) (c) (italics added).

24. Ibid., 101.5614 (6).

25. Ibid., 102.166 (5) (b).

26. Florida Division of Elections, Rule 1S-2.027, "Clear Indication of Voter's Choice on a Ballot," (1) (b) (c) (g), www.flcourts.org.

27. Ibid., (4) (d), (e) 3.

28. Martin Merzer, Joni James, and Alfonso Chardy, "It's Deja Vote: More Problems at the Polls Delay Voters, Primary Results," *Miami Herald*, September 11, 2002, p. 1A; Joni James, "Florida Asks U.S. to Help in Next Vote," *Miami Herald*, September 19, 2002, p. 1A.

29. Alfonso Chardy, Tere Figueras, and Martin Merzer, "Leahy Blames Unskilled Workers," *Miami Herald*, September 13, 2002, p. 1A.

30. Alfonso Chardy, Beth Reinhard, and Martin Merzer, "A Winner Waits as Chaos Grows," *Miami Herald*, September 14, 2002, p. 1A.

31. For much of this material I have relied on the marvelous study of election reform in the United States since November, 2001, *What's Changed, What Hasn't, and Why,* an annual report of inestimable value issued by the Election Reform Information Project, www.electionline.org.

32. Election Reform Information Project, *What's Changed, What Hasn't, and Why*, p. 62.

Appendix A:
Chronology of the Bush-Gore Dispute

November 7   Election Day U.S.A. A very close contest is forecast between Vice President Al Gore and Governor George Bush.

Numerous complaints arise because of Palm Beach County's butterfly ballot.

November 8   It is clear that the presidential election's outcome hinges on Florida. An automatic machine recount of the state's vote is ordered under state law, because George Bush's margin over Al Gore is less than 0.5 percent—1,784 votes.

November 9   Gore asks for manual recounts in Broward, Miami-Dade, Palm Beach, and Volusia Counties.

Voters file numerous lawsuits in Palm Beach County demanding a revote because of the butterfly ballot.

November 11   Volusia County begins a full manual recount (then postpones it a day); Palm Beach County starts its sample count.

George Bush and a group of Florida voters go to federal district court seeking an immediate stay of, and a temporary injunction against, hand counting of votes in Florida.

November 12   The Palm Beach County canvassing board votes 2-1 to do a full manual recount.

November 13   Federal District Judge Donald Middlebrooks rules against the Bush stay and injunction. (Two days later, the Eleventh Circuit Court of Appeals also refuses an emergency stay, though agreeing to hear the case later.)

November 13   Director of the Florida division of elections, Clay Roberts, writes to canvassing boards, stating that manual recounts are appropriate only if there are failures in the vote-tabulating equipment.

Partly because of the memo, the Broward County canvassing board votes 2-1 not to do a full manual recount.

In a separate memo, Roberts states that all returns must be in to the Florida Elections Canvassing Commission by the statutory deadline, 5 P.M. November 14.

Volusia, Palm Beach, and Broward Counties, joined by Vice President Gore, go to Leon County Circuit Court seeking an injunction to prevent enforcement of the deadline.

November 14   State Attorney General Robert Butterworth sends a memo stating that finding voter error is a proper cause for recounts.

The Broward County board changes its mind and decides to do a full manual recount.

The Palm Beach County board decides to hold off its recounts, and go to the Florida Supreme Court for guidance on the recount issue.

The Miami-Dade County canvassing board decides 2-1 not to do a full manual recount.

In the injunction suit, Circuit Judge Terry Lewis rules that the Florida secretary of state must exercise sound "discretion" in deciding whether to accept election returns after November 14. Secretary Katherine Harris writes to the canvassing boards asking for their reasons for submitting late returns.

November 15   Harris refuses the counties' requests and certifies totals (including Volusia's completed hand count) showing a 300-vote lead for George Bush. She says final certification will take place after the overseas absentee ballots are counted on November 18.

November 16   Gore appeals the actions of Secretary Harris to Judge Lewis.

November 17   Judge Terry Lewis upholds Harris's exercise of her discretion in deciding certification; Gore appeals to the Florida Supreme Court.

November 17   The Florida Supreme Court accepts Gore's appeal, combines it with the Palm Beach case, and forbids the secretary from promulgating a final certification until the court acts.

The Miami-Dade canvassing board reverses itself and agrees to do a full manual recount.

November 18   The overseas absentee ballots are counted, increasing Bush's lead to 930.

November 20   Oral arguments are held before the Florida Supreme Court.

November 21   The Florida Supreme Court rules unanimously that manual recounts to uncover voter intent are valid under Florida law, that Secretary Harris abused her discretion in refusing to accept manual recounts after November 14, and that as a matter of "equity," canvassing boards have until November 26 to submit the recounts.

Bush immediately appeals to the United States Supreme Court.

November 22   Miami-Dade County's canvassing board decides unanimously to abandon its manual recount for lack of time.

November 24   The United States Supreme Court accepts certiorari in Bush's appeal, *Bush v. Palm Beach County Canvassing Board*.

November 25   Broward County completes its manual recount, showing a gain of 567 votes for Gore.

November 26   The court deadline comes at 5 P.M., and Palm Beach County misses it. Harris certifies George Bush the winner of Florida by 537 votes.

November 27   Gore files his contest complaint in Leon County Circuit Court.

December 1   Oral arguments are held in the United States Supreme Court in *Bush v. Palm Beach County Canvassing Board.*

                The Florida Supreme Court definitively ends the butterfly case, refusing all relief.

December 2   Contest trial begins before Judge N. Sanders Sauls.

December 4   The U.S. Supreme Court vacates the Florida Supreme Court decision and sends it back to the Florida court for clarification.

                Judge Sauls rules against Gore on every point in the contest trial.

December 5   The Florida Supreme Court agrees to hear arguments in Gore's contest appeal.

December 6   The Eleventh Circuit Court of Appeals turns down Bush's request for a temporary injunction to bar any more manual recounts.

December 7   The Florida Supreme Court hears arguments in Gore's contest appeal, *Gore v. Harris.*

December 8   The Florida Supreme Court orders a statewide recount of all undervotes; Bush immediately appeals to the United States Supreme Court.

December 9   By a 5-4 vote, the U.S. Supreme Court orders a stay of all counting until it decides *Bush v. Gore.*

December 11   Oral arguments in *Bush v. Gore.*

December 12   With the U. S. Supreme Court decision not handed down during the day, the Florida House of Representatives votes to name its own slate of electors, then sends its work to the senate.

At 10 P.M., the U.S. Supreme Court decides by a 5-4 vote that Florida's recount standards violate the equal-protection clause of the Fourteenth Amendment, and that there is no time to fix the problem, since the Florida legislature meant for election litigation to end by December 12.

December 13   Vice President Gore concedes.

December 18   The Electoral College meets. George W. Bush is elected president with 271 electoral votes. Al Gore gets 266 (with an elector from the District of Columbia refusing to cast a ballot).

Appendix B:
The U.S. Presidential Election of 2000:
Electoral and Popular Vote Totals by State

	Electoral Votes		Popular Votes	
	Gore	Bush	Gore	Bush
Alabama	0	9	692,611	941,173
Alaska	0	3	79,004	167,398
Arizona	0	8	685,341	781,652
Arkansas	0	6	422,768	472,940
California	54	0	5,861,203	4,567,429
Colorado	0	8	738,227	883,748
Connecticut	8	0	816,015	561,094
Delaware	3	0	180,068	137,288
D.C.	2	0	171,923	18,073
	(1 elector abstained)			
Florida	0	25	2,912,253	2,912,790
Georgia	0	13	1,116,230	1,419,720
Hawaii	4	0	205,286	137,845
Idaho	0	4	138,637	336,937
Illinois	22	0	2,589,026	2,019,421
Indiana	0	12	901,980	1,245,836
Iowa	7	0	638,517	634,373
Kansas	0	8	399,276	622,332
Kentucky	0	8	638,923	872,520
Louisiana	0	9	792,344	927,871
Maine	4	0	319,951	286,616
Maryland	10	0	1,144,008	813,827
Massachusetts	12	0	1,616,487	878,502
Michigan	18	0	2,170,418	1,953,139
Minnesota	10	0	1,168,266	1,109,659
Mississippi	0	7	404,614	572,844
Missouri	0	11	1,111,138	1,189,924

Montana	0	3	137,126	240,178
Nebraska	0	5	231,780	433,862
Nevada	0	4	279,978	301,575
New Hampshire	0	4	266,348	273,559
			(Nader, 22,198)
New Jersey	15	0	1,788,850	1,284,173
New Mexico	5	0	286,783	286,417
New York	33	0	4,112,965	2,405,570
North Carolina	0	14	1,257,692	1,631,163
North Dakota	0	3	95,284	174,852
Ohio	0	21	2,186,190	2,351,209
Oklahoma	0	8	474,276	744,337
Oregon	7	0	720,342	713,577
Pennsylvania	23	0	2,485,967	2,281,127
Rhode Island	4	0	249,508	130,555
South Carolina	0	8	566,039	786,892
South Dakota	0	3	118,804	190,700
Tennessee	0	11	981,720	1,061,949
Texas	0	32	2,433,746	3,799,639
Utah	0	5	203,053	515,096
Vermont	3	0	149,022	119,775
Virginia	0	13	1,217,290	1,437,490
Washington	11	0	1,247,652	1,108,864
West Virginia	0	5	295,497	336,475
Wisconsin	11	0	1,242,987	1,237,279
Wyoming	0	3	60,481	147,947
Totals	266	271	51,003,894	50,459,211

Appendix C:
Map of the Disputed State and Counties: Florida, 2000

FLORIDA

DUVAL

VOLUSIA

PALM BEACH

BROWARD

DADE

Appendix D:
Official Results in Florida by County

County	Bush/Cheney (REP)	Gore/Lieberman (DEM)	Nader/LaDuke (GREEN)
Alachua	34,124	47,365	3,226
Baker	5,610	2,392	53
Bay	38,637	18,850	828
Bradford	5,414	3,075	84
Brevard	115,185	97,318	4,470
Broward	177,902	387,703	7,104
Calhoun	2,873	2,155	39
Charlotte	35,426	29,645	1,462
Citrus	29,767	25,525	1,379
Clay	41,736	14,632	562
Collier	60,450	29,921	1,400
Columbia	10,964	7,047	258
Desoto	4,256	3,320	157
Dixie	2,697	1,826	75
Duval	152,098	107,864	2,757
Escambia	73,017	40,943	1,727
Flagler	12,613	13,897	435
Franklin	2,454	2,046	85
Gadsden	4,767	9,735	139
Gilchrist	3,300	1,910	97
Glades	1,841	1,442	56
Gulf	3,550	2,397	86
Hamilton	2,146	1,722	37
Hardee	3,765	2,339	75
Hendry	4,747	3,240	104
Hernando	30,646	32,644	1,501
Highlands	20,206	14,167	545

Hillsborough	180,760	169,557	7,490
Holmes	5,011	2,177	94
Indian River	28,635	19,768	950
Jackson	9,138	6,868	138
Jefferson	2,478	3,041	76
Lafayette	1,670	789	26
Lake	50,010	36,571	1,460
Lee	106,141	73,560	3,587
Leon	39,062	61,427	1,932
Levy	6,858	5,398	284
Liberty	1,317	1,017	19
Madison	3,038	3,014	54
Manatee	57,952	49,177	2,491
Marion	55,141	44,665	1,809
Martin	33,970	26,620	1,118
Miami-Dade	289,533	328,808	5,352
Monroe	16,059	16,483	1,090
Nassau	16,404	6,952	253
Okaloosa	52,093	16,948	985
Okeechobee	5,057	4,588	131
Orange	134,517	140,220	3,879
Osceola	26,212	28,181	732
Palm Beach	152,951	269,732	5,565
Pasco	68,582	69,564	3,393
Pinellas	184,825	200,630	10,022
Polk	90,295	75,200	2,059
Putnam	13,447	12,102	377
Santa Rosa	36,274	12,802	724
Sarasota	83,100	72,853	4,069
Seminole	75,677	59,174	1,946
St. Johns	39,546	19,502	1,217
St. Lucie	34,705	41,559	1,368
Sumter	12,127	9,637	306
Suwannee	8,006	4,075	180
Taylor	4,056	2,649	59
Union	2,332	1,407	33
Volusia	82,357	97,304	2,910
Wakulla	4,512	3,838	149
Walton	12,182	5,642	265
<u>Washington</u>	<u>4,994</u>	<u>2,798</u>	<u>93</u>
Sub Total	2,911,215	2,911,417	97,426
Fed Abs	1,575	836	62
Total	2,912,790	2,912,253	97,488
Percent	48.8%	48.8%	1.6%
Recount Completed			

Cases Cited

A.L.A. Schechter Poultry Corporation v. United States, 295 US 495 (1935).
Bain Peanut Company of Texas v. Pinson, 282 US 499 (1931).
Baker v. Carr, 369 US 186 (1962).
Baker v. Curry, 802 F. 2d 1302 (11th Cir. 1986).
Bayne v. Glisson, 300 So. 2d 79 (1974).
Beckstrom v. Volusia County Canvassing Board, 707 So. 2d 720 (1998).
Board of Trustees of University of Alabama v. Garrett, 148 LEd 2d 866 (2001).
Boardman v. Esteva, 323 So. 2d 259 (1976).
Bouie v. City of Columbia, 378 US 347 (1964).
Broward County Canvassing Board v. Hogan, 607 So. 2d 508 (Fla. 4th DCA 1992).
Brown v. Allen, 344 US 443 (1953).
Brown v. Board of Education, 347 US 483 (1954).
Bush v. Gore, Application For Stay 148 LEd 2d 553 (2000).
    Decision 148 LEd 2d 388 (2000).
Bush v. Palm Beach County Canvassing Board, Order Granting Certiorari 148 LEd 2d 478 (2000).
    Decision 148 LEd 2d 366 (2000).
Carpenter v. Barber, 198 So. 49 (1940).
Chappell v. Martinez, 506 So. 2d 1007 (1988).
Chevron USA v. Natural Resources Defense Council, 467 US 837 (1984).
City of Boerne v. Flores, 521 US 507 (1997).
Cleburne v. Cleburne Living Center, Inc., 473 US 432 (1985).
Cooper v. Aaron, 358 US 1 (1958).
Cuomo v. Nuclear Regulatory Commission, 772 F. 2d 972 (D.C. Cir. 1985).
Darby v. State, 75 So. 411 (1917).
Delahunt v. Johnston, 671 N.E. 2d 1241 (1996).
Dred Scott v. Sandford, 19 Howard 393 (1857).
Duffy v. Mortenson, 497 N.W. 2d 437 (1993).
Duncan v. Poythress, 657 F. 2d 191 (5th Cir. Unit B 1981).
Employment Division v. Smith, 494 US 872 (1990).
Erie Railroad Company v. Tompkins, 304 US 64 (1938).
Fairfax's Devisee v. Hunter's Lessee, 7 Cranch 603 (1813).
F.C.C. v. Beach Communications, Inc., 508 US 307 (1993).
Flack v. Carter, 392 So. 2d 37 (Fla. 1st DCA 1980).

New Orleans v. Dukes, 427 US 297 (1976).

Nuccio v. Williams, 120 So. 310 (1929).

O'Brien v. Election Commissioners of Boston, 153 N.E. 553 (1926).

Palm Beach County Canvassing Board v. Harris, Interim Order (Nov. 16, 2000).
  Stay Order (Nov. 17, 2000).
  Decision 772 So. 2d 1220 (2000).
  On Remand 772 So. 2d 1273 (2000).

Planned Parenthood of Southeastern Pennsylvania v. Casey, 505 US 833 (1992).

Plessy v. Ferguson, 163 US 537 (1896).

Powers v. Ohio, 499 US 400 (1991).

Pullen v. Mulligan, 561 N.E. 2d 585 (1990).

Reynolds v. Sims, 377 US 533 (1964).

Roe v. Wade, 410 US 113 (1973).

Royster Guano Co. v. Virginia, 253 US 412 (1920).

Rutan v. Republican Party of Illinois, 497 US 62 (1990).

Saenz v. Roe, 526 US 489 (1999).

Shapiro v. Thompson, 394 US 618 (1969).

Siegel v. LePore, 120 F. Supp. 2d 1041 (S.D. Fla. 2000).
  234 F. 3d 1162 (11th Cir. 2000).
  148 LEd 2d 478 (Order Denying Certiorari Before Judgment).
  234 F. 3d 1163 (11th Cir. 2000).

Smith v. Tynes, 412 So. 2d 925 (Fla. 1st DCA 1982).

Stanton v. Stanton, 421 US 7 (1975).

State ex. rel. Clark v. Klingensmith, 163 So. 704 (1935).

State ex. rel. Davis v. Hildebrant, 241 US 565 (1916).

State v. Smith, 144 So. 333 (1932).

Stone v. Powell, 428 US 465 (1976).

Taylor v. Martin County Canvassing Board, 2nd Judicial Circuit of Florida (Nov. 8, 2000).
  Appeal 773 So. 2d 517 (2000).

Touchton v. McDermott, 120 F. Supp. 2d 1055 (M.D. Fla: 2000).
  234 F. 3d 1130 (11th Cir. 2000).
  234 F. 3d 1133 (11th Cir. 2000).

Trimble v. Gordon, 430 US 762 (1977).

United States v. Butler, 297 US 1 (1936).

United States v. Lopez, 514 US 549 (1995).

United States v. Morrison, 529 US 598 (2000).

United States v. Virginia, 518 US 515 (1996).

U.S. Term Limits, Inc. v. Thornton, 514 US 779 (1995).

Vance v. Bradley, 440 US 93 (1979).

Werhan v. State, 673 So. 2d 550 (1996).

Wiggins v. State, 144 So. 62 (1932).

Selected Bibliography

The Other Disputed Election: 1876

Haworth, Paul. *The Hayes-Tilden Disputed Election of 1876* (New York: Russell & Russell,1966).

Polakoff, Keith Ian. *The Politics of Inertia* (Baton Rouge: Lousiana State University Press, 1973).

Shofner, Jerrell H. "Florida Courts and the Disputed Election of 1876," 48 *Florida Historical Quarterly* (July 1969), p. 26.

———. "Florida in the Balance: The Electoral Count of 1876," 47 *Florida Historical Quarterly* (October 1968), p. 124.

———. "Fraud and Intimidation in the Florida Election of 1876," 42 *Florida Historical Quarterly* (April 1964), p. 321.

Woodward, C. Vann. *Reunion and Reaction: The Compromise of 1877 and the End of Reconstruction* (Boston: Little Brown, 1966).

The 2000 Election in Florida: General Works

Correspondents of *The New York Times. 36 Days: The Complete Chronicle of the 2000 Presidential Election Crisis* (New York: Times Books, 2001).

Dionne, E. J., and William Kristol (eds.). *Bush v. Gore: The Court Cases and the Commentary* (Washington, D.C.: Brookings Institution Press, 2001).

Gillman, Howard. *The Votes That Counted: How the Court Decided the 2000 Presidential Election* (Chicago: University of Chicago Press, 2001).

Greene, Abner. *Understanding the 2000 Election* (New York: New York University Press, 2001).

Greenfield, Jeff. *"Oh Waiter! One Order of Crow!": Inside the Strangest Presidential Finish in American History* (New York: Putnam, 2001).

Jacobson, Arthur J., and Michael Rosenfeld (eds.). *The Longest Night: Polemics and Perspectives on Election 2000* (Berkeley: University of California Press, 2002).

Kaplan, David A. *The Accidental President* (New York: William Morrow, 2001).

Merzer, Martin, and the Staff of *The Miami Herald. The Miami Herald Report: Democracy Held Hostage* (New York: St. Martin's Press, 2001).

The Political Staff of *The Washington Post*. *Deadlock: The Inside Story of America's Closest Election* (New York: Public Affairs, 2001).

Posner, Richard. *Breaking the Deadlock* (Princeton, N.J.: Princeton University Press, 2001).

Rakove, Jack (ed.). *The Unfinished Election of 2000* (New York: Basic Books, 2001).

Sabato, Larry (ed.). *Overtime! The Election 2000 Thriller* (New York: Longman, 2002).

Tapper, Jake. *Down and Dirty: The Plot to Steal the Presidency* (Boston: Little Brown, 2001).

Toobin, Jeffrey. *Too Close To Call: The Thirty-Six Day Battle to Decide the 2000 Election* (New York: Random House, 2001).

Zelnick, Robert. *Winning Florida: How the Bush Team Fought the Battle* (Stanford: Hoover Institution Press, 2001).

About the Rehnquist Court and Its Justices

Belsky, Martin (ed.). *The Rehnquist Court: A Retrospective* (New York: Oxford University Press, 2002).

Boles, Donald. *Mr. Justice Rehnquist, Judicial Activist: The Early Years* (Ames: Iowa State University Press, 1987).

Brisbin, Richard A. Jr. *Justice Antonin Scalia and the Conservative Revival* (Baltimore: Johns Hopkins University Press, 1997).

Culp, Jerome McCristal Jr. "Understanding the Racial Discourse of Justice Rehnquist," 25 *Rutgers Law Journal* (1994), p. 597.

Friedman, Lawrence. "The Limitations of Labeling: Justice Anthony M. Kennedy and the First Amendment," 25 *Ohio Northern University Law Review* (1993), p. 225.

Gerber, Scott. *First Principles: The Jurisprudence of Clarence Thomas* (New York: New York University Press, 1999).

Gottlieb, Stephen E. *Morality Imposed: The Rehnquist Court and Liberty in America* (New York: New York University Press, 2000).

Halberstam, Malvina. "Ruth Bader Ginsburg: The First Jewish Woman on the Supreme Court," 19 *Cardozo Law Review* (1995), p. 1441.

Hanks, Liza Weiman. "Justice Souter: Defining 'Substantive Neutrality' in an Age of Religious Politics," 48 *Stanford Law Review* (1996), p. 906.

Irons, Peter. *Brennan v. Rehnquist: The Battle for the Constitution* (New York: Knopf, 1994).

Koehler, David. "Justice Souter's 'Keep-What-You-Want-and-Throw-Away-the-Rest' Interpretation of Stare Decisis," 42 *Buffalo Law Review* (1994), p. 859.

Maltz, Earl M. "Justice Kennedy's Vision of Federalism," 31 *Rutgers Law Journal* (2000), p. 761.

Maveety, Nancy. *Justice Sandra Day O'Connor: Strategist on the Supreme Court* (Lanham, Md.: Rowman & Littlefield, 1996).

Pressman, Carol. "The House That Ruth Built: Justice Ruth Bader Ginsburg, Gender and Justice," 14 *New York Law School Journal of Human Rights* (1977), p. 311.

Rosen, Jeffrey. "The Humility of Justice Breyer," *New Republic*, January 14, 2002, p. 21.

————. "The Tempting of Antonin Scalia, *New Republic*, May 5, 1997, p. 26.

Savage, David G. *Turning Right: The Making of the Rehnquist Court* (New York: Wiley, 1992).

Schultz, David A., and Christopher Smith. *The Jurisprudential Vision of Justice Antonin Scalia* (Lanham, Md.: Rowman & Littlefield, 1996).

Sickels, Robert J. *John Paul Stevens and the Constitution: The Search for Balance* (University Park, Pa.: Pennsylvania State University Press, 1988).

Simon, James F. *The Center Holds: The Power Struggle Inside the Rehnquist Court* (New York: Simon & Schuster, 1995).

Smith, Christopher. "Supreme Court Surprise: Justice Kennedy's Move Toward Moderation," 45 *Oklahoma Law Review* (1992), p. 459.

Symposium. "The Jurisprudence of Justice Ruth Bader Ginsburg," 20 *Hawaii Law Review* (1998), p. 581.

Thomas, Andrew Peyton. *Clarence Thomas* (San Francisco: Encounter Books, 2001).

Van Sickel, Robert. *Not a Politically Different Voice: The Jurisprudence of Sandra Day O'Connor* (New York: P. Lang, 1998).

Yarbrough, Tinsley. *The Rehnquist Court and the Constitution* (New York: Oxford University Press, 2000).

By the Rehnquist Court Justices

Breyer, Stephen G. *Breaking the Vicious Cycle: Toward Effective Risk Regulation* (Cambridge, Mass.: Harvard University Press, 1993).

————. *The Legal Profession and Public Service* (Washington, D.C.: National Legal Center for the Public Interest, 2000).

————. "Liberty, Prosperity, and a Strong Judicial Institution" 61 *Law and Contemporary Problems* (1998), p. 3.

————. "Our Uncertain Constitution," Madison Lecture, 77 *New York University Law Review* (2002), p. 245.

Ginsburg, Ruth Bader. "Access to Justice: The Social Responsibility of Lawyers," 7 *Washington University Journal of Law and Policy* (2001), p. 1.

————. "Informing the Public About the U.S. Supreme Court's Work," 29 *Loyola University Chicago Law Journal* (1998), p. 275.

————. "Speaking in a Judicial Voice," in Norman Dorsen (ed.), *The Unpredictable Constitution* (New York: New York University Press, 2000).

————. "Women's Progress in the Legal Profession in the United States," 33 *Tulsa Law Journal* (1997), p. 13.

Kennedy, Anthony M. "Judicial Ethics and the Rule of Law," 40 *St. Louis University Law Journal* (1996), p. 1067.

O'Connor, Sandra Day. *Lazy B: Growing Up on a Cattle Ranch in the American Southwest,* with H. Alan Day (New York: Random House, 2002).

————. "Portia's Progress," in Norman Dorsen (ed.), *The Unpredictable Constitution* (New York: New York University Press, 2000).

————. "Set-Asides Violate the Equal Protection Clause" (Excerpt from *City of Richmond v. J. A. Croson*, 488 US 469, 1989), in Russell Nieli (ed.), *Racial Preference and Racial Justice* (Lanham, Md.: Rowman & Littlefield, 1991), p. 237.

————. "Taking a Seat Among the Brethren" (Grolier Educational Corporation, 1981, audio cassette).

Rehnquist, William. *All the Laws But One: Civil Liberties in Wartime* (New York: Knopf, 1998, 2000).
———. *Grand Inquests: The Historic Impeachments of Justice Samuel Chase and President Andrew Johnson* (New York: Morrow, 1992).
———. "The Notion of a Living Constitution," 54 *Texas Law Review* (1976), p. 693.
———. *The Supreme Court* (New York: Knopf, 2001).
Scalia, Antonin. "The Dissenting Opinion," *Journal of Supreme Court History* (1994), p. 33.
———. *A Matter of Interpretation: Federal Courts and the Law* (Princeton, N.J.: Princeton University Press, 1997).
———. "Originalism: The Lesser Evil," 57 *University of Cincinnati Law Review* (1989), p. 849.
———. "The Rule of Law as a Law of Rules," 56 *University of Chicago Law Review* (1989), p. 1175.
Stevens, John Paul. "Banning Indecency on the Internet Is Unconstitutional," in Paul A. Winters (ed.), *The Information Revolution: Opposing Viewpoints* (San Diego: Greenhaven Press, 1998).
———. "Interpreting Our Written Constitution" in *The Great Debate* (Washington, D.C.: The Federalist Society, 1986), p. 27.
———. "Minority Teachers Serve on Important Purpose" (Excerpt from *Wygant v. Jackson Board of Education*, 476 US 267, 1986), in Russell Nieli (ed.), *Racial Preference and Racial Justice* (Lanham, Md.: Rowman & Littlefield, 1991), p. 263.
Thomas, Clarence. *Confronting the Future* (Washington, D.C.: Regnery Gateway, 1992).

Bush v. Gore: The Supreme Court Case

Alexander, Larry. "The Supreme Court, the Florida Vote, and Equal Protection," 38 *San Diego Law Review* (2001), p. 1077.
Baddour, David Bryant. "Could Florida 2000 Happen Here? The Application of the Equal Protection Clause to North Carolina's 'Intent of the Voter' Standard in the Aftermath of the 2000 Presidential Election," 79 *North Carolina Law Review* (2001), p. 1804.
Baker, James A. III. "*Bush v. Gore's* Legacy: Observations on the Florida Electoral Dispute," 13 *Stanford Law and Policy Review* (2002), p. 15.
Balkin, Jack. "*Bush v. Gore* and the Boundary Between Law and Politics," 110 *Yale Law Journal* (2001), p. 1407.
Bragow, Stephen G., and Barbara A. Perry. "The 'Brooding Omnipresence' in *Bush v. Gore*: Anthony Kennedy, the Equality Principle, and Judicial Supremacy," 13 *Stanford Law and Policy Review* (2002), p. 19.
Bugliosi, Vincent. *The Betrayal of America* (New York: Thunder's Mouth Press/Nation Books, 2001).
Campos, Paul. "The Search for Incontrovertible Visual Evidence," 72 *University of Colorado Law Review* (2001), p. 1039.
Carcieri, Martin D. "*Bush v. Gore* and Equal Protection," 53 *South Carolina Law Review* (2001), p. 63.
Chermerinsky, Erwin. "*Bush v. Gore* Was Not Justiciable," 76 *Notre Dame Law Review* (2001), p. 1093.

Choper, Jesse. "Why the Supreme Court Should Not Have Decided the Presidential Election of 2000," 18 *Constitutional Commentary* (2001), p. 335.

Dershowitz, Alan M. *Supreme Injustice: How the High Court Hijacked Election 2000* (New York: Oxford University Press, 2001).

Dworkin, Ronald. "A Badly Flawed Election," *New York Review of Books,* January 11, 2001, pp. 53–55.

Farnsworth, Ward. "'To Do a Great Right, Do a Little Wrong': A User's Guide to Judicial Lawlessness," 86 *Minnesota Law Review* (2001), p. 227.

Fried, Charles, and Ronald Dworkin. "'A Badly Flawed Election': An Exchange," *New York Review of Books*, February 22, 2001, pp. 8–10.

Gabel, Peter. "What It Really Means to Say 'Law Is Politics': Political History and Legal Argument in *Bush v. Gore*," 67 *Brooklyn Law Review* (2002), p. 1141.

Goldstein, Leslie Friedman. "Between the Tiers: The Newest Equal Protection and *Bush v. Gore*," 4 *University of Pennsylvania Journal of Constitutional Law* (2002), p. 372.

Greenhouse, Linda. "Thinking About the Supreme Court After *Bush v. Gore*," 35 *Indiana Law Review* (2002), p. 435.

Hasen, Richard. "A 'Tincture of Justice': Judge Posner's Failed Rehabilitation of *Bush v. Gore*," 80 *Texas Law Review* (2001), p. 137.

Herz, Michael. "The Supreme Court in Real Time: Haste, Waste, and *Bush v. Gore*," 35 *Akron Law Review* (2002), p. 185.

Kesovan, Vasan. "Is the Electoral Count Act Unconstitutional?" 80 *North Carolina Law Review* (2002), p. 1653.

Klarman, Michael. "*Bush v. Gore* Through the Lens of Constitutional History," 89 *California Law Review* (2001), p. 1721.

Krotoszynski, Ronald Jr. "An Epitaphios for Neutral Principles in Constitutional Law: *Bush v. Gore* and the Emerging Jurisprudence of Oprah!" 90 *Georgetown Law Journal* (2002), p. 2087.

Lee, Robert W. "The Florida Election Canvassing System," 26 *Nova Law Review* (2002), p. 851.

Levinson, Sanford. "The Law of Politics: *Bush v. Gore* and the French Revolution," 65 *Law and Contemporary Problems* (2002), p. 7.

Lund, Nelson. "The Unbearable Rightness of *Bush v. Gore*," 23 *Cardozo Law Review* (2002), p. 1219.

Norton, Helen. "What *Bush v. Gore* Means for Elections in the 21st Century," 2 *Wyoming Law Review* (2001), p. 419.

Seidman, Louis Michael. "What's So Bad About *Bush v. Gore*? An Essay on Our Unsettled Election," 47 *Wayne Law Review* (2001), p. 953.

Sunstein, Cass M., and Richard A. Epstein (eds.). *The Vote: Bush, Gore and the Supreme Court* (Chicago: Chicago University Press, 2001).

Symposium. "Federal Courts and Electoral Politics," 82 *Boston University Law Review* (2002), p. 608.

Symposium. "The Law of Presidential Elections: Issues in the Wake of Florida," 29 *Florida State University Law Review* (2001), p. 325.

Symposium. "Litigating the Presidency: The Election 2000 Decision and Its Ramifications for the Supreme Court," 61 *Maryland Law Review* (2002), p. 505.

Tribe, Laurence. "*Bush v. Gore* and Its Disguises: Freeing *Bush v. Gore* from Its Hall of Mirrors," 115 *Harvard Law Review* (2001), p. 170.

Tushnet, Mark. "Renormalizing *Bush v. Gore*: An Anticipatory Intellectual History," 90 *Georgetown Law Journal* (2001), p. 113.

Index

About the Book

Florida 2000 offers a clear, but also nuanced, account of the legal and constitutional issues surrounding the disputed presidential election. Combining original sources with analyses, Mark Whitman traces the major developments in the Bush-Gore struggle.

Section introductions and commentaries synthesize the often complex material, while editor's notes provide context for each selection. The appendixes include a comprehensive chronology of events, maps, and detailed election returns for both the state and the entire country.

Mark Whitman is professor of history at Towson University. His publications include *The Irony of Desegregation Law: 1955–1995* and *Removing a Badge of Slavery: The Record of Brown v. Board of Education.*